inclusive
EDUCATION

inclusive EDUCATION

A practical guide to supporting diversity in the classroom

Tim Loreman, DipT, Grad DipEd, MEd, PhD
Faculty of Education, Concordia University College of Alberta

Joanne Deppeler, BEd, MEd, PhD, MAPs
Faculty of Education, Monash University

David Harvey, MA, PhD, MAPs
Faculty of Education, Monash University

RoutledgeFalmer
Taylor & Francis Group

LONDON AND NEW YORK

First published in 2005 by Allen & Unwin
83 Alexander Street, Crows Nest NSW 2065, Australia

First published in the UK in 2005 by RoutledgeFalmer
2 Park Square, Milton Park, Abingdon OX14 4RN

Simultaneously published in the USA and Canada by RoutledgeFalmer
29 West 35th Street, New York, NY 10001

RoutledgeFalmer is an imprint of the Taylor & Francis Group

British Library Cataloguing in Publication Data
A catalogue record for this book is available from the British Library

Paperback ISBN 0 415 35669 5
Hardback ISBN 0 415 35668 7

Library of Congress Cataloging in Publication Data
A catalogue record for this book has been requested

Typeset in 10.5/12 pt Sabon by Bookhouse, Sydney, Australia
Printed and bound in Singapore by South Wind Productions

10 9 8 7 6 5 4 3 2 1

Foreword

What is the purpose of school? This is a question that draws many answers. And those answers point to different types of practices in the school and classroom. I've been thinking about this question for many years. In countries that consider themselves political democracies, most schools have mission statements that read something like, 'becoming a citizen in a democracy', 'lifelong learner', 'developing skills to be a valuable member of the community'. Yet, too many schools continue to structure their operations to assure another message—that democracy and community are only for some. The ongoing, systematic segregation of students by ability, race and class sends a powerful and well-learned message—one that needs to be revised.

Throughout the world, many people are developing a different vision for our communities. They see communities as groups where all members are valued, and all are included. These same people see how inclusive community building must start in our schools. Unless we teach our children how to live and work together, not only tolerating but valuing differences in culture, ethnicity, language, background and, yes, even dramatically different cognitive, social-emotional, and sensory-physical abilities, we almost always teach the opposite—systematic forms of segregation, oppression and elitism.

The champions of this view of schooling realise that having children with substantial differences learning together in an inclusive classroom is not about being 'nice' to 'those' people. Rather it's a fundamental condition for a good school, one that pays attention to both excellence and equity. But can you have both equity and excellence together? Loreman, Deppeler and Harvey clearly state that we can. The message comes through clear—excellence cannot exist without equity.

Inclusive Education is an important book because it adds a clear voice that helps teachers, administrators and parents visualise in concrete form truly inclusive instruction. The approach the authors have taken is helpful from many perspectives as it gives readers strategies and tools. I'd like to point out a few of these. Firstly, the issue of who we are discussing: children with 'diverse educational needs'. The authors use the platform of two points on the continuum: students with disabilities and those who are considered gifted and talented. They recognise well that creating an effective inclusive classroom requires the range of intellectual and behavioural functioning to be accommodated. This is a very important perspective.

Secondly, they combine practical, clear strategies with concrete stories that illustrate how to make such approaches real. These strategies are based on sound research, which the authors share. However, their focus is on practical strategies rather than acting as a review of the literature. This perspective will be appreciated by teachers who need answers to questions like: 'What do I do on Monday?' Thirdly, the authors are clear about their viewpoint. This is not a text that reviews the 'options' in the way schools deal with children in a pseudo-objective manner. Rather, they state clearly their view of a good school: one that includes all children in learning well together. Yet, they also recognise the absolute importance of beliefs, values and attitudes and provide opportunities to explore the cognitive and emotional dimensions of this important foundation.

Fourthly, the authors describe strategies from the perspective of a practicing general education teacher regarding how to develop individualised programs for students and then design inclusive instruction so that these programs can be implemented as part of the general education curriculum. They discuss the practicalities of collaboration as a form of teacher support, organising the classroom, and, most importantly dealing with the social-emotional needs of students by promoting positive behaviour and social competence. They communicate well to teachers who live this world of diversity in their practice.

In 1997, I joined with a small group of people to create a new vision of schools. We identified six principles of what we now call 'Whole Schooling': empowering citizens for democracy; including all; authentic-multilevel instruction; building community; supporting learning; and partnering with parents and the community (see www.wholeschooling.net). We created the Whole Schooling Consortium involving teachers, schools, parents, administrators and university faculty, now an international network. From this perspective, we are happy to see useful documents and tools that help educators and parents move towards schools based on these principles. *Inclusive Education* provides a powerful, value- and research-based, practical set of tools, ideas, and strategies to equip those on the journey towards schools that truly do link equity and excellence, schools we call 'Whole Schools'. May you enjoy and appreciate this text as I have.

Michael Peterson, PhD
Professor and Coordinator, Wayne State University, USA
Whole Schooling Consortium

Contents

Differences hold great opportunities for learning. Differences offer a free and abundant renewable resource. I would like to see the compulsion for eliminating differences replaced by an equally compelling focus on making use of these to improve schools. What is important about people and about schools is what is different, not what is the same.

R. Barth (1990), 'A special vision of a good school' in *Phi Delta Kappa*, 71, pp. 514–15.

For Lizz, Holly, Tom, Mum and Dad.

T.L.

For John and Marge for their support and positive examples of lifelong learning.

J.D.

For Bronwyn, our children and grandchildren, in the hope that the educational experiences of the latter group reflect the aims we had in mind when writing out our ideas in this book.

D.H.

Preface

Inclusion means full inclusion of children with diverse abilities (that is, both giftedness and disabilities) in all aspects of schooling that other children are able to access and enjoy. It involves 'regular' schools and classrooms genuinely adapting and changing to meet the needs of all children as well as celebrating and valuing differences (Loreman and Deppeler 2001). This book is based on research on inclusion, and how information from that research can be used to influence inclusive practices in classrooms in a positive way. It is written for pre-service teachers or working classroom teachers who want some tips and strategies on how to better include diverse learners across the wide variety of regular classroom activities. It is written with a range of age groups in mind, and should be relevant to children from the first year of school through to the final year of high school. The practices and strategies suggested are as universal as possible, and are relevant across a wide variety of school systems and contexts.

Teachers are busy people. It is for this reason that we have gone to considerable effort to make this book accessible. Where possible we have tried to avoid large sections of text in favour of a more user-friendly approach, including text boxes, examples and blank forms that can be copied and used. Those wanting a more in-depth treatment of a particular subject are encouraged to seek out materials listed in the further reading sections at the end of each chapter.

In this text we have deliberately made an effort to omit or reduce the emphasis on some of the features common to other texts written on the subject of inclusion. For example, many texts base discussion of inclusive practices around categories of disability, often featuring specific chapters on how to educate students with severe and multiple disabilities or those with sensory impairments. While there is some discussion on the categorisation of diverse learners in Chapter 2, we have chosen not to structure this book in this way. We believe that what category of disability or ability a child belongs to is largely irrelevant and often unhelpful, and we do not wish to reinforce that thinking in our text. What is important is that teachers view each child as an individual with unique strengths and needs regardless of what diagnosis they might have, or what category they might fit into.

Similarly, chapters on specific curriculum areas such as literacy and numeracy are not included. Literally hundreds of existing texts address these areas, and there is little that this book could contribute to this already large body of work. Rather, our emphasis is on process. We examine the process of assessing, planning, implementing and evaluating inclusive curriculum and learning. This process can be applied to all curriculum areas, including literacy and numeracy, with equal success.

We would like to point out from the outset that there is no formula for how to 'do' inclusion, and readers looking for easy solutions are likely to be disappointed by any text on this subject. What this text offers instead is a range of helpful advice, tips, strategies and structures that have been used widely in the past and have been found to be effective in the research literature. The text is essentially organised chronologically, beginning with philosophy and issues surrounding identification of diverse learners, and then moving on to assessment, programming, classroom teaching and social issues. Readers should, however, feel free to pick and choose the elements of this book that are helpful within their individual contexts. Inclusion is about problem solving, and readers should use the elements of this book as tools to help them overcome some of the barriers to the inclusion of diverse learners present in their schools and classrooms.

Teachers in regular schools already have the skills they need to successfully include diverse learners. This book will hopefully help teachers to recognise and use these skills in order to produce a more effective and caring educational environment for all learners.

Tim Loreman, Joanne Deppeler
and David Harvey 2004

1

The case for inclusion

This chapter sets out to provide you with enough background information on the theory and practice of inclusion to enable you to use the rest of the book in an informed way. It by no means serves as a comprehensive review of the theoretical underpinnings to the current movement towards inclusion, but rather is intended to provide a broad portrait of what inclusion is, why it is important, and some of the main issues teachers and schools are dealing with today.

KEY IDEAS IN THIS CHAPTER
- defining inclusion
- concerns about inclusion:
    - teacher training
    - curriculum
    - resources
    - school organisation
- benefits of inclusion for children with diverse abilities
- benefits of inclusion for children without disabilities
- one school works towards inclusion: a case study

What is inclusion?

As university researchers and teacher educators with a background and interest in the education of children with diverse abilities, we are often in the position to speak with groups of other educators about inclusion. We sometimes find that these educators are misinformed and confused about inclusion. What exactly is inclusion and why is it important? Part of the confusion strikes at the heart of the matter and arises from the meaning of the term itself. We believe that inclusion, by its very nature, cannot exist in environments where some children are educated separately or substantively differently to their peers. It is perhaps easier to provide examples of what is not inclusion. Educating children part-time in special schools and part-time in regular schools is not inclusion. Educating children in special, mostly segregated, environments in regular schools is not inclusion. Educating children in regular classes, but requiring them to follow substantially different courses of study in terms of content and learning environment to their peers, is also not inclusion (unless all children in a class follow individual programs). We often hear educators speak of these examples as 'inclusion', furthering the confusion (Loreman and Deppeler 2001).

Inclusion means full inclusion of children with diverse abilities in all aspects of schooling that other children are able to access and enjoy. It involves regular schools and classrooms genuinely adapting and changing to meet the needs of all children, as well as celebrating and valuing differences. This definition of inclusion does not imply that children with diverse abilities will not receive specialised assistance or teaching outside of the classroom when required, but rather that this is just one of many options that are available to, and in fact required of, all children (Loreman and Deppeler 2001).

'Integration' and 'inclusion' are two terms that are often used interchangeably by teachers and schools, as if they were synonymous. Some teachers speak of their school's integration program as being an inclusion program, while other schools working towards inclusion use the term integration. There are, however, important differences between the two terms. One simple distinction that can be made is that integration involves coming from the outside. Integration programs aim to involve children with diverse abilities into the existing classes and structures within a school. They endeavour to 'normalise', to help a child fit in to a pre-existing model of schooling. Inclusion differs in that it assumes that all children are a part of the regular school system from the very beginning of school. The need, therefore, for children to adapt to a school setting is not an issue as they are already a part of that system. One goal of inclusion is for every school to be ready in advance to accept children with diverse abilities. This may involve not only a change in the way our schools are structured and work but also a change in the attitudes of many special and regular education teachers, who view their job as to educate a certain 'type' of child. Most schools advocate the use of a child-centred approach to education, which implies that all teachers should be willing to meet the needs of all children (Loreman 1999).

Box 1.1: Elements of inclusion

Sailor and Skrtic (1995, p. 423) list the following elements in their definition of inclusion:

- inclusion of all children with diverse abilities in schools they would attend if they had no disability
- representation of children with diverse abilities in schools and classrooms in natural proportion to their incidence in the district at large
- zero rejection and heterogeneous grouping
- age- and grade-appropriate placements of children with diverse abilities
- site-based coordination and management of instruction and resources
- 'effective schools' style decentralised instructional models.

Any teacher who has had experience with children with diverse abilities in regular classrooms will tell you that including these children can be a difficult and complex matter. Teachers need to be highly skilled and motivated to be successful. This is not, however, an argument against inclusion. It is because inclusion demands such high levels of teaching competence and organisational changes aimed at promoting effective learning that it is so important for schools. Improving learning through the development of outstanding educational practice should be a primary aim of every teacher and school (Loreman and Deppeler 2001).

Initially, many of the educators we support through consultation and professional development want two things of us. Many of you reading this book probably have the same questions. Firstly, they want to know if inclusion *really works* in schools. Secondly, they want to know *how to make inclusion work* in their schools. The answers to both questions are complex, and often disappoint those looking for quick, straightforward answers.

Inclusion in schools does not always work. Instances of inclusion not working are well documented (Kauffman and Hallahan 1995b; Fox and Ysseldyke 1997). There is, however, sufficient research evidence to suggest that inclusion, even of children with the most severe disabilities, can work if schools have a culture of shared values and are genuinely committed to improving their practice (Giangreco et al. 1993; Farmer 1996; Yasutake and Lerner 1997; Grenot-Scheyer et al. 2001; Loreman 2001). As an individual teacher you are not always in the position to promote a culture of shared values in your school, but you can improve your own classroom practice to promote better inclusion and in doing so act as an example of what is possible for others. We hope this book will help you to do that.

Box 1.2: Reasons why school inclusion may not work

Rationale   The benefits of inclusion have not been communicated to those involved in the process.

Scope   The changes necessary for inclusion to work are either too ambitious to begin with, or too limited.

Pace   Required changes are either implemented too quickly or too slowly, allowing enthusiasm for the change to drop off.

Resources   Adequate resources are either not provided to ensure inclusion can work, or resources are not allocated in a way that is helpful.

Commitment   Long-term commitment to inclusion is not fostered. It is seen as a 'fad'.

Key staff   Staff members who are crucial to the success of inclusion may be either not committed, or taking on too much of the workload. This might alienate other staff members.

Parents   Parents are not included in the school as collaborators.

Leadership   School leaders are either too controlling, too ineffectual, or do not encourage staff to progress to higher goals.

Relationship to other initiatives   Inclusion is dealt with in isolation from other school initiatives.

(Source: Hargreaves 1997)

The second question from educators, 'How can I make inclusion work at my school?', also cannot be answered easily or simply. Inclusion is context dependent, and as such there is no formula for how to successfully include children with diverse abilities that can be applied to all schools. Inclusion works best with teachers who understand and demonstrate effective teaching and learning practices within a framework of collaboration and support from the school community. Even without that support from the school community, however, there is a lot you can do as an individual teacher to make your classroom more inclusive.

In order to make inclusion successful, you must become good at problem solving. Of course, the problem is not the individual child. Rather, the problem rests with the school and how it is going to meet the needs of all children. Coming up with creative solutions to problems as they arise, based on sound pedagogical platforms, shared values and positive leadership represents the best way for schools and classrooms to become more inclusive. Solving problems often comes naturally to teachers who are called on to solve any number of problems in their interactions with children and adults every day.

Box 1.3: Reasons for successful school inclusion

Rationale All school staff have been involved in the development of the rationale for inclusion and the benefits of inclusion for all students are clearly communicated.

Scope The school has started off small (one or two students) and has been careful to learn from its mistakes and successes before moving incrementally forward to including other students.

Pace The pace of implementation for inclusion will vary from setting to setting. Frequent collaboration with all involved parties and regular review of the pace of change will help to ensure success.

Resources Where extra resources are available they are accessed. Schools also must be creative about the best way to use resources to support inclusion. The provision of adequate resources will help to ensure commitment from those implementing inclusion.

Commitment Collaboration between all parties involved in inclusion will help to ensure long-term commitment. When team members are involved in an initiative they take more ownership of it, and have more of a vested interest in its success.

Key staff Key staff members are viewed as leaders and motivators whose job it is to ensure equal collaboration between all members of the school community. They are not seen as being any more responsible for the success of inclusion than any other staff member.

Parents Parents are welcomed in the school as collaborators, and supported so that their views, knowledge and skills are used and valued by school staff.

Leadership School leaders facilitate collaborative school teams working towards inclusion, support individual team members and ensure that ideas are acted upon.

Relationship to other initiatives Inclusion is viewed as an integral part of general school improvement and relationships to other initiatives are clearly outlined.

(Sources: Hargreaves 1997; McGregor and Vogelsberg 1998)

Questions and concerns from educators about barriers to inclusion frequently include:

- inadequate teacher training
- not being able to deliver an appropriate curriculum for children with diverse abilities
- not having enough resources to help them
- the way their schools and classrooms are organised.

Teacher training

Teachers and researchers often express concerns about training when discussing the abilities of teachers to cater for the diverse needs in inclusive classrooms. Research suggests that these concerns may be well founded.

Secondary teachers in Victoria, Australia, were found to lack the skills required to modify curriculum for children with diverse abilities and were reported to be in urgent need of training in this area in a study conducted by Grbich and Sykes (1992). These teachers reported using curricula that had undergone only a little adjustment, mainly as the result of their own competence, time, and support. A later study by Loreman (2001) found that the situation had changed little in nearly a decade. Westwood (1997) describes the 'tyranny of time' in classrooms trying to include children with disabilities where teachers simply do not have adequate time to plan and deliver sound programs. These concerns have also been raised by Lloyd et al. (1996), who report that teachers in New Zealand were unable to modify curriculum to accommodate the perceived educational needs of children with disabilities despite being aware of those needs. In another study, inclusion was found to fail because, in part, teachers were unable to meet the demands of modifying and delivering an appropriate curriculum to children with disabilities (Fox and Ysseldyke 1997).

Teacher training would seemingly be a solution to this problem. In a study involving teachers in the USA it was found that only 29 per cent of general educators felt that they had enough expertise or training in inclusion (Hobbs and Westling 1998). In light of this and other research findings, these authors suggest that 'the degree of success of inclusion can be related to several factors, perhaps the most important being teachers' preparation, attitudes, and opportunity for collaboration' (p. 13). Australian research into the practice of inclusion found that 'the majority of staff in post-primary schools stressed an urgent need for special training or additional specialist support to help them modify curricula for integrated students' (Grbich and Sykes 1992, p. 321).

A significant concern that might be addressed through further training is teacher attitudes towards children who have diverse abilities. Positive attitudes towards children with diverse abilities are essential to the success of inclusion programs; these attitudes, however, can, and need to, be fostered through training and positive experiences with children with diverse abilities (Hobbs and Westling 1998). Forlin et al. (1996) found that negative attitudes from Western Australian teachers towards children with disabilities increased with the severity of the disability. This negative attitude, however, was found to decrease with teacher experience and further training. Additional training in how to teach children with diverse abilities leads to improvements in individual attitudes and then improvements in the school ethos towards educating children with diverse learning needs (Idol 1997). This takes the focus away from the commonly held belief that the child must change to meet the requirements of the school and places the onus back on the school to become more accepting of difference. It then becomes the responsibility of the school to adapt to personal characteristics of the child, such as severity of disability or perceived 'deficits', and schools with better trained staff are more able to do this (Cosden et al. 1990; Forlin et al. 1996).

While we encourage teachers to undertake extra training when they can, we also believe that due to the uniqueness of every teaching situation, teachers can better learn from each other in a collaborative and supportive school atmosphere. Collaboration with colleagues as a way to better cater for the needs of all children in a school is discussed throughout this book.

Curriculum

Issues surrounding curriculum provision to children with diverse abilities and their peers in inclusive settings are central to successful inclusion (Margolis and Truesdell 1987; Clough 1988; Gormley and McDermott 1994; Carpenter 1997; Cole and McLeskey 1997; Loreman 1997). The idea that children with diverse abilities should be provided with individualised programming has been incorporated into the legislation or policy of almost every Western country (OECD 1994a), and individualised education programs are widely accepted as an appropriate tool for educating children with diverse abilities. Nevertheless, the efficacy and morality of individualised plans are rarely questioned.

Classrooms are now expected to provide instruction in well-defined learning problems related to the specific needs of the child with diverse abilities, while also ensuring that they are included in the regular program as much as possible (Madden and Slavin 1983; Strickland and Turnbull 1990). Under this system, children with diverse abilities may be viewed as being fundamentally different from their peers in how they learn and what they need to know. The paradigm of modification of the regular curriculum is based on a number of assumptions about children with diverse abilities. These include that children with disabilities often learn at slower rates (Ryndak and Alper 1996; Department of Education Victoria 1998), are unable to perform the required assessment tasks (Ryndak and Alper 1996), and often require more practice and repetition to consolidate learning (Department of Education Victoria 1998). Teachers of children with disabilities are seen as requiring specialised training and expert assistance to appropriately educate the child with a disability (Alter and Goldstein 1986; Margolis and Truesdell 1987; Cheney and Demchak 1996).

Supporters of individualised education argue that ensuring a child's specific educational goals are targeted and met can be done through the effective use of an individualised educational program (Manley and Levy 1981; Madden and Slavin 1983; Alter and Goldstein 1986; Strickland and Turnbull 1990; Cheney and Demchak 1996). The overriding principle behind individualised program planning for a child with a disability is to remediate difficulties as efficiently as possible (Pugach 1982; Evans and Vincent 1997). The careful and systematic structuring of appropriate educational goals for a child with diverse abilities through the adaptation and modification of the regular curriculum is viewed by many as an excellent method of providing an appropriate education while also allowing for inclusion in a regular class (Madden and Slavin 1983; Strickland and Turnbull 1990; Cheney and Demchak 1996; Department of Education Victoria 1998).

While modification of curriculum to suit the individual child with diverse abilities is a widely accepted practice, it does have its critics. Critics view this type of process as a means of singling out as 'other' and marginalising people with diverse abilities in order to exercise control over them through special programs (Corbett 1993; Danforth 1997; Evans and Vincent 1997). It is also criticised for presenting children with diverse abilities with a curriculum that is too prescriptive. Such a tightly constructed plan of learning is seen by critics as leaving little opportunity for a child to direct his or her own learning and, as a result, the instruction becomes teacher centred (Goodman and Bond 1993). Individualised goals frequently focus on specific skills rather than cognitive aspects of learning (Weisenfeld 1987; Collet-Klingenberg and Chadsey-Rusch 1991; Goodman and Bond 1993). Often these skills are applicable to only a limited number of situations. There is some evidence to suggest that narrow skill development such as this is the overriding focus of the curriculum for children without disabilities (Collet-Klingenberg and Chadsey-Rusch 1991; Goodman and Bond 1993).

Slee and Cook (1994) advocate change in the school system. They call for a change in the focus of the debate on school failure from the pathological to the interactional. They argue that instead of trying to remediate 'deficits' in individuals, we should be trying to change the system to be more accommodating of children of all abilities.

School cultures are determined by their structural, pedagogical and curricular arrangements, and it was these aspects that became the focus for forging an inclusive and enabling culture for girls and women in education—so, too, with those thought to be disabled (Slee and Cook 1994, p. 22).

The view of Slee and Cook (1994) that schools should be changing to meet the wider needs of all children is supported by Clough (1988), who calls for a reformed curriculum broad enough to suit the needs of children with a wide range of abilities. Clough (1988) sees 'special education' as primarily a curriculum problem and argues 'that it is only through a greater understanding of the curriculum that we may hope to break through to an understanding of individual problems' (p. 327). While these calls for change were made some time ago, they are just as relevant today, as school systems have changed very little in that time.

We believe there is some middle ground to be found in this debate. It is possible to provide instruction targeted towards the strengths and needs of the individual child, while at the same time remaining inclusive in terms of the daily curriculum and activities conducted in a classroom. This book is based on that premise.

School resources

The need for additional funds to be provided to schools for the purposes of educating children with diverse abilities and impairments has long been recognised by researchers (O'Grady 1990; O'Shea and O'Shea 1998). As far back as 1988. Gow et al. (1988) identified 'expensive and often wasteful systems of service delivery' (p. 15) as being one of the barriers to effective integration in Australia. Idol (1997) admits that inclusion programs are expensive, but outlines ways schools can achieve more effective cost accommodations. These include utilising support staff to work with a number of children in a classroom, reconsidering how funds are spent and making changes where possible, using funding from other special programs within the school that already support children with diverse abilities, and site-based decision making. A British study by O'Grady (1990) found that inclusive schools could be more cost effective than special schools through savings on administration and buildings.

Three different models of special education funding delivery in Europe have been identified by Meijer et al. (1999). Two of these models commonly in use both inside and outside of Europe are known as the 'input based' model, and the 'throughput' model. With the input-based model, funding is 'based on need, as determined by the number of children eligible for special needs education according to certain criteria' (p. 80). With the throughput model the 'allocation of money is not linked to particular children but rather to tasks to be carried out or services to be delivered' (p. 80). Both models attract criticism from Meijer et al. (1999), who outline a third model suggesting that funding should be decentralised with schools automatically receiving a level of extra funding proportionate to their entire child population in their global budgets. Local authorities would then ensure that the needs of children with disabilities within schools are adequately met.

There seems to be a perception amongst some teachers that the extra funding provided to support children with diverse abilities is inadequate (regardless of the amount provided), and that an increase in that funding would assist in solving any number of problems they are currently experiencing (Loreman 2001). But is this necessarily the case? Does extra funding improve the quality of the school experience for an included child with diverse abilities? A study of funding in Norwegian inclusive schools examined the effect of varying levels of funding to support children with disabilities from various municipalities (Vislie and Langfeldt 1996). This study found that 'the quality of the organisation seems to influence a school's ability to deliver service as much as the level of resources needed' (p. 69). Vislie and Langfeldt (1996) recognised the importance of schools with a broad educational vision as well as staff that cooperated with one another in including children with diverse abilities effectively. Ainscow and Sebba (1996) also questioned the provision of large amounts of extra funding, remarking that it 'tends to reduce the school's capacity to use support creatively, since it encourages teachers and parents to see assistants as being attached to individuals rather than as a resource for the class or school' (p. 11). A recent study in some Australian schools conducted by Loreman (2001) raised questions about the need for increasing funding to support inclusion. While this issue is currently under further investigation, initial findings indicated that schools receiving lower levels of funding were coping as well (or better) with inclusion than schools with much higher levels of funding.

We believe that while it is true that financial resources are often required to improve inclusion and assist in the daily care and well-being of some children, extra funds alone are not sufficient to ensure successful inclusion. We hope to provide you with strategies for inclusion that do not necessarily require large amounts of additional funds to implement.

Organisational structures

The ways in which our many schools are organised and classes are structured are often not conducive to effective learning for the majority of the children they serve. This is especially apparent in secondary schools (Jorgensen 1998; Kennedy and Fisher 2001). Teachers are often faced with inflexible timetables that schedule them with children for brief periods of time during which little can be achieved, especially with those children who might require longer to complete tasks or to organise themselves to begin learning after transition. In becoming more inclusive, schools will need to examine the ways in which they work. How should children be grouped to enable them to learn most effectively? Ultimately, it is probable that structural and organisational changes made to allow schools to become more inclusive will benefit all children, not just those with diverse abilities (Jorgenson 1996; Jorgensen 1998; Kennedy and Fisher 2001).

While there is often little an individual teacher can do about the way a school is structured and organised, what occurs in the classroom is influenced to a high degree by the teacher. This book will discuss ways schools can be better organised for inclusion while maintaining a primary focus on the individual classroom.

The benefits of inclusion: some myths exploded

The best thing about inclusion is that when it is done well, everyone wins. This includes children with and without disabilities or giftedness, teachers (in terms of improved practice), and the wider school community (in terms of building a more accepting school climate). There are, however, some long-held beliefs that children with diverse abilities will disrupt classes and impair the learning of other children in a class, teachers will be unable to cope with the extra tasks expected of them, and children with diverse abilities will ultimately receive an inferior education and possibly come through the process with damaged self-esteem. A growing body of research, however, seems to indicate that many of these beliefs are founded more on preconceived notions than on any solid experience or evidence. In any case, the benefits of inclusion would seem to far outweigh any disadvantages. The benefits of inclusion can best be examined in terms of outcomes. That is, what is the end result of including children with diverse abilities in regular schools? Positive outcomes of inclusion that have been identified in the research literature are outlined below.

Benefits of inclusion for children with disabilities

There are many benefits of inclusion for children with diverse abilities. McGregor and Vogelsberg (1998), in a comprehensive review of the literature in this area, list these as:

- Children with disabilities demonstrate high levels of social interaction with non-disabled peers in inclusive settings when compared with segregated settings. This is especially true if there is adult support to encourage socialisation, and if children with diverse abilities are included in their natural proportion to the community in general.
- Social competence and communication skills of children with diverse abilities are improved in inclusive settings. This is believed to be closely associated with greater opportunities for social interaction with non-disabled peers, who act as models for children still developing age-appropriate social and communicative competencies.
- Children with disabilities in inclusive settings often have a more rigorous educational program, resulting in improved skill acquisition and academic gains. Some research has suggested that the educational program for children with diverse abilities in inclusive settings is generally of a higher standard than in segregated settings, and children in these settings spend more time engaged in academic tasks and demonstrate improved academic outcomes.
- Social acceptance of children with diverse abilities is enhanced by the frequent small-group work nature of their instruction in inclusive classrooms. Children get to see beyond the disability when working in

small groups, and begin to realise that they have much in common with children with disabilities.

- Friendships more commonly develop between children with disabilities and those without disabilities in inclusive settings. Research has found that children in inclusive settings have more durable networks of friends than children in segregated settings. This is especially true of children included in their local neighbourhood school, where they can more easily see friends outside of school hours. Teachers have also been found to play a critical role in facilitating these friendships.

Other benefits of inclusion for children with disabilities have been noted in the literature. These include:

- Inclusion assists in the development of general knowledge for children with disabilities (Davern and Schnorr 1991).
- Children with disabilities who are included in regular schools tend to become adults who spend more time in leisure activities outside of the home, spend more time in leisure activities with adults without disabilities, and spend more time in community work settings than do their counterparts educated in segregated settings (Alper and Ryndak 1992).
- Graduates from inclusion programs have been found to earn up to three times the salary of graduates from segregated programs, and cost half as much to support in the community (Alper and Ryndak 1992).

The arguments supporting inclusion are compelling. The opposing argument that children with diverse abilities receive an inferior standard of education in an inclusive setting, or are somehow socially disadvantaged, is difficult to sustain. Inclusion, however, has benefits that reach beyond children with disabilities.

Benefits of inclusion for children without disabilities or giftedness

In many ways children without disabilities or giftedness benefit from inclusion just as much as children with diverse abilities. While some have tried to argue that inclusion does not always benefit these children (Kauffman and Hallahan 1995a), the evidence that has been provided to support this notion is largely anecdotal, and is unsubstantiated by the bulk of the research literature. The following benefits of inclusion for children without disabilities or giftedness have been substantiated in the literature:

- The performance of children without disabilities or giftedness is not compromised by the presence of children with diverse abilities in their classes (Sharpe et al. 1994; Davis 1995; McGregor and Vogelsberg 1998).

The perception that children with diverse abilities can disrupt a class is largely unsubstantiated in the research literature. Indeed, one study found that children with disabilities not only spent comparable levels of 'engaged time' during classes as their non-disabled peers, but caused no losses of instructional time. Indeed, losses of instructional time were attributed to administrative interferences, transitions between activities and to children without disabilities (Hollowood et al. 1995).

- Children without disabilities or giftedness can benefit from improved instructional technologies in the classroom (Rogan et al. 1995). Some children with diverse abilities will require the use of technology to help them learn, such as specialised computer software or hardware to assist them in their work. Other children can benefit from the presence of these technologies, and can use them when they are not required by the child with diverse abilities.

- Children without disabilities or giftedness can benefit from increased funds in the classroom. Blackman (1992) argues that extra funds and resources removed from 'special programs' can be used in the regular classroom to enhance the learning of both children with diverse abilities and their peers. These funds can be used in a variety of ways to provide additional learning experiences that benefit all children, such as guest speakers, experiences outside of the school, or classroom-based resources chosen for the child with diverse abilities that are also made available for the use of all children.

- Children without disabilities or giftedness benefit from higher classroom staff ratios (Blackman 1992; Jakupcak et al. 1996). Frequently, extra funding for children with diverse abilities is directed towards the provision of additional staff, either specialist teachers or paraprofessionals. In either case, the presence of an extra adult in the classroom opens up a wide range of possibilities for all children. How these additional staff can be used to benefit all children is discussed in more detail later.

- Children without disabilities or giftedness involved in peer-tutoring situations can benefit from improved self-esteem and mastery of academic content (Alper and Ryndak 1992). These children tend to demonstrate improved self-concept, growth in social cognition and the development of personal principles (Cooper et al. 1986; Davis 1995; Staub and Peck 1995). Furthermore, it has been found that peer tutors demonstrate a higher mastery of academic content in a given area than do their peers who are not involved as tutors (Alper and Ryndak 1992).

- Children without disabilities or giftedness have the opportunity to learn additional skills such as Braille or sign language (Alper and Ryndak 1992). These skills can be taught in a meaningful context and represent an opportunity for growth not often available to children who are not educated with others with diverse abilities (McGregor and Vogelsberg 1998).

- Children without disabilities or giftedness can learn to value and respect children with diverse abilities in inclusive classrooms. They learn to see past the disability or giftedness and the associated social stigmas when placed in inclusive classes (Alper and Ryndak 1992; Gormley and McDermott 1994; Davis 1995; Staub and Peck 1995).

Case study: Angela, aged 16

This case study is presented as a snapshot of a school trying to adopt an inclusive approach to education. It is extracted from a broader study by Loreman (2001), with a school being examined and evaluated in terms of the experience of one child with a disability. While the school has by no means perfected the 'art' of inclusion, it is included here as an example of inclusion being realised at the school level. It is also an example of the need for schools and teachers to be continuously revising and adjusting how they work in order to maintain an inclusive environment.

Student information

Name: Angela

Age: 16   **Year in school:** 11   **Included in school year:** 11

School: Catholic girls secondary (years 7–12)

School region: Metropolitan; lower socio-economic area

School outcomes: Small percentage of graduates attend university. The majority enter the workforce after secondary school, or pursue studies in a technical or community college setting.

Family background: Family immigrated to the city from a non-English speaking country in 1980. Family maintains cultural and language ties to country of origin, while also making an effort to integrate into a multicultural society. Parents employed in blue collar jobs. Both are supportive of Angela furthering her education in an inclusive environment and pursuing leisure interests typical of teenage girls.

Disability: Intellectual. Significant developmental delays noted from early infancy. Full-scale IQ of 60. Receptive language ability at 8-year-old level with reading level at Grade 4. Difficulty experienced in most academic areas, particularly language tasks, visual processing and problem solving. Moderate deficit in short-term auditory memory. Verbal response time of 15–60 seconds (possibly the result of seizure medication).

At the time this study was conducted Angela took a reduced number of subjects towards completing a regular year 11 course of study. These subjects were English, maths, materials technology and information technology. Six double periods per week were set aside as private study time to allow Angela an opportunity to catch up on her work. She used this time either to work on her own or to seek assistance from the special-education teacher. As the school did not employ paraprofessionals, the special education teacher also attended some of Angela's classes with her to provide support. Interviews indicated that untrained volunteers were also sometimes used in classes to provide extra assistance for the entire class, including Angela. Angela was described by her teachers as a pleasant and patient child to teach, although her disability did mean that she frequently required extra attention in class. Once she felt comfortable with a new teacher she would politely request help as required.

Both Angela and staff made mention of the good relationship between children and staff at the school. One staff member remarked, 'Learning, or part of the platform of learning, is that young people develop good relationships with their teachers and with each other. That, I think, is fairly strongly an element of the school.' It appeared that the positive relationship between children and teachers extended to the wider school community, not just those with disabilities. Comments made in a recent survey of past children compiled by the school recognised the support and kindness shown to children by school staff. Angela's mother also recognised the effort school staff have made in supporting her daughter. She remarked that 'she has got the help of [special-education teacher] always, and she is having some extra help at the moment. I can [not] say anything about that school because there is not the money in the world that I can pay them.' While building a good relationship and offering staff support were seen to be important elements at the school, support for Angela also came from her classmates. Angela, her teachers and her mother remarked on how her class supported her. One participant remarked that 'all the girls have been very supportive with [Angela]. They care about her.' This support from the class ranged from understanding that Angela sometimes needed more help from the teacher to actually helping her themselves through informal peer tutoring.

Angela had a very positive attitude toward her school, her classmates and her teachers. She said she enjoyed going to school and was interested in what was being taught to her. So positive was her attitude to school that she made the comment, 'I don't like holidays that are too long. I get bored . . . I was bored in summer. I just wanted to go back to school.' According to her teachers, she was also prepared to attempt difficult tasks before asking for help. When asked what she liked about each of her subjects, the common denominator was that she felt some sense of achievement in each class. She enjoyed making things in materials technology, solving problems in maths and typing successfully in computers. Some staff at the school indicated that an effort was made to treat Angela the same as the other children and to not make her feel she was different. They indicated that although work was modified, an attempt was made to provide Angela with an experience as close to the rest of the class as possible. Some teacher interviews indicated that Angela took responsibility for her own work and would ask for help only after trying to do it herself first. This idea of giving Angela the responsibility of work was also supported in her home.

Angela also viewed the extra help she was getting at the school in a positive light. In particular, she felt that the help given to her by the special-education teacher was a pivotal element in her success at the school, and this view was supported in the interviews with other participants. Angela indicated that spending time with the integration teacher helped her understand difficult concepts and pieces of work. At no stage did Angela mention any kind of perceived stigma associated with getting extra help at school. The special-education teacher at the school performed a number of roles, all of which were reported to be helpful by both Angela and staff. These included acting as a consultant to teachers, coordinating and training volunteers, assisting with modifying curriculum, support in the classroom and direct teaching.

The school claimed to operate within a culture of caring, kindness, and mutual respect and support. When asked about how this culture came about and why the school was a caring environment in which to work and learn, participants in the study had more difficulty in answering. The principal remarked, 'It does come back to relationships. We don't tolerate people shouting at kids and we don't tolerate people being unkind to each other. At the base of that is probably some sort of a notion of justice.' The principal also cited an emphasis on teamwork at the school as a contributing factor to the school culture:

> You're going to use team-based approaches to things. You're going to use . . . group learning settings that are going to recognise the mix of abilities that are within any learning setting. You're going to recognise that the differences amongst people are things that should be celebrated. After all, in a group some are going to be able to contribute really well and provide leadership and rich insights into certain things, where some aren't. Flip the activity around and do something else and it all might be quite different.

Other reasons given for the positive culture in the school included the selection of a caring staff, good leadership from the principal and the fact that the school is a school for girls. One participant felt that because it was a school for girls, more 'feminine' qualities of cooperation and understanding were emphasised. Whether being a Catholic school made a difference to the culture of caring was a matter for debate. Some participants felt the pastoral aspect had no influence at all, while others felt that there was a moderate and positive effect on the school culture.

Angela received a significant amount of help with schoolwork at home. In particular, her mother frequently helped her with her daily homework. Her mother also tried to relate what Angela learned at school to home where possible. One example of this was getting Angela to help with cooking or asking her to read road signs when they were out in the car. Staff from the school reported that this extra support at home gave Angela a significant advantage at school. Angela's mother saw her role as being a support to Angela with her work and also as a source of encouragement: 'My role is to try to encourage her. That is what I try to do always . . . to encourage her to learn.'

The school received special funding in a conventional manner through the Catholic Education Office. Being a Catholic school, and therefore considered by the government to be a private school, the extra funding provided to Angela amounted to about 25 per cent of what she would have received had she attended a public school. While her school could not be considered wealthy, this funding was perceived by only two teachers to be inadequate. Most teachers indicated that resources were adequate to support the learning of Angela and other children with diverse abilities at this school. Given the low level of special funding, however, teachers were often expected to teach Angela with no extra staff support. Generally staff felt that they were able to cope with the specialised assistance required by Angela and meet the needs of the class alone. This was confirmed by brief classroom observations where teachers were seen to be coping with directing the rest of the class while helping Angela. A peer tutor was used in one class, while Angela received some support from a group of her peers in another. One teacher was not even aware that Angela had a disability at the start of the year, but managed to include her successfully into the class with little assistance once she had discovered what her specific needs were. Some staff mentioned time as being a limiting factor. They felt that they could be better teachers both for Angela and the rest of the class if they had more time, because it takes quite a lot of time each lesson to assist Angela and to get her started with work. Sometimes, if the topic was challenging for the entire class, there was less time to spend with Angela. At the time of the study the school was working at some organisational changes to try and assist teachers in dealing with issues of time.

After experiencing difficulties making friends and being teased in her primary-school years, Angela finally made a friend in her first year of secondary school. While she was described by her mother and teachers as always being shy and preferring the company of adults, Angela managed to make more friends her own age as she progressed through secondary school. According to Angela, this was achieved by her making a conscious decision to approach other girls in the schoolyard and through proactive support from school staff. At the time of the study Angela had one 'best friend' whom she saw outside of school, as well as a small group of acquaintances at school. Her best friend was described as being very different to Angela, very outgoing and confident. The girls spent their time involved in common teenage activities such as going to see movies or listening to music. Interviews indicated that Angela was the victim of teasing from other children in primary school and in her first year at secondary school from one child. Teachers dealt with this at the time following a parent complaint. At the time this study was conducted Angela did not get teased and was left alone by children who were not her friends.

The most likely post-school option for Angela at the time of the study was seen by Angela, her mother and her teachers as continuing education through a program for people with disabilities at the local community college prior to entering the workforce. This program has a focus on social and life skills. Concern was expressed by staff members at the school at the lack of post-school options for children with intellectual disabilities such as Angela.

Box 1.4: Ways in which Angela's school was inclusive

- welcoming environment for children with disabilities
- flexible scheduling available, allowing private study sessions
- Angela's available subject choice was the same as for all other children
- assistance provided by special-education teacher and volunteers only as required
- opportunities for formal and informal peer tutoring
- positive staff attitudes towards inclusion
- positive school leadership from principal
- school fostered an ethos of caring and respect for individual differences
- curriculum was modified as required
- friendship development supported by staff
- team-based approach to inclusion was used
- parents involved as partners.

How to include children with diverse abilities in regular schools and classrooms

The remainder of this book is dedicated to providing you with background information, practical advice, tools and strategies to assist you to include children with diverse abilities in your classroom. As can be seen in Angela's case study above, whole-school commitment is an extremely important element of inclusion, and is a preferable context within which to teach, but we understand that the level of commitment to inclusion varies from school to school. This does not mean, however, that you cannot try your best to be inclusive in your own classroom. We hope that the information in this book will prove helpful to you even if you operate in a school that is not particularly committed to inclusion.

As you read further, bear in mind that inclusion is context dependent. Your experience with a particular group of children will be different from the experience of others. This is because schools and classrooms differ from one another in many ways, and the ways in which you teach and structure your classroom will be different from the ways in which other teachers work. Because of this, there is no single 'correct' way of including children with diverse abilities. You will need to decide what is best for the children you teach. We hope that you are able to adapt much of what is written in this book to your own teaching situation as you modify the ways in which you work to become more inclusive.

KEY TERMS FROM THIS CHAPTER

Inclusion   Full inclusion of children with diverse abilities in all aspects of schooling that other children are able to access and enjoy.

Integration   Programs that aim to involve children with diverse abilities into existing classes and structures within a school.

Children with diverse abilities   Children who demonstrate significantly different performance on tasks when compared to the majority of their peers.

FURTHER READING

Foreman, P.J. (2001), *Integration and Inclusion in Action*, Sydney: Harcourt Brace & Company.

Jorgensen, C.M. ed. (1998), *Restructuring High Schools for All Students: Taking Inclusion to the Next Level*, Baltimore: Paul H. Brookes.

Lipsky, D.K. and Gartner, A. (1994), 'Inclusion: What it is, what it's not and why it matters' in *Exceptional Parent*, September pp. 36–38.

Stainback, S. and Stainback, W. (1996), *Inclusion: A Guide for Educators*, Sydney: Paul H. Brookes.

Who are our children with diverse learning needs?

International standards on human rights are based on the idea of full participation of all persons in society on equal terms and without discrimination (United Nations 1993). During the past two decades, equity legislation throughout the world, but particularly in Westernised countries, has significantly affected how schools provide education for all students. These laws address the issue of discrimination and make discrimination on the basis of disability against the law. In education this means that students with disabilities must have the same educational opportunities as others. This chapter discusses definitions and criteria for determining disabilities and the various purposes for diagnosis.

KEY IDEAS IN THIS CHAPTER
- defining disabilities
- disabilities discrimination
- defining giftedness
- do labels really matter?
- standardised assessment: intelligence tests

Definitions

Historically, policy and legislation changes have been influenced by the redefining of disability, particularly during the 1970s and 1980s. Three categories of definitions of disability have been used in education, namely, functional limitations, medical and socio-political (Bernell 2003; Hahn 1985; Jeon and

Haider-Markel 2001). Each definition has a different emphasis and type of policy, therefore each has different financial and support implications for those with disabilities.

Functional limitations definitions emphasise the limitations or inability of the person to perform a particular activity or activities. Definitions can be broad (limited in daily living activities) or narrow (the specific type and amount of employment-related skills the person can perform) (Bernell 2003) and also call attention for the need for occupational training and income support (Jeon and Haider-Markel 2001). Medical definitions emphasise the person's condition, involves an assessment of their medical condition and describes each disability in a separate category, e.g. cerebral palsy, spinal cord injury. Medical definitions require objective measures that determine who does and does not meet the specific criteria for each category. Medical definitions of disabilities have implications for increased expenditures for health care and research and are often supported by philanthropic groups with an interest in particular disabilities (Bernell 2003; Jeon and Haider-Markel 2001). Socio-political definitions emphasise the failure of the environment to adapt to persons with disabilities. From this perspective policy attempts to affect the external environment so that persons with disabilities do not face discrimination (Jeon and Haider-Markel 2001). 'Disabilities are regarded as no different than other bodily attributes such as skin color, gender or age, all of which have been used as a means of differentiation and discrimination throughout history' (Hahn 1985, p. 93).

Box 2.1: Three definitions of disability

Functional limitations   Emphasises the limitations of a person based on their function-ing, and can include occupational capacity.

Medical   Emphasises classification of a person according to objective indicators of health-related conditions.

Socio-political   Emphasises the failure of the environment to adapt to persons with dis-abilities. Emphasis is shifted from the person to their surroundings.

Under the Individuals with Disabilities Education Act (IDEA), the term 'child with a disability' is taken to mean a child with mental retardation, hearing impairments (including deafness), speech or language impairments, visual impairments (including blindness), serious emotional disturbance (hereinafter referred to as 'emotional disturbance'), orthopedic impairments, autism, traumatic brain injury, other health impairments, or specific learning disabilities; and who, by reason thereof, needs special education and related services. Further:

> Disability is the functional consequence of an impairment or change in body or human functioning. The extent to which disability affects a person's life depends very much upon the environments in which a person lives—social, cultural, psychological and physical (*IDEA* 1997).

Definitions make a difference

Definitions of disability affect how problems are defined and what evidence is collected, therefore they determine the alternative solutions that are considered and who participates in the decision making. Inclusive educational policies are consistent with socio-political definitions—a student with disabilities should be viewed no differently to any other student with different physical attributes including race, gender, size, etc.

Example 1: Using medical definitions—special education model

Schools in which policies reflect medical definitions may view a student with a disability as having 'a problem'. Evidence gathered typically involves medical and health professionals in psychological or other 'general assessment and takes place outside of the context in which the learning takes place' (Deppeler 2003, p. 17). A professional, such as a special-education teacher or psychologist, who is considered to have expertise with the problem, typically suggests alternative solutions. Solutions are often similar across schools and involve programs suggested for the particular disability. Finally, the adopted solution may be a program that is delivered separately from the rest of the student's peers. Many of these programs are not consistent with curriculum models being employed within the school and are therefore unlikely to transfer easily to classrooms and integrate with existing school programs.

We believe strongly in the principles of inclusive schooling. We therefore have *not* included the criteria used to define the multitude of categories of disability from a medical approach. When individual students do not make academic progress or continue to be marginalised, the process can often be repeated several times throughout the student's schooling. The process is separate from the school community and therefore has very little chance of success (Deppeler 2003, p. 17).

Example 2: Using socio-political definitions—inclusive education model

In inclusive schools, communication and collaboration amongst teachers, parents and students and sometimes others from the wider community can determine how to reduce barriers for students with disabilities and increase facilitators for learning.

First, priorities are established for the student. Evidence-gathering typically involves interviewing, observing the student in various contexts in the school, and examining student work. Evidence collection may also involve the teacher critically reflecting on his or her classroom practices through video-recording or feedback from a colleague. Evidence-gathering could also include policy-document analysis or observation of school practices for determining the participation of students in social aspects of schooling. In every instance the evidence is critically examined, alternative solutions are generated and decisions made collaboratively. Solutions are likely to be different from school to school as decision making occurs in response to the specific priorities and variables important for that particular school context. 'This model also can involve "expert" professional input but it becomes part of the shared decision-making and in response to the collaborative process—but is not reliant upon it' (Deppeler 2003, p. 19).

What is the legal definition of disability?

The term 'disabilities' as used in legislation can be very broad and include some conditions not usually thought of as disabilities (see Box 2.2), as well as impairments to vision and hearing, speech and language disorders, intellectual and learning disabilities, serious emotional disturbance, physical and multiple disabilities, and other health impairments.

Box 2.2: What is a disability?

The definition of disability as seen by the Human Rights and Equal Opportunity Commission (1994) is typical of those found in the legislation of many countries and has implications for disability discrimination and funding:

- loss of physical or mental functions, e.g. a person who has quadriplegia, brain injury, epilepsy or who has a vision or hearing impairment
- loss of part of the body, e.g. a person with an amputation or a woman who has had a hysterectomy
- infectious and non-infectious diseases and illnesses, e.g. a person with AIDS, hepatitis or TB, a person with allergies or who carries typhoid bacteria
- the malfunction, malformation or disfigurement of a part of a person's body, e.g., a person with diabetes or asthma or a person with a birthmark or scar
- a condition which means a person learns differently from other people, e.g., a person with autism, dyslexia, attention deficit disorder or an intellectual disability
- any condition which affects a person's thought processes, understanding of reality, emotions or judgment or which results in disturbed behaviour, e.g. a person with a mental illness, neurosis or personality disorder.

Disability discrimination legislation aims to eliminate discrimination against people on the basis of disability, to ensure that people with disabilities have a right to equal treatment before the law and to promote community understanding that people with disabilities have the same fundamental rights as the rest of the community (see Box 2.3).

Box 2.3: What is disability discrimination?

The Human Rights and Equal Opportunity Commission in 1994 defined types of discrimination as:

Direct discrimination is less favourable treatment

Less favourable treatment means the person with a disability is disadvantaged and does not have the same opportunity or choices as a person without a disability.

Indirect discrimination is about unfair exclusion

Unfair exclusion happens when a condition stops a person with a disability from doing something. It must be a condition which:

- has to be complied with
- generally people without a disability can comply with
- the person cannot comply with
- is unreasonable in the circumstances.

Discriminatory questions—includes asking for information which

- can be used to discriminate against the person
- would not be asked of a person without a disability in the same situation.

To label or not to label?

The labelling of students by categories of disability is controversial. In order to understand this controversy we must first ask the question, 'Why and for what purpose are children with disabilities to be identified by a label?' Many parents and educators argue that labels are necessary because they provide a common understanding of the needs of the student and therefore students who are not labelled may not be adequately supported. Further, this group argues that labels promote additional funding for students and their families not available to students without disabilities, and for targeted research programs. Other parents and professionals believe that labels are associated with negative stereotypes, harm students' views of themselves and do not directly contribute to the planning of teaching or curriculum for individual students. Further, this group view disability as a socially and culturally constructed concept and the categorisation and labelling of students according to medical and psychological definitions as disabling. Categorisation and labelling may sometimes be helpful, sometimes detrimental. The cases of Ben and Jeff illustrate some of the perceived advantages and disadvantages of labelling.

Case study: Ben, aged 9 years

Ben's mother was concerned that her son was being bullied at school and that he didn't seem to have any friends. She believed Ben was 'gifted' and that because of his advanced development, he found many classroom activities 'boring'. She blamed the school for not providing sufficient challenges. She also believed that it was his giftedness that caused him difficulties in relating to his peers and to speak in an adult manner. Ben's teacher was also concerned that Ben had very few friends. She observed that he only related to his peers on his terms and could be very bossy and inflexible. She believed that his peers thought of him as 'odd'. She believed that because Ben was an only child and his mother was a single parent he didn't have any appropriate male role models and was 'spoiled'. Although he wasn't skilled at any sport, she had encouraged him to participate in team activities. She noted he often became upset when he felt the other children were not playing by the rules. She noted Ben was generally well behaved in class and completed his work. In some areas his performance was of a very high standard (for example, his general knowledge was excellent—he knew lots of facts) but he was very slow with written work and his handwriting was particularly poor. She also noted that he had regular but infrequent episodes, where he became very upset and would scream and cry, when it was very difficult to calm him down. The teacher indicated she did not know what caused these episodes. Ben was referred for a psychological assessment.

The psychological assessment report indicated that Ben's test performance was at average to advanced levels of cognitive development, but his verbal abilities were substantially higher than his non-verbal abilities. It was also noted that Ben had some difficulties in solving socially meaningful problems. Based on these results and in conjunction with the background information provided by Ben's mother and teacher, further assessment of his social competence was recommended. Using the Gillian Asperger's Disorder Scale (GADS), the psychologist reported that Ben's pattern of behaviour indicated a number of features characteristic of Asperger disorder. This is a pattern of autistic behaviour that includes difficulties in relating to peers as well as other people, the presence of obsessive behaviours such as routines or preoccupation with certain topics, and difficulties in the use of language to communicate flexibly with other people. Delayed motor milestones and clumsiness are additional characteristics. Overall, the disorder causes significant impairment in social functioning, yet because of good language and cognitive skills, is frequently not recognised until later in childhood. Ben's mother and teacher felt the diagnosis was helpful in understanding why Ben was having difficulties in school. A change in direction occurred. Rather than blaming Ben and his mother for his 'odd' behaviour, or the school for not providing sufficient challenges, emphasis was placed on *how* the school and home might support Ben in processing information about people and their emotional and social responses and in further developing his social competencies.

Case study: Jeff, aged 8 years

Jeff enjoyed school and had many friends in his classroom. He played with them outside during breaks, and saw them after school and on weekends. Jeff was generally regarded as a 'popular' member of the class by his peers. He was liked by his teacher and was regarded as a classroom leader. Academically, Jeff had many great ideas for projects and always actively participated in class discussions. He was verbally fluent and loved to give oral reports, entertaining his classmates with his humour. Jeff disliked reading and rarely brought books home. He tended to avoid most reading and writing tasks in class. Samples of his writing revealed he could spell only a handful of words other than his name. As a consequence, his written work did not often reflect his understanding of the subject and he was experiencing difficulties completing library research for projects. Jeff was referred for a psychological assessment.

The psychological assessment report indicated that Jeff's pattern of performance was consistent with a diagnosis of 'learning disabilities'. As a consequence, further resources were provided to support him. A teacher aide was funded to work with Jeff in his classroom for two half-days per week. Jeff was scheduled to join a small group for reading support for one hour a day, three times a week, during class time. Jeff indicated to his parents he hated going to the 'dumb readers' group. He complained that his friends never got to sit with him when the aide was there and asked why he 'couldn't do the same group work—like he did before'. Jeff started complaining about stomach pains before school—needing to stay home because he was sick. In class, Jeff avoided doing literacy tasks by telling jokes and disturbing others, or by not having the necessary materials. He began to feel disconnected from what his friends were doing in class when he missed large sections of regular classroom work due to his remedial classes. He was less enthusiastic about class projects and rarely participated constructively in class discussions. Jeff's teacher no longer regarded him as a leader in the classroom. Although Jeff was still popular with many of his classmates, he was viewed by others as a 'boy who was always getting into trouble'. Jeff was involved in several fights on the playground with boys who had apparently teased him about his reading and calling him 'stupid'. Although Jeff made some specific measurable reading gains, his label of 'learning disabilities' resulted in a loss of confidence and social status that went far beyond any reading improvement.

Defining the term 'disability' and the classification and labelling of students into categories of disability remains controversial. Society can place barriers in the way of persons with disabilities, impeding their achievement and full participation. As with *all* students, the fundamental purpose of identification is to support the educational needs of the individual. We need to think of the individual person first—rather than their disability (see Box 2.4).

Box 2.4: *When talking about disabilities…*

Legislation such as US *Individuals with Disabilities Education Act* (IDEA) puts the person first and the use of the term *disability* second. Use expressions that put the person ahead of the disability and avoid expressions that put the person after the disability. As an example:

Use:	Rather than:
the man who is blind	the blind man
the woman who is deaf	the deaf woman
the student with disabilities	the disabled student
the child with physical disabilities	the crippled
the boy with an intellectual disability	the mentally retarded
the girl with learning disabilities	the learning disabled student
the student who is emotional and/or has a behavioural disorder	the mentally ill student and/or the mental patient
the boy who uses a wheelchair	the wheelchair boy
people with and without disabilities	disabled people and normal people

Society can place barriers in the way of persons with disabilities, impeding their achievement and full participation. Handicap is the social or environmental consequence for persons with disabilities—exclusion. If the societal environment is inclusive then the person with disabilities will not have a handicap.

(Deppeler 1998, p. 35)

What is disability discrimination?

In the United States the *Americans with Disabilities Act of 1990* (ADA), the *Individuals with Disabilities Education Act 1997* (IDEA) (Public Laws 94–142;

101–476 and 105–17) and in Australia, the *Disabilities Discrimination Act* 1992 (DDA), address the issue of discrimination and make discrimination on the basis of disability against the law. These laws are aimed at enhancing the quality and equity of education for *all* students.

Students with disabilities must have the same educational opportunities as others. Educators must not make assumptions about what a student can or cannot do on the basis of their disability. If a student can meet the necessary entry requirements of a school, college, university or other training or educational institution, that student must have the same chance as anyone else to study. Students with disabilities also must have access to the same benefits offered to other students, including:

- a positive atmosphere for learning
- camps, counselling services
- choices of courses and subjects (Deppeler 1998).

What is giftedness?

For several decades concepts of giftedness have been associated with controversy. There are those who contend that differences in IQ scores represent a largely genetic and fixed *ability* construct. A more modern view of giftedness is one of developing expertise (Sternberg 1986).

Teachers, parents and others often behave as though giftedness is a single and universally accepted concept. They speak of the 'gifted child' and the 'gifted program'. In fact, there are many different concepts and ways of viewing giftedness. The historical changes in the notions of what constitutes intelligence have been reflected in the beliefs about giftedness, and in the definitions and identification procedures adopted over time. Early notions were one-dimensional and equated giftedness with high intelligence, and the identification of gifted students usually relied on intelligence tests (IQ) or on the actual performance of a high achiever (achievement tests). Modern approaches to intelligence are multi-dimensional. They involve more complex notions of cognitive competency and include multiple components not necessarily assessed in standardised tests, such as Gardner's (1983) theory of multiple intelligences or Sternberg's (1986) triarchic intelligence model. Increasingly, these newer, broadly based views of intelligence are considered across a diverse range of human endeavours and contexts, and across an individual's life span. These approaches provide new insights into ways of identifying and thinking about gifted students. Abilities are viewed as having interactive genetic and environmental components and gifted levels of abilities as forms of developing expertise (Sternberg 1986).

To identify or not to identify?

First, we must ask the question of why gifted children need to be identified. It is usually argued that children who are not identified early may not be adequately stimulated or challenged and therefore their gifts will not develop (Perleth 2000). Identification of both the 'nature and level of gifted students' talents and aptitudes' is also considered important for curriculum and instruction as general educational is far less effective than 'programs that address specific talents and interests' (Feldhusen 2000, p. 271). As with *all* students, the fundamental purpose of identification is to support the educational needs of individual students.

In spite of the growth in our understanding regarding intelligence and giftedness, it is accepted that gifted students may not always be easy to identify. Schools, therefore, should select from a range of different quantitative and qualitative methods to suit the specific circumstances. The identification process can include several methods.

Standardised assessment: what do intelligence tests test?

Individual intelligence tests, such as the Wechsler and the Standford-Binet series, assess an individual's intelligence based on their performance on a set of specific tasks. The relationship between the individual's performance and their age is expressed as a ratio, or intelligence quotient (IQ).

In each standardised test the individual differences are related to mathematically derived factors. Different theorists have developed tests associated with different factors. In spite of the multitude of intelligence tests available, many with similar names for specific factors or abilities, *these tests do not necessarily measure the same abilities*. Part of the confusion concerning definitions of intelligence, and the various tests to measure it, results from the fact that there is no objective method for deciding: *Which abilities should be included on a test to represent intelligent behaviour?* As a consequence, IQs obtained from different tests may not be interchangeable.

It is unlikely that any single intelligence test will ever be capable of adequately measuring all the possible attributes that are classified as intelligent behaviour. Intelligence tests measure only a small aspect of what might be considered intelligent behaviour, and therefore IQ should not be expected to predict all aspects of intelligent behaviour. (Refer to Chapter 3 for further information on psychological assessment and understanding psychological reports.)

Does high IQ predict future academic success?

From the many studies covering a wide range of cognitive abilities it can be concluded that several of the abilities named in various tests appear to relate to academic learning and predict performance in specific subjects. Children with high IQ scores tend to:

- earn higher grades
- have higher scores on achievement tests
- stay in school longer
- be more likely to earn tertiary qualifications (Pendarvis et al. 1990).

This positive correlation between high IQ and indices of school performance is usually interpreted to mean that intelligent children (those who are identified by high IQ scores) learn more rapidly and efficiently and so perform better in school. This interpretation is not necessarily correct.

It is at least as likely that indices such as grades and performance on achievement tests are measures of similar cognitive skills and therefore the environmental and social influences that contribute to high IQ also contribute to high grades and high achievement test scores (Ceci 1990). In other words, environmental and social influences that contribute to high IQ may also contribute to high grades and high achievement test scores.

Environmental and social influences on IQ

Since many of the items on conventional intelligence tests are measures of acquired knowledge, it has been suggested that these tests are a reflection of the child's opportunities through social class and the home environment. These are likely to be far more powerful determinants of future professional and economic success than IQ (Ceci 1990).

Studies have indicated that while intellectually gifted students may demonstrate a weakness and/or average score on any subtest, the variation is often centred on a few subtests (Hollinger and Koesek 1986). For example, in one recent study a group of Australian children appeared to be most advanced on subtests that shared a dependency on accumulated knowledge of general, social and word information (Deppeler 1994).

Different cultural groups may place greater or lesser values on the relevance of acquiring particular types of knowledge. For example, some Australian children may have acquired print and letter knowledge before coming to school. This knowledge may be more advantageous in learning the school-based skill of reading than the sophisticated knowledge acquired by some Aboriginal children about indigenous cultural skills such as story telling (Davidson and Freebody 1986, 1988).

It is important to remember that the same test may make different demands on different individuals depending on their background experiences and opportunities to learn. It is imperative that we consider these factors and how they may affect individual test performance.

Conventional intelligence tests do not need to be completely abandoned; they may still provide useful information about an individual's current and various levels of performance on a set of standardised tasks.

Remember: only use intelligence tests with an informed understanding of their limitations.

Other predictors of outstanding achievement

The results of research clearly show there is no one predictor of outstanding achievement. While high intelligence is necessary for achievement in school it is not sufficient. Outstanding achievement results from a highly complex interaction of individual cognitive, motivational, emotional and personality traits, and environmental factors (Trost 2000). There are other critical components of giftedness that are not assessed by intelligence tests and that are educationally important. Some of these are listed in Box 2.5. Remember though, an individual student's gifted performance may:

- occur in a single content area or be in more than one of the content areas
- persist over their life time or may be more intermittent
- be in one or more areas and they may also have an area in which their performance is more typical of their peers (average performances) or even be more typical of students much younger than themselves (difficulties).

Box 2.5: Components of performance

Learning style

Aspects of individual learning styles of students vary (Dunn and Price 1980; Griggs 1991). Learning preferences and skill patterns may characterise gifted underachievers and learning disabilities among the gifted as well as other students with learning difficulties (Whitmore 1980; Redding 1990; Schofield 1993). Higher academic achievement and more positive attitudes may result when the instructional environment matches the individual student's learning preferences (Dunn 1983, 1989; Yong and McIntyre 1992).

Motivation

Students' management and control of their effort on academic and other tasks have been proposed as an important component of competent performance (Ames and Ames 1989) and regarded as necessary for outstanding performances (Ericsson 1994; Feldhusen 1986; Sternberg and Davidson 1986).

Cognitive and metacognitive strategies

The different strategies that students use for learning, remembering and understanding, and for planning, monitoring and modifying their cognition have been found to foster higher levels of achievement (Brown et al. 1983; Pressley et al. 1987).

Knowledge

The knowledge of a particular area influences the development of effortful strategies and metastrategies, memory efficiency and cognitive competence (Chi and Ceci 1987; Bjorklund and Harnishfeger 1990; Bjorklund and Schneider 1996; Schneider and Weinert 1990). Gifted performances in one area have not always guaranteed gifted performances in another but a large and well-structured knowledge base is considered to be a basic function of all achievement.

(Adapted from Deppeler 1994).

Complex identification

Students may give indications of advanced ability, but not perform to that indicated potential. The teacher and/or parent may request testing or assessment of abilities by a psychologist or guidance officer. These students are often referred to as underachieving (Whitmore 1980; Redding 1990). Students may not always be able to demonstrate their capabilities through gifted performances for a variety of reasons, as suggested in the case studies following. (Refer also to the 'Observation and investigation' suggestions later in this chapter.)

Case study: Quynh, aged 9 years

Quynh is a new arrival in the country. She is a talented and creative poet and story-teller. Her English written composition and oral language may not always reflect her creative ideas.

When examining a piece of writing from a new arrival or a student for whom English is a second language, teachers may need to look beyond the obvious because the student's written expression may not express the depth of the ideas they wish to convey.

Case study: Stephen, aged 12 years

Stephen's levels of ability are very uneven. His performance in non-verbal, spatial and reasoning areas is well in advance of his peers, he has many excellent ideas for construction when using Lego and has good computer skills. However, Stephen has had a history of middle-ear infections and still experiences marked difficulties in retaining and processing auditory information, particularly in noisy environments. This is reflected in his written language and other literacy competencies, which are much less advanced than most of his classmates. He is often distracted during listening and literacy activities in the classroom and is said by his teachers to be 'disruptive'. Stephen is less likely to be disruptive and more likely to demonstrate gifted performances in 'hands on' learning environments where he is actively involved.

When the learning environment does not match a student's preferred learning style or when the learning activities are either 'too easy' or 'too difficult', the student will most likely be off-task and disruptive.

Some students have not had the same opportunities for learning before coming to school as many of their classmates. This may have occurred for a number of different reasons, the most common including:

- economic disadvantage
- family attitudes towards traditional schooling
- disruptive family circumstances
- gender bias in the available activities
- a cultural background that is very different from the context of the classroom.

Case study: Sally, Martin and Angelique, aged 8 years

Sally has not had the same social opportunities as many other children for developing friendships. Martin and Angelique have had limited literacy experiences, and no opportunities to use a computer or to use construction materials such as Lego. As a consequence, these children may not have acquired knowledge in a number of areas relevant to the curriculum. Sally, Martin and Angelique may not be able to demonstrate gifted performances until they have had adequate exposure to particular activities.

Teachers need to identify the content knowledge that may be a prerequisite to particular activities as a part of planning for their students.

Case study: Matthew, aged 11 years

IQ and achievement testing indicates Matthew is intellectually and academically well in advance of his peers. He is a reflective adolescent and a talented artist who also enjoys music and sport. Matthew generally has a very slow rate of productivity and is inclined to complete the minimum for most of his class assignments. His 'underachievement' appears to be directly related to his level of *interest*. He is highly motivated, and consistently demonstrates gifted performances, in only a narrow range of art, music and sporting activities. Matthew also needs additional time to complete and select activities.

Gifted performances may only occur when a student is motivated to achieve because of their special interest in the activity.

Is it important to use the gifted label?

Categorisation and labelling may sometimes be helpful; they may also have detrimental consequences for even well-adjusted and able students. The cases of Carl and Narissa illustrate some of the perceived advantages and disadvantages of labelling.

Case study: Carl, aged 11 years

'Before I had an assessment and they said I was gifted or somethin' . . . I was always gettin' in trouble. After me Mum got me tested the teachers let me do some different work. I got to use a video camera for my report and 'cause my writin' and spellin' aren't very good, I also get extra time on the computer. I used to hate school . . . I like some of the science stuff. Hey! I did a real cool project with capacitors an' resistance and I won a prize at Science Talent Search.'

(Source: an interview with Carl, who has a history of difficulties with literacy learning)

A student who may have previously been viewed and supported on the basis of a negative label, e.g. behaviour problem and literacy difficulties, might receive benefit from being seen as gifted.

Case study: Narissa, aged 14 years

'*Gifted and talented.* The three words that, in the past two years have turned my life upside down. Since being assessed, expectations of me have never run so high. Teachers who had never paid too much attention to me started watching me like hawks. My parents to this day continue to quip "all we ask is that you do your best". Nevertheless, the fact is that what they consider to be "my best" has changed. I have found myself pushed into extension programs, seminars and workshops for able students. I now live in constant fear of Individual Differences Departments, who have given me *too much attention and too much extension* . . .

'So parents and teachers alike, my advice to you would be to let your kids be kids. Nobody needs to live with a label. Use extension only if it is sought, or else it will be wasted. Be prepared to help extend your child but don't pressure them to achieve any more than they have been. Encourage, but don't push. I lived the first 13 years of my life without a label and for that I am truly grateful.' By Narissa, an able and talented teenager.

(Source: *Gifted and Talented: Blessing or Curse? Parenting Strategy,* Krongold Centre, September 1995)

Labelling can have detrimental consequences for even well-adjusted and able students.

Learning environments that promote gifted performances

Students are more likely to demonstrate gifted performances in a learning environment that:

- supports and encourages the exploration of different learning styles
- provides a wide range of enriching learning experiences
- allows students to extend their learning in areas of interest, including breadth and depth as well as opportunities to accelerate their learning
- includes supports or scaffolds for students in areas where their performance is 'average' relative to their performances in other areas
- provides a curriculum that is flexible, integrated and responds to student diversity.

What can I learn from the classroom?

Teachers have many opportunities to observe students engaging in teaching and learning sequences. Some instructional practices may result in a student displaying a gifted performance, other instructional practices may not; some may facilitate a student's engagement and learning performance, while some may indeed place barriers and reduce a student's opportunities for engagement and learning.

The important question is not whether a student can be classified as gifted or having a disability but rather: 'How do the instructional practices in my classroom affect the engagement and performance of the students? What evidence can I collect in order to answer this question?'

Observation and investigation

The regular and careful observation of student behaviours can provide a number of starting points for teachers in determining what may be contributing to a student's engagement or performance in the classroom. All of these starting points will need further investigation. Teachers may observe any of the following situations and can investigate further by following the suggestions in brackets.

Situation:	Investigate:
• a student's performance is advanced (faster or at a greater depth) compared to that of his/her classmates.	→ student's performance with a more challenging curriculum

Situation:

- a student experiencing literacy difficulties may need structured support to access content or be given alternative ways for displaying their knowledge, otherwise they may not be able to engage or demonstrate gifted performances

- a student's effort and motivational output may vary across subjects and learning formats and can have a direct effect on their performance

- a student's interest in a particular learning sequence is more likely to result in increased engagement and improved performance

- a student's breadth and depth of knowledge will influence their application of problem-solving strategies and their level of performance.

- more positive attitudes and higher academic achievement are likely to result when the individual student's preferred learning and/or thinking styles matches the instructional environment

- the strategies students use for learning, remembering and understanding for planning, monitoring and organising their learning can enhance higher levels of performance; conversely, students who may have advanced understanding but who are lacking in organisational skills may not be able to demonstrate their competencies.

- a student's social skills can prevent or enhance collaboration, performance and engagement with peers

Investigate:

→ the use of scaffolds to support writing, reading or cooperative learning on engagement and level of performance

→ student's performance across different activities and topics

→ the student's preferred activities outside school interests through observation and interviews

→ the student's prerequisite skills and knowledge—what opportunities has the student had to learn about the particular topic?

→ the level of student's engagement and performance across activities that require different kinds of student input, e.g. listening, talking, active construction, drama, analysis, etc.

→ whether the student knows *how* to do the task? Does the explicit teaching of the requirements and/or steps for completing a piece of work improve performance?

→ whether the student has the social competencies to engage and perform in the activity

Teachers need to carefully consider all of these aspects when making identification decisions based on individual student performances. Observation of these student behaviours is also of crucial importance when designing teaching and learning sequences across the curriculum (see Chapters 6 and 7).

The challenge for the future

The field of gifted education is changing along with the field of special education and disabilities education. Our conceptions of intelligence have changed along with a shift in focus: from categorical labelling and separate education to a more responsive approach to individual students within the social context of their schools.

The challenge is to respond positively to *all* student performances, including individual excellence, within a context that values diversity.

KEY TERMS

Disability   Is the functional consequnce of an impairment or chang in body or human functioning.

Diability Discrimination   Is less favourable treatment or unfair exclusion on the basis of a person's disability.

IQ Intelligence Quotient   The relationship between an individual's performance on a standardised intelligence test and their age is express as a ratio or IQ.

FURTHER READING

Katzman, L. (2003), 'Minority Students in Special and Gifted Education' in *Harvard Educational Review*, 73(2), pp. 225–39.

Seigel, L.S. (1999), 'Issues in the definition and diagnosis of learning disabilities: A perspective on Guckenberger v. Boston University' in *Journal of Learning Disabilities*, 32(4) pp. 304–24.

Attitudes and inclusion

Teaching is one of the few professions that brings the professional into contact with the whole range of children from five through to 16–18 years of age. The only exceptions to this range are a very small group of children enrolled in special facilities due to the seriousness of a physical, psychological, cognitive or health impairment.

Since the policy of inclusive schooling, and its forerunner policies 'integration' and 'mainstreaming' were implemented, some of those same young people who formerly would have been educated in a special facility will now have been enrolled in their local, regular, school. The result is that teachers have a much wider range of children and young people with whom they deal.

Teachers can build up expectations of behaviour within the age groups because they interact and observe them over long time spans. Other professions know how clients or patients are likely to behave only within their narrow realms of focus, but teachers are second only to parents in terms of observing children in natural environments. Their opinions then about children should be both realistic and informed.

KEY IDEAS IN THIS CHAPTER
- attitudes—what they are
- values
- ideologies
- facing disability
- realistic planning

Is history repeating itself?

The policy of inclusion is in a sense a return to the original concept of universal compulsory education for all. In the state of Victoria, Australia, for example, the 1872 *Education Act* made it mandatory for all children of a certain age to be enrolled in a school. The Act stipulated that it should be *all* children and that education should be free, compulsory and secular. Regrettably, the Act also set out that children were to progress through the grades following an end-of-year examination on the work that was supposed to have been covered during the year. If a child failed to progress they were held back to repeat that year, and so on until they passed. Further to be regretted was the policy that teachers would be paid according to how well they had done their job, a payment by results system. The outcome was that children with disabilities, especially those with impairments that affected their learning, were not progressing, and teachers were becoming frustrated by the lack of progress and its consequent effects on their salaries and promotion prospects.

The Act was amended in 1874 and children who were deemed 'ineducable' could be excluded from the requirement that they attend a school. A medical doctor in Moonee Ponds, a suburb of Victoria's captial Melbourne, had a daughter who was included in the group who could not attend a local school. After failing to win government support, he set up a private special facility in 1881 for his daughter and other children in similar situations. Only after the success of this venture became evident did the idea of special-education facilities to cater for those excluded from the normal provisions become officially accepted—in 1907. It has taken almost a century to see the original concept of the importance of education for all in regular schools to be reintroduced and become, once again, official policy.

This increase in range confirms the fact that teachers are now likely to see more diverse children and young people, irrespective of their physical state or condition. This is almost unique amongst professional groups. Of the other professions one could say that dentists see the range, but only when dental treatment is called for; GPs see the range, but only when the children are sick or injured; only teachers see the same children for significant amounts of time, five days a week.

Despite the changes in official policy, the changes in enrolment patterns in most schools will be relatively small. The numbers of children with disabilities new to regular schools are probably less than five per cent overall and teachers can reasonably expect that the children or young people they teach will be healthy, normally functioning and able. The majority of the population of children and young adolescents develop according to well-known processes and in predictable patterns. Even if there is a significant disability it will affect only part of the person. Intellectual disability may affect learning and social competence but physical development is unlikely to be seriously affected. Nevertheless, two questions need to be asked:

- What barriers are likely to prevent a teacher addressing the educational needs of the one or two children whose developmental patterns or medical histories differ from the majority and how can a teacher make sure they then progress?

And, very importantly:

- What is the key to ensuring that a teacher is comfortable or professionally secure in approaching the task of running an inclusive classroom?

The answers to these questions come back to thinking about the attitudes with which teachers approach their tasks. There is obviously a need to consider the professional aspects associated with practical organisation of the classroom, the planning of lessons, modifications of curricula, and the evaluation of learning (see Chapters 4, 6, 7, 8 and 9), but most important is the need to consider the attitudes of teachers to those who are different.

Positive teacher attitudes are essential to making inclusion work (Sharma and Desai 2002), but our attitudes are based on a number of underlying components discussed in this chapter. If we are to maintain a positive attitude ourselves, and assist others we work with also to develop positive attitudes, it is important to recognise and understand these components.

Attitudes

Attitudes are basic and pervasive aspects of human life. Without the concept of attitude, we would have difficulty construing and reacting to events, trying to make decisions, and making sense of our relationships with people in everyday life (Vaughan and Hogg 2002). Our attitudes are made up of the groups of feelings, likes, dislikes, behavioural intentions, thoughts and ideas we all have about the people and things we encounter in our everyday lives. They can, however, be thought of as a threefold entity comprising thoughts, feelings and actions. How widespread this grouping of the three aspects is in our thinking is commented on by McGuire (1989), namely:

> The trichotomy of human experience into thought, feeling and action, although not logically compelling, is so pervasive in Indo-European thought (being found in Hellenic, Zoroastrian, and Hindu philosophy) as to suggest that it corresponds to something basic in our way of conceptualization,

perhaps . . . reflecting the three evolutionary layers of the brain: cerebral cortex, limbic system, and old brain (p. 40).

Irrespective of their source, our attitudes clearly affect our thoughts, our feelings and what we do; indeed, it could be said that they actually determine what we think, feel and do. They are relatively permanent and the more we know about a person's attitudes the more we can predict how he or she will behave in relevant situations. Allport (1954) suggested that an attitude is basically a readiness to respond in a particular kind of way, but attitudes also are very emotional, because they reflect the ways we evaluate people (including ourselves) and things. They guide us in deciding whether we like or dislike someone or something and whether we are going to approach or avoid whatever has attracted our attention.

Attitudes are very important to us. They serve the same function as stereotyping and categorisation of people or events. They help us make sense of the world. We use them as short-cuts in helping us decide how to react to things that happen in our lives, or to people we meet, or to political questions we must answer.

Attitude formation is a direct result of the socialisation experiences we have had since our childhood, and come about as a result of the experiences we have had in life, the information we have picked up from other sources, or as a result of our own thinking processes. Because they are learned rather than innate, they are just as amenable to change as any other learned behaviour.

Values

Underlying our attitudes is our system of values. Similar to attitudes, values are enduring beliefs about what is right, and about what principles of living ought to guide our behaviours. They exist 'in the mind' but they show themselves in the way we behave and in the way they influence our emotional responses to events.

Values are concerned with life goals rather than being beliefs about the specific things or events or people to which our attitudes relate. They refer to overriding concerns about what is right in life and play a major role in the establishment of personal goals.

The philosopher Richard Robinson (1964) argued that there are five basic values that should guide one's living: life, beauty, truth, reason and love. Another philosopher, James Griffin (1986), suggested they should be: accomplishment, autonomy, liberty, health, understanding, enjoyment and deep personal relations. There are no universally accepted lists of values but irrespective of whether we can consciously describe them, our values serve to give a structure to the attitudes we hold.

Our values can change. Sometimes events occur that challenge the values we hold and challenge them in such a way that we just cannot go on living in the same old way. Take the case of someone who suffers a major loss. This loss could be the death of a spouse or a child or a close friend. It could be that one loses control of a bodily function, or loses a limb, or is diagnosed with an illness that is progressive or chronically debilitating. The challenge to us as the person involved is that the value we once placed on the love and comfort of the lost one, or on being independent, healthy and whole, is no longer applicable and we must come to terms with the newly experienced loss or absence. We feel devalued. Accepting the loss means we need to move from the *devaluating* position to one of viewing it as *non-devaluating*. This is not the same as saying we just resign ourselves to the facts, or we just ignore them. It means that we need to make changes to our value system.

If we take the case where we have to come to terms with significant changes to our physical systems, how can these changes come about? Let us take the example of the loss of a limb and use the fourfold analysis of value change advocated by Dembo et al. (1956) and outlined in Wright (1983).

First, we know that during periods of crisis, one's psychological and physical resources are focused on the loss itself. This shock reaction, or period of mourning, is a time when the realisation dawns that the things we once did, without thought, are now denied to us. How intense these feelings are and how long they last cannot be defined, as the reactions are very personal and deep seated. The period of mourning is, however, important in that it gives time to prepare for the challenges involved in successfully managing the transition from what *was* to what *is now*.

Second is the need to enlarge the scope of one's values to see that what has been lost can be replaced by values that are not dependent on the use of the limb; that one's personality need not change and that values such as kindness, wisdom, effort and cooperativeness still apply. To achieve this aim, physique and its importance to us must be subordinated relative to other values, that is, the sense of devaluation of ourselves will diminish insofar as personality and other aspects of personal traits become more important.

Third, there is a need to recognise that the newly acquired disability does not necessarily influence everything we do. It may be a physical fact with effects that are far-reaching but the physical facts relate only to specific things we can or cannot do. They do not define us, and even if they are an impediment to doing some things, these impediments may well be due to societal barriers as much as they may be due to personal limitations. If the loss means we now need a wheelchair to get around, we have to learn how to negotiate barriers that once we could ignore. Dembo et al. (1956) call this third stage 'containing disability effects'.

Fourth is a demand that we aim for a transformation of comparative status values into asset values. Comparative status values refer to those attributes of a person that are looked at, by them or others, in terms of a scale of better or worse. This means that whatever is being judged (be it beauty, physical strength, intelligence) is seen as being 'below' or 'above' a presumed standard, with the distinct possibility that perceptions of other characteristics of the person are also being judged by the same measure. Therefore, where the focus may be on appearance, there is the tendency to think that where the person is 'above' on the main characteristic, that is, 'more attractive than most' then he or she must also be brighter, stronger and nicer than other people. The alternative is to look at physique (or any other characteristic) not in terms of its comparative status but in terms of its usefulness or intrinsic value. The focus is on the value of the attribute, not in comparison to other people, but to the person. A prosthesis or a wheelchair can be appreciated for its usefulness without inherently indicating dysfunction. Although we applaud winners and tend to ignore those who come second, not every event in life can be rank-ordered. For some contestants, just to compete may be reward enough. Perhaps the last word should go to Shakespeare:

In nature there's no blemish but the mind;
None can be called deformed but the unkind:
Virtue is beauty, but the beauteous evil
Are empty trunks, o'erflourished by the devil.
(*Twelfth Night, Act III, Scene 4*)

Ideologies

Just as important as values are the ideological views we hold of what life should be about and how society should be organised. Ideological statements, sometimes referred to as philosophical statements, concern the overall goals for a society or group. Two commonly opposed ideologies concern the differences between those who believe that individual freedoms override the demands required by national security irrespective of the political conditions prevailing at the time and those who do not. We can also think about the ongoing debates about private ownership versus government ownership of public services.

Policies of inclusion are related to the ideological view that schools should provide for the needs of all the children, whatever the level of their ability or disability in their communities. These issues are those espoused by governments that have introduced the formal policies on which inclusion is based, but as

Foreman (2001) points out, there is no specific requirement that teachers agree with the policy, just that they must be prepared to provide for the needs of all students in their grades irrespective of any diagnosis of 'difference'. Clearly an attitudinal system and ideology that are in sympathy with the overall aims will make for better outcomes for all concerned.

Just as important in ensuring inclusive practice works is the underlying belief that all children can learn and be taught. This is a major principle that goes right against the ideas that led to the development of special-education provisions and places major responsibilities on schools to adjust programs to reflect its utility. Previous approaches to education included categorising children as being either educable or ineducable. Behind this system lies the implicit belief that we should not waste education on those who will not profit from our efforts. The principle that all children can learn and be taught, however, must be seen in light of what it does not say as much as in light of what it does say. The principle does not say that all children can learn at the same rate, nor in the same volumes. In Chapter 4, on assessment, we make the point that individual differences in many areas can be identified and that these differences are likely to have some effects on how children learn. The tests that show up these individual differences do not say that learning cannot take place. They can guide teachers in determining just what should be taught and the time frames that may be needed in order to achieve acceptable levels of achievement.

Facing disability

Differences of the sort that set challenges to teachers range from the frankly obvious, as in conditions such as cerebral palsy or spina bifida meningomyelocele or Down syndrome, to the not so obvious, as in learning disability and some forms of intellectual disability or developmental delay or giftedness.

Although we can be, or pretend to be, blasé about any or all of the more obvious disabilities, it is rare for anyone to be able to approach individuals with a frankly obvious disability without pause. So threatening to our self-image are some forms of disability that we can find ourselves trying out any one or more of a series of strategies to deal with our very private and very personal reactions. We may try to withdraw from interaction, at least in public places.

Imagine yourself in a shopping mall in the food hall and you see a friend or reasonably close acquaintance with another person. You begin to walk towards them but suddenly notice the other person is clearly disabled and being fed by your friend. It is not a usual sight and you pause; it is not often you find an adult or adolescent being fed in public. You recall that your friend has taken on a part-time role as a carer of persons with serious disabilities. You begin to wonder if you will go ahead and greet them. To withdraw in this way is to deny the fact of friendship, but we justify our behaviour by repressing anxious thoughts about being unfaithful to our friend. After all, we really shouldn't interrupt our friends while they are working!

You find that you cannot withdraw but must interact with the person with your friend. In that case it is tempting to go overboard in one's willingness to be introduced and begin a conversation. False bonhomie, effusiveness and over-reacting are common techniques to hide embarrassment and we use them often. Freud called this sort of response a *reaction formation*, that is, an unconscious impulse is consciously expressed by its behavioural opposite. By such means, 'I hate you' is expressed as 'I love you'. Or we might try to be jokey and look for a laugh—humour can be very close to the truth and it helps deflect our anxieties about what and how we should react.

Even those who have chosen to go into occupations where interaction with people with disabilities is the norm need time to build up resources and skills to be able to initiate and maintain normal personal relations. How medical students react to seeing their first cadaver in anatomy classes has been the subject of considerable research, but once they get over their initial shocks they must get on with their dissections and learning (Dinsmore et al. 2001). In this example, and in any work that involves close interaction with 'difference', the ability to get on with work is accomplished by the adoption of a professional 'distance'. The focus is placed on the task or on an aspect of the individual that prevents the ego of the professional person feeling threatened. With experience, they can cope with making the distinction between the problem and the person, a task made easier for medical professionals because of the constancy of their work.

Medical professionals, though, do not have the last say on how to interact with persons with disabilities. The Medical School at the University of Bristol in the United Kingdom has introduced workshops in communication, led solely by presenters who are themselves disabled, in which students are encouraged to talk about their own experience of disability (Wells et al. 2002). The presenters cover a range of disabling conditions including visual, speech, hearing and learning difficulties, and the direct teaching by disabled presenters is said by the students to have been highly valued. Their list of key teaching elements is divided into three sections, of which attitudes is number one, followed by skills and knowledge. First topic on the list of subjects dealt with in the seminars is a consideration of the students' own attitudes, including their emotions, values and reactions to disability and persons with disabilities.

Unlike medical students, teachers are not usually accustomed to dealing with frank difference in the same way medical students must be prepared for it. Our expectations about the young people with whom we deal are that they will be essentially healthy, 'all together' and whole. That is what characterises the majority of persons found in normal populations, and normal populations are the basis of a teacher's regular life. But the policies of inclusive schooling mean we must be prepared to face the fact that, sooner or later, we will find that not all our students meet standard health, or physical, criteria. It is in relation to these students that we need to consider our reactions and personal behaviours in the way we think about them.

How does one react to a frank or obvious disability?

Being brought face to face with obvious and serious disability threatens our sense of security and makes us feel anxious. Being faced with reminders that not every person is a 'perfect example of a normal body' can lead to a desire to ignore the facts and deny the existence of impairments/disabilities. Such attitudes are evident in communities where residents object to the fact that a bus with the words 'Spastic Society' or 'Crippled Children's Society' on its sides drives down their street each day to collect or return a neighbour's child for school. How difficult is it for most people to talk to a person in a wheelchair?

Our natural reactions in life include screening out disturbing information and focusing instead on something that does not threaten our sense of wholeness. Whether it is because we are generally unfamiliar with how to talk with a person who is obviously different, or whether we somehow identify with the person and imagine how it would be to have the same affliction, or whether there is some deeper psychological reason for our discomfort, may not be known. What is known is that it is quite common in considering persons with disabilities to focus on the impairment as if it was the only important thing about that person. Warren (1980) comments that 'the testimony of authors writing from the perspective of handicap very frequently draws attention to the fact that it is "the other" who creates significant problems; very often physical difference seems to concern the observer more than it does the subject' (p. 79).

Although these reactions may be common, perhaps normal, they disguise the fact that we are thinking of ourselves, not of the person with the disability. Our thoughts may cover a multitude of emotions that may include pity, concern, worry, disappointment or even revulsion, but such reactions are a *projection* of our own insecurities, not emotions the person stirs in us.

Healthy emotions are addressed to the person; they see beyond the impairment to the person (Greenway and Harvey 1980). The impairment that causes the disability does not define the child; it defines only a part of the child. Bodenheimer (1974) describes a deaf and visually disfigured girl in psychotherapy and her progress towards coming to terms with the disfigurement and the disability:

> This fact is of principal importance to the therapeutic attitude in the situation described here. The child was able to attain distance towards *something*, could talk about *something*, and thereby distinguish herself from *something*. This *something* always meant something that could be casually referred to as 'suffering' only until she was able to convert or transmute that *which she herself was* into something she *had* or *has* and would from now on and always, irrevocably and unchangeably, have and keep. The basic change lies in the fact that she now *has it* and no longer *is it* (pp. 107–8).

The anecdote sums up the experience whereby the child was able to develop a self-image that was not dominated by the impairments and disfigurement; an outcome achieved by the therapist focusing on her and not her appearance. That indeed is the key to coping with those first reactions to impairment, disfigurement or obvious indicators of disability.

Go back to the earlier section in this chapter in which we introduced Dembo et al.'s (1956) analysis of value change (p. 42). That same process applies as much to an observer as it does to the person with the disability. The first reaction of an observer to frank disability is often one of shock, an affront to our expectations as we adjust our perceptions so that we are neither unreasonable nor unrealistic in terms of our expectations for this child. Second, we need to appraise the situation and avoid taking this one characteristic as an indication of all other aspects of this person. Physique, if the problem is physical, must be subordinated relative to other values that characterise this child. Third, the programming side of the teacher must take the physical status and the whole environment into account to see that impediments to learning are not due to the physical structures or systems of the school. The disability may be a fact of life but countering its effects is the task of the teacher. Fourth, we need to look at asset values pertinent to the child and hold back on conveying to this child or the class any idea that he or she is disabled and therefore 'unabled'.

Once the child is seen as a person the same as others in the group, the focus moves from the disability to the person who wants to learn. The teacher's task is to find the ways whereby the things to be learned can be achieved; a task that may require modification of curriculum materials or reorganisation of the room, or whatever. The important issue is that the values underlying one's commitment to the tasks of teaching are not compromised.

Plan realistically

There is no intention here to suggest that the way to cope with meeting disability is to deny its existence or its effects on a person's capacity to learn or interact in the social setting of the school. No good purpose will be served if the fact of the disability is denied. What is intended is that the child's needs be seen in realistic fashion without the overlay of emotional investment that will disguise the true extent of individual difference or ways in which the disability has led to handicap.

Warren (1980) notes the word 'handicap' has an interesting history. It appears to derive from the construction 'hand in cap', which related first to a lottery game in the seventeenth century in which stakes to be forfeited were held in a cap in the hand. In the eighteenth century it became the term applied to the act of penalising the better horse in horse racing, and from there it became a noun to define the actual penalty itself. In modern times it has become more generally used to convey the notion of disadvantage. Warren noted that 'all original senses of the term involved penalty or disadvantage in a *contest*; a rather ominous notion for human existence in contemporary times, and one that has some obvious support—we even speak colloquially of the "rat race"' (pp. 77–78).

The etymology of the word allows us to see the child with a disability as fighting against the odds. How high those odds are depends on many factors, of which type and severity of impairment are two of immediate concern. Irrespective of these factors, the principle of the teacher's role as assisting the young person not to allow the problem to impede development is attractive. The metaphor does not lie only with the child with the particular disability; in the inclusive classroom it allows a picture of the teacher monitoring the learner, all learners, irrespective of physique, internal bodily systems, psychological adjustment or intelligence.

Inclusion does not mean that handicap does not exist. If a disability handicaps performance in any significant way then in those areas a specific attack needs to be made on how the problem can be overcome. This may mean modifying curriculum demands and hence the need for a critical, objective assessment of skills and strengths that can be built up. It may mean devising and teaching strategies the child can use when faced with the situations they find difficult. Focusing on these practical aspects of the learner's needs will have the effect of lessening thinking about the disability and more on the achievement of goals and increasing abilities. It will also change the teacher's attitudes. Inclusion will be seen not as an insurmountable challenge but as a process of learning that affects everyone in the class and school. Modifications of a program to suit one individual will be found to benefit others as well, and inclusion will lead to greater satisfaction for all.

Irrespective of the emotions we may experience in meeting with people with disabilities or getting to know them well enough to see beyond the superficial appearances, when it comes to making classrooms work there are two overriding attitudes that matter most. The first is the belief that all children can learn. The second is that teachers who believe they can make a difference, do.

KEY TERMS FROM THIS CHAPTER

Attitudes   The groups of thoughts, feelings and actions that affect how we react to individuals and to groups of people.

Values   What we think is right and proper and the long-term basis on which we make decisions.

Ideologies   Our beliefs about what life should be and how society should be organised.

FURTHER READING

McGuire, W.J. (1989), 'The structure of individual attitudes and attitude sytems' in *Attitude Structure and Function*, A.R. Pratkanis, S.J. Breckler, and A.G. Greenwald eds, Hillsdale, NJ: Erlbaum, pp. 37–69.

Vaughan, G.M. and Hogg, M.A. (2002), *Introduction to Social Psychology*, Frenchs Forest, NSW: Pearson Education.

Psychological and teacher-based assessment

Assessment is part and parcel of teaching. In its broadest terms, assessment concerns the determination of whether learning has taken place or whether further instruction is required. In the case of children with disabilities it is also likely to involve formal assessments of intelligence, language, and neurological or motor development. Teachers need to know what to make of the different pieces of information and recommendations emanating from such assessments, information usually provided in the form of written reports, sometimes supplemented by personal communications between the teacher and the person who carried out the assessment.

From the teacher's point of view reports vary considerably in terms of both content and quality. This wide variation is due to the different audiences writers have in mind and the different reasons for the assessments in the first place. A report by a paediatrician could have been written for another medical specialist or a general practitioner and contain numerous terms and expressions that mean little to anyone outside those professions yet the report could still contain information that a teacher could use.

This chapter is divided into two sections, the first dealing with formal assessments, which are usually conducted by psychologists, the second with teacher-based assessment you can use in your own classroom.

KEY IDEAS IN THIS CHAPTER
- intelligence tests—what are they and what are they good for?
- components of the most common intelligence scales for children
- qualitative assessment
- teacher-based assessment
- curriculum-based assessment
- portfolio assessment

Educational reports

Educational psychologists will produce many of the reports used by schools. Teachers can expect that the content of these reports will be classroom friendly and contain information directly useful in understanding individual children and planning curriculum activities. If this is not case, then teachers should contact the report writers to clarify what is written and/or ask further questions about the meaning of the results for their classroom.

A lack of recommendations about how the report's information can be directly used in the classroom does not mean the writer doesn't care about the outcomes. It may well be due to a reluctance on the part of the professional writing it to interfere with the professional responsibilities of the teacher. Most professionals recognise that what can be accomplished in the one-to-one setting in which most formal assessments are conducted will not be so easy where a teacher has to think about the needs of 20+ other children at the same time. The best way to overcome this difficulty is for the teacher to talk with the professional concerned and to build up a partnership in which the different perspectives can be joined to best meet the needs within particular classrooms.

Most psychological reports for children with disabilities are based on intelligence test and formal academic-achievement test results. It is important that teachers understand the purposes of these tests and how their results can be applied in their classrooms.

Intelligence tests

The first piece of information a report will give will be a statement saying why the assessment was done and what tests were used in the process. This information is useful in that teachers can be sure that the matters they are concerned with will have been addressed.

The next piece of information to be gleaned from a psychological report will be the test results. This section of a report will give the teacher two types of information, the first being the formal test results and the second being the personal impressions formed by the psychologist while the testing was being conducted. We will look at the formal or quantitative aspects of assessment first, then consider the qualitative impressions.

Most educational-testing reports will show a composite score for the intelligence test administered as either the Full-Scale IQ or the General Intellectual Ability score or the Composite Standard Age Score. Which of these is reported will depend on the test used. The Wechsler Preschool and Primary Scale of Intelligence (WPPSI), the Wechsler Intelligence Scale for Children-III

(WISC-III), the Wechsler Intelligence Scale for Children-IV (WISC-IV) and the Wechsler Adult Intelligence Scale-III (WAIS-III) all yield a Full-Scale IQ. If the Stanford-Binet Intelligence Scale, Fourth Edition (SB-IV), the Standard-Binet Intelligence-Fifth Edition (SB-V) or the Woodcock-Johnson III Test of Cognitive Abilities (WJ-III) are used, there will be the equivalent of an IQ termed Standard Age Score.

The IQ is an important item, but if not properly understood it can be very misleading; indeed, it is because of its ambiguity that the SB-IV and the WJ-III no longer use it—they have replaced it with the term Standard Age Score (SAS). IQ is a term that has been in use for the past 100 years and it continues to serve the same purpose now as it did in the beginning. The mathematical equations have changed but to all intents and purposes nothing else has. An IQ is a statistical device for identifying where, on a continuum that works in two directions from a midpoint defined as 100, an individual compares with his or her same-age peers on a cognitive-ability test. The 100-point is the average of the population on which the test was put together and is itself based on the notion that the results of measuring most naturally occurring phenomena amongst a large population sample will plot onto a normal curve.

The normal curve

The normal curve, sometimes referred to as the bell curve, (see Figure 4.1) allows us to make comparisons between people because when we know a person's score (or test result) we can know not only whether that individual is below or above the average but also how far below or above it they may be. In order for this to be true, the test norms must have been based on the results of a properly organised and selected reference group that is similar to the population with which we work. When we are sure the original population is similar to ours, then we can use the norms and compare how well our person has performed relative to others of the same age.

Most people score fairly close to the average point, with smaller numbers of scores tapering off towards the tails of the spread. How far the numbers spread can be found by calculating the standard deviation of scores from the average. Once we know this standard deviation, and in the case of intelligence tests we do, we know more accurately how far from the average an individual's IQ is. Because approximately 68 per cent of the population is within the limits of one standard deviation below or above the average, 68 per cent of the population will have an IQ between 85 and 115. Approximately 14 per cent of the population will have IQs ranging from 116 to 130, with another 14 per cent having IQs ranging from 70 to 86, that is, their scores will be between one and two standard deviations from the average. The remainder of the population, approximately 4 per cent, will be found three (or more)

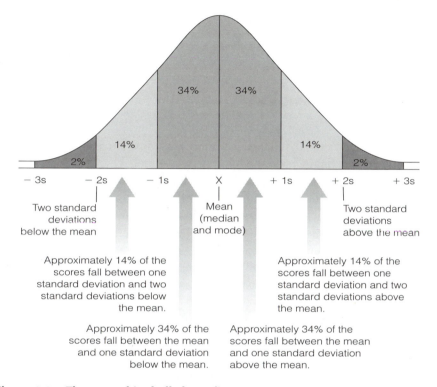

34%   34%

14%   14%

2%   2%

− 3s   − 2s   − 1s   X   + 1s   + 2s   + 3s

Two standard   Mean   Two standard
deviations   (median   deviations
below the mean   and mode)   above the mean

Approximately 14% of the   Approximately 14% of the
scores fall between one   scores fall between one
standard deviation and two   standard deviation and two
standard deviations below   standard deviations above
the mean.   the mean.

Approximately 34% of the   Approximately 34% of the
scores fall between the mean   scores fall between the mean
and one standard deviation   and one standard deviation
below the mean.   above the mean.

Figure 4.1:   The normal (or bell-shaped) curve

standard deviations either below or above the average, that is, they will have IQs below 70 or above 130.

The reports sent to schools may show single-figure IQs (see Figure 4.2) but the information teachers should take most notice of is the 10-point range, for example, 95–105 rather than 100, that all reports should include. Using this range to report IQs acknowledges that the score obtained at any specific time a test is administered cannot reliably be judged as entirely accurate. If the same test was given on another day, the individual is very likely to give slightly different responses, be a little slower (or faster), may be a little more tired (or alert), or may just feel better (or worse) than the other time. These variations are natural, they are planned for, and they do not invalidate the general trends in cognitive ability that intelligence tests show.

Some reports may talk about 90 per cent or 95 per cent confidence intervals and explain that we can have 90 per cent or 95 per cent confidence that the true score for this person is somewhere within that 10-point range. This information, while correct, need not bother too many teachers. It is a further

If the mean is 3.0 (X = 3.0) and the standard deviation is 1.0 (s = 1.0) the scores are as follows:

0.0	1.0	2.0	3.0	4.0	5.0	6.0
(− 3s)	(− 2s)	(− 1s)	(X)	(+ 1s)	(+ 2s)	(+ 3s)

Figure 4.2: Single-figure IQ scores

acknowledgement that all intelligence-test results must be treated as indicators of ability, not the final word on what a person can do.

The practice of not using a single-figure IQ is important because the single figure hides the fact that there is much naturally occurring variation in human performance. This lack of understanding leads to many thinking that an IQ obtained at one point in their life defines their intellectual status, and many other things about them, for ever afterwards. This is not so, and there are many reasons why some people's IQs will vary tremendously over time. These reasons could include differences in home life, effects of illness or neurological trauma, changes of country or changes in educational opportunities, to name just a few. An IQ needs to be interpreted in the light of many different factors.

Box 4.1: What does an IQ tell us or not tell us?

- An IQ does *not* tell us anything about a person's emotional state—although emotional states can and do affect performances on intelligence tests.
- An IQ does *not* tell us anything about a person's motivation to do (or not do) well at any given task—although lack of motivation will adversely affect a person's performance on a test.
- An IQ does *not* tell us anything about how a person copes with problems in living, such as relationships, money worries, career aspirations or a host of similar factors.
- IQs indicate, relative to age, how well persons can analyse and problem solve, how good their memories are, to what extent they are able to exercise good judgment and how well they can deal with abstractions.
- IQs are important for teachers because the things they tell us about a person's cognitive abilities are about skills and abilities that are important in traditional school-type work.

Percentile ranks

Another item or column on the opening page of an educational report based on intelligence tests records the results in terms of percentile ranks. A percentile rank is a way of showing how well an individual has performed on the test compared to others of the same age. This way of reporting assumes that if 100 randomly chosen people from the same population and age took the test, then the result of one person reported as a percentile shows how many people in that group of 100 would score higher, and conversely, it shows how many would have scored lower.

- If the IQ was 100, then that person would be at the 50th percentile; half of the group would have scored higher and half lower.
- If the IQ was 115, he or she would be at the 84th percentile; 16 people in the comparison age group would have scored higher and 83 would have scored lower.
- If the IQ was 85 it would be at the 16th percentile; 84 would have scored higher and 15 would have scored lower.

Percentile ranks reflect the fact that approximately 68 per cent of the population cluster around the average point, with the spread between scores in that cluster pushing people close together, but as the extremes are reached the distance between points on the scale becomes greater.

- An IQ of 105 is at the 63rd percentile and an IQ of 109 at the 73rd percentile, a difference of 10 percentile ranks but only 4 IQ points.
- An IQ of 127 is at the 90th percentile and an IQ of 145+ at the 99.9th percentile, a difference of 10 percentile ranks but 18 (or more) IQ points.

IQs above 145 are all accorded a percentile rank of 99.9 or >99.9 in recognition of the fact that such high scores are quite rare. It is not normal for percentile ranks to be reported in a range but the same caveats about variation in test results still apply.

The pieces of intelligence

Since Alfred Binet's time much research has gone into understanding and measuring the development of intelligent behaviour, and the original Binet–Simon test (see Box 4.2) has been extensively revised. Although the global or composite score is usually reported and the information can be taken as a useful indicator of overall ability, it is rarely interpreted as anything more than that. Teachers need specific information about a child's cognitive abilities in planning school activities, much more specific than is available from a single score.

If a Wechsler scale (other than the WISC-IV) or the SB-V are being used it is quite common for two further IQs to be reported: a Verbal IQ (VIQ) and a Performance IQ (PIQ). These two IQs are also useful indicators of ability in the two domains, but the information found in the separate indexes will be more helpful.

Box 4.2: A little piece of history

The first intelligence test published by Alfred Binet and Theodore Simon in 1905 in Paris yielded a single-figure IQ, all that was then required. Binet's work took place at the time that universal compulsory education for all children was being introduced within the Western world. One outcome of that movement was the realisation that children do not all learn at the same rate and that schools needed to take these different patterns of learning into account. Schools at the time were not able to react to this need and selected individuals were often deemed to be incapable of learning in regular classrooms. For many, it was decreed that they needed to be catered for in special, usually institutionalised, settings.

Binet's test was devised to classify those who should be in regular schools and those who should not, in the light of educational practices of the time, be enrolled.

Binet was not just interested in keeping children out of regular schools if it seemed they could not cope with their demands—he was also concerned to ensure that children wrongly considered ineducable were not denied the opportunity to learn. In one institution looking after the needs of 25 children in Paris he identified five who were incorrectly diagnosed as 'idiots', the term then used to describe those with severe intellectual disabilities.

Modern versions of intelligence tests break their results down into discrete categories of cognitive skills. When grouped together they form clusters of subtest scores that can be reported as Standard Age Scores. These clusters have a mean of 100 and standard deviations of 15 and can be interpreted in much the same way as an IQ. Different tests have different names for the types of intellectual behaviours involved but they are usually quite similar in content and all have direct relevance to teachers and teaching.

Underlying the different categories is the idea that there are a number of different abilities that make up intelligence. We cannot at this time be certain about how many there are, but some of the more commonly accepted ideas include the concepts of 'crystallised intelligence' and 'fluid intelligence' (Cattell 1963). Crystallised intelligence relates to the way we can recall and use information built up over time and that is relatively stable. Knowledge of words and history and social comprehension come into this category. Fluid intelligence refers to mental operations that we use when faced with novel tasks that we cannot react to automatically. Two other important concepts are 'quantitative knowledge' and 'speed of mental processing'. The use of numbers and being able to perform mental operations on quantities are seen as qualitatively different from other mental operations, hence quantitative knowledge is seen as a separate aspect of intelligence. Speed of mental processing combined with eye–hand coordination is also seen as a separate intellectual requirement.

The Wechsler scales

The Wechsler scales, the most used intelligence tests in clinics and schools, have four clusters of subtest scores called indexes. They are a sufficient illustration of how useful these separate scores can be and illustrative of how valuable, separate aspects of intelligence can be to teachers. The four are a Verbal Comprehension Index, a Perceptual Organisation/Perceptual Reasoning Index, a Processing Speed Index and a Freedom from Distractability/Working Memory Index. When reading a report on a WISC-III, WISC-IV or WAIS-III assessment, these four index scores need to be checked out to see what information they can provide teachers.

Verbal Comprehension Index

This score is based on subtests that measure verbal conceptualisation, general knowledge and expression of ideas verbally, and serves as a measure of crystallised intelligence. To do well on this section a student must be able to comprehend what is involved in listening to an oral question and be able to answer it by calling on knowledge stored in long-term memory. It also involves the ability to look at common objects, or ideas, and see how different classes or examples can be linked in some, usually abstract, manner. For example, a desk and a couch are related in that they are both items of furniture. These abilities are closely linked to reading, writing and oral expression, all of which are important in class activities. The subtests are all sensitive to socio-cultural and language influences.

Perceptual Organisation/Perceptual Reasoning Index

This index is based on activities that test non-verbal and visual motor co-ordination, all aspects of fluid intelligence. To do well, a student must be able to look at visual stimuli, which may be pictures in a comic book or a coloured design, and then manipulate a series of pictures or blocks or parts of a puzzle to make a complete story or a specific design. In every case the objects can be manipulated, either mentally or physically, in a manner that will allow the student to see when a correct solution has been found. The tasks must be completed within set time limits and the student is aware that they are being timed. These subtests set problems of a kind not usually taught in school, but the information they convey about the attitudes of a student, or the mood at time of testing, and the ability to work within time constraints yet still concentrate on the tasks, is important. They also indicate whether there are any major visual–perceptual problems that may need further investigation.

Processing Speed Index
This index uses subtests which indicate speed of thinking and ability to process information, manipulate whatever is important about it and recall details in order to complete a task. This index is related to concentration on written tasks, an activity closely related to schoolwork. Completing these tasks is related to the kind of attention and sense of mastery of symbolic material that a successful student needs. Failure suggests that teaching strategies aimed at improving writing speed and planning may be required.

Freedom from Distractability/Working Memory Index
This index is concerned with the ability to deal with numbers and similar material presented orally, the ability to manipulate the information mentally, and not to be distracted by other noises, movements or ideas. The numbers or word-based problems need to be handled sequentially, and for successful completion a student must have an adequate non-distractible attention span. The tasks involve working with numbers, as in solving mental arithmetic problems or recalling strings of numbers and repeating them in correct order. There is a clear link between these tasks and schoolwork.

The four index scores enable a teacher to work out where an individual student has particular strengths and where there are weaknesses that may need following up. They may also enable a teacher to understand why instructions aren't always followed, or why errors are made in the placement of words on a page or figures in a column of arithmetic problems. If each index is considered separately, a clear picture of a student's academic performances can be built up with consequent clues about where curriculum emphases should be placed.

Stanford-Binet area scores

The Stanford-Binet Intelligence Scale, 4th Edition, is a test that is used often, either as the first test of choice or as a check to the results obtained from another, such as a Wechsler-based instrument. The SB-IV is in the process of being superseded by a new fifth edition with some different subtests but with the same overall purposes. It is strongly recommended that between the administration of any single intelligence test there be gap of at least two years. This precaution overcomes the possibility that children can learn how to do a test, with the consequence that the second test is likely to be influenced by the earlier experience and yield invalid results. Sometimes this two-year period is unrealistic and in such cases a second test is called for. A Stanford-Binet Intelligence Scale, if not used as the primary test form, serves the purpose well.

The SB-IV and SB-V yield a composite score that, as with a Wechsler Full Scale IQ, serves as a general indication of level of intellectual performance.

The area scores are the ones of most use to teachers. They are similar to the Wechsler index scores.

Verbal Reasoning/Knowledge
This section tests crystallised abilities and, as with the Wechsler Verbal Comprehension Index, gives the student the chance to use pieces of information and ideas picked up over their earlier years. Formal schooling, reading, talking with people, thinking about things that happen in life, all contribute to this area score. It is a good indicator of how well a child has learned before starting school and during their school life.

Abstract/Visual Reasoning/Visual Spatial Reasoning/Fluid Reasoning
These scores reflect fluid intelligence and use geometric shapes and figure-based symbols to set problems to be solved. To do well it is important to be able to see what is presented, visualise images, cope with different shapes and work out novel ways to solve problems. Few school activities relate to these tasks but they can indicate levels of confidence and motivation to succeed.

Quantitative Reasoning
Quantitative, Number Series and Equation Building comprise this subset and as with Verbal Reasoning is believed to test crystallised intelligence. The Examiner's Handbook suggests that this area score can be interpreted as 'an academic ability factor' because of its value as a predictor of outcomes in schooling. It requires a capability with numbers and arithmetic, and the ability to make sense out of randomly presented material.

Short-term Memory/Working Memory
Short-term memory/working memory is assessed with visually presented material and orally presented material. Successful completion requires attention and the use of visual or verbal strategies for information storage, retrieval and recall. It is closely related to much that goes on in classrooms.

A report based on the SB-IV or SB-V should include a discussion of all the areas and comment on the individual's strengths and weaknesses.

Qualitative assessment
Administering a standardised intelligence test is something educational psychologists do very often. The concept of standardisation means that the test is always given in the same order, using the same instructions and the same equipment. These rules are needed in order to allow fair comparisons between people in the same age groups.

The same standardised test rules also mean the psychologists administering them are able to note behaviours of people being tested and to assess whether, in the tester's judgment, there are behaviours that would invalidate the test results. Such observations are more than just a validation or confirmation of the test outcomes, for through making these observations the tester can learn a great deal about the personality of the client. Delaney and Hopkins (1987) describe the administration time as a clinical interview in itself, 'a conversation guided by a purpose' (p. 89). The insights gained from the administration, informed by the experiences of the tester with similar-aged children, can often yield useful information that can be passed on to a teacher. Some examples of the kind of informal assessments, in this case taken from the SB-IV, that can be made include:

- attention—was the child absorbed in the task or easily distracted?
- were activity levels normal or overactive/hyperactive?
- did the child initiate activity or wait to be told?
- was the child quick to respond or was urging needed?
- did the child appear socially confident or insecure?
- was the child realistically self-confident or distrustful of ability?
- was the child persistent or easily discouraged?
- was the child needing minimum of commendation or needing constant encouragement?

In many cases teachers will note the comments in a report and be able to recognise that that is exactly how the child operates in their class. Such confirmation is useful, as are any new insights the report yields. How useful these insights can be is illustrated by Delaney and Hopkins (1987):

> . . . while testing one child, an examiner made the important discovery that this six-year-old had obviously learned how to avoid the effort of problem solving by manipulating a question-and-answer session. The examinee's teacher later confirmed that she was so sympathetic with the examinee's inability to respond—she looked like she was trying so hard to respond—that she would go on to another child. This examiner's insight was more important to future behavior modification than the examinee's ability score. And during the test session the examiner used this insight and refused to allow the examinee's strategy to succeed. The examiner eventually determined that the examinee's ability was substantially above that which might otherwise have been assumed (pp. 89–90).

Achievement tests

Intelligence or cognitive-ability tests are useful indicators of general ability but teachers also need to know about significant strengths and weaknesses in school achievement. There is some controversy, however, about the value of cognitive-ability tests that measure processes underlying learning to identify where specific teaching is required in order to overcome obvious weak areas. There is no doubt, though, about the value of achievement tests to show the outcomes of teaching in terms of the specific skills required in order to do well in school. There are numerous tests used to measure these skills. For illustration, we will look at the Wechsler Individual Achievement Test (WIAT-II).

Wechsler Individual Achievement Test (WIAT-II)

This test was designed to measure academic achievement of students from the first grade in school to senior secondary school and is directly linked to the WISC-III in a way that makes it very useful in matching expected levels of achievement with intelligence scores. It is a test that covers oral expression, listening comprehension, written expression, basic reading skill, reading comprehension, mathematics calculation and mathematics reasoning. The test scores can be used to assist in the diagnosis of problem areas and guide the teacher in planning curriculum interventions.

Reading

The reading scores are based on three categories. Word Reading assesses phonological awareness and decoding skills, as in naming letters of the alphabet, identifying and generating rhyming words, matching sounds with letters and reading aloud from a graded word list. Reading Comprehension reflects reading instruction in classrooms including matching written words with their representative picture, reading passages and answering questions about the content, and reading passages aloud and answering comprehension questions. The third, Pseudoword Decoding, assesses the ability to apply phonetic decoding skills by reading aloud a list of nonsense words designed to mimic the phonetic structure of words in the English language.

From these reading-related subtests, and all the other subtests in the WIAT-II, a number of scores are generated allowing comparisons for each child by age and/or by grade. These scores include: a Standard Score (mean = 100, standard deviation = 15, both the same as the WISC-III and WISC-IV); a percentile rank indicating the number of individuals of the same age or grade who scored the same or lower; and an age or grade equivalent score.

Mathematics

The mathematics section assesses skills in numerical operations and mathematical reasoning. Numerical Operations consider the ability to identify and write numbers in one-to-one correspondence counting, solving written problems and solving equations in addition, subtraction, multiplication and division. Mathematical Reasoning tasks look at the ability to count, identify geometric shapes, interpret graphs, identify mathematical patterns, and solve problems related to statistics and probability.

Written Expression

There are five written expression tasks. The results of these subtests show teachers the value of the kind of information that can be obtained from tests like the WIAT-II. Alphabet Writing counts the number of lower-case letters written in 15 seconds. Word Fluency counts the number of words able to be generated in 60 seconds. Sentences assesses how well one sentence combines two or more smaller examples into one, or how well a sentence can be made up following exposure to verbal or visual stimulus items. In the paragraph task the student must demonstrate a grasp of the mechanics of Paragraph writing, good organisation and sensible use of vocabulary. Essay is a task in which the mechanics of an essay, the organisation of argument, the development of themes and the use of vocabulary are individually assessed. The actual tests administered are based on age and grade level but only children in grades above Grade 6 are administered Word Fluency, Sentences and Essay.

In relation to Essay, the marking sheets enable analysis by four categories. They are: Mechanics—spelling errors, punctuation errors and multiple spellings; Organisation—sentence structure, topic sentence, sequencing, linking words and phrases, as presented in a letter to the editor that uses introductory sentences or paragraph, has a concluding sentence or paragraph and uses the organisation of the essay to persuade the reader; Theme Development—the essay has at least three supports for the position taken, contains evidence to back up the argument, keeps to the topic, makes an argument rather than just answers a question, and contains counter-arguments; Vocabulary notes whether words used are specific, or varied and if unusual expressions are used to capture the reader's attention or add spark to the writing.

Not only does the WIAT-II give a report on the actual achievements of the examinee with nine individual subtests as well four composite scores (reading, mathematics, written language and oral language) and a total composite score, it also enables a direct comparison between the scores on each with the score that could be predicted from the WISC-III or WISC-IV intelligence scale. This information, called an Ability–Achievement Discrepancy Analysis, identifies where a difference is significantly different in terms of the proportion of the general population that also show this same pattern of results. The implication of this difference and level of variation from the general population is that where it is significantly different then that is an area requiring some form of intervention in school.

The WIAT-II does not give information that is not potentially available to any teacher. What it does is categorise performance on the different skills in a way that few teachers have time to do. Informally, but without being able to give a formal diagnosis, a teacher may know many of the things about a student that the tests display. That does not mean the testing is wasted time, because the test results allow the teacher to formalise his or her thinking about students and their specific attributes. Once this is done, then program or curriculum matters can be attended to in a much more informed manner. To have one's impressions of a student confirmed by a formal assessment can boost a teacher's confidence. If there is anything unexpected in the results, then this too can be turned to professional advantage and the ensuing changes in classroom programs can be to everyone's benefit.

Teacher-based assessments

While formal intelligence and achievement tests can be useful for gaining extra funding for students with diverse abilities, and in some instances for assisting with programming, they often do not help teachers discover what a child already knows and what a child needs to learn in relation to the curriculum. In order to successfully program for any student, teachers must first know the 'starting point' from which they can teach. The best way for teachers to discover what their students know and can do is through teacher-based assessments. There are some commercially produced assessments available for teachers to use; however, the most effective assessments for the classroom are often those developed by individual teachers themselves.

Remember that the results of assessments can be used in two ways:

- to compare a child's performance to other children his/her age
- to compare a child's performance to his/her own past performance.

Inclusive classrooms are those which primarily compare a child's progress with his/her own past performance in a variety of different areas across the curriculum. These are the most helpful types of assessments for teachers. Consider the standardised intelligence tests discussed earlier in this chapter. They can provide a teacher with information on general ability trends and provide a percentile rank and IQ score, but they do not tell a teacher much about what exactly needs to be taught. A combination of curriculum-based assessment and portfolio assessment can be helpful in giving teaching and learning some direction.

Curriculum-based assessment

The concept of curriculum-based assessment is now well established in many education systems, and is widely used as the basis for measuring the performance of all students in a classroom regardless of their ability. While curriculum-based assessment is recognised as good practice generally, it is also an excellent means of assessing the progress of diverse learners.

Curriculum-based assessment involves using curriculum objectives as a basis for measuring what a child is able to do. In some parts of the world where the curriculum is highly structured and prescriptive, the task of curriculum-based assessment is made easier. In Edmonton, Canada, for example, teachers in the public school system teach using what is known as the 'Program of Studies'. This outlines what is to be taught in each school year, and breaks the learning goals down into smaller objectives for teachers to teach. In this case a curriculum-based assessment is made easier because a teacher simply needs to match a child's performance with the criteria outlined in the Program of Studies. In other parts of the world curriculum is more flexible and teachers have more scope to invent their own teaching goals and objectives based on contextual factors, which include culture, location, resources, and student background and development. In these instances a teacher would need to create his or her own set of criteria in order to conduct a curriculum-based assessment. What you will need to do in order to conduct curriculum-based assessment will depend on your own situation and the requirements of the education authority you work for.

Salvia and Hughes (1990) suggest these eight steps when conducting curriculum-based assessments:

1 specify reasons for decisions
2 analyse the curriculum
3 formulate behavioural objectives
4 develop appropriate assessment procudres
5 collect data
6 summarise data
7 display data
8 interpret data and make decisions.

1 Specify reasons for decisions

Teachers should be able to justify what they do in every area in which they work, including assessment. In order to conduct a worthwhile assessment the teacher should be able to outline why the assessment is being done, why this method has been chosen for the assessment, and how the outcomes of the assessment will be used.

Decisions will need to be made throughout the assessment process, and these decisions should always be justifiable in terms of their consistency with good educational practice and the classroom context in which the decisions are being made.

2 Analyse the curriculum

Whether your curriculum is highly structured and prescriptive (as in the Canadian 'Program of studies' example discussed above), or more unstructured and at the discretion of individual schools or teachers, you will need to conduct an analysis of the curriculum you use to determine what is to be measured. This involves methodically working through any curriculum documents and identifying exactly what skills, knowledge and attributes a child is expected to have developed in order to be considered as having 'mastered' that curriculum area or topic.

Depending on the nature of your original curriculum document, these skills, attributes and knowledge areas may need to be listed on a separate piece of paper as follows:

Example: Skills, knowledge and attributes identified from this week's mathematics curriculum topic of 'sorting'

- children should be able to sort beads according to colour
- children should be able to sort beads according to shape
- children should be able to sort beads according to size
- children should be able to work out which 'odd shape' bead does not belong in a particular group of like beads.

3 Formulate behavioural objectives

Once you have determined what children need to learn according to the curriculum, you can begin to set some specific behavioural objectives. Behavioural objectives are discussed in greater detail in Chapter 6; in brief, however, a behavioural objective sets the parameters for your assessment. A good behavioural objective will tell you exactly what a student needs to demonstrate, where, when, how often and under what conditions, in order to be considered to have 'mastered' a skill, knowledge or attribute area.

A behavioural objective for one of the identified areas in the example above would include what the child needs to demonstrate along with any other factors that would contribute to the child being considered to have 'mastered' the curriculum objective. It could be recorded as follows:

Example: A behavioural objective

By the end of the week children will have demonstrated that they can sort four different coloured beads according to colour three times during Friday's mathematics class. Colours will be interchanged and will include red, brown, yellow, blue, white, black, green, purple, pink and orange.

This type of objective can be easily measured. Either the child does demonstrate the ability to sort the beads three times on Friday or he/she does not.

4 Develop appropriate assessment procedures

Once you have outlined *what* you are going to assess, you will need to decide *how* to conduct the assessment. Classroom assessments generally work best when they are conducted within the natural context of classroom activities. Classroom assessments that involve more 'formal' types of approaches, where the child is removed from the learning context, tend to be disruptive. The child should demonstrate the acquisition of skills, knowledge or attributes in the context in which he/she has learned it.

Based on a qualitative research technique known as 'triangulation' (Denzin 1978), it has been suggested that a thorough curriculum-based assessment should involve assessment over three separate days using three separate types of 'test' (Taylor 2000). While this would be an ideal situation and would most certainly result in the development of a better picture of a student's true mastery of an area, it is impractical for the modern inclusive classroom. We believe that in an inclusive classroom, usually with well over 20 children, the reality is that most teachers would only have the time to conduct a curriculum-based assessment on a particular area on one or, at best, over two occasions. This is acceptable as long as teachers are aware that this results in a more limited view of a child's true learning.

Box 4.3: Classroom assessment procedures

Some ideas for conducting assessments include:

- when conducting an activity with the whole group, ask all children to demonstrate the skill at the same time. Observe them and check off names on a checklist
- arrange children to work in small groups. Over the course of a lesson visit each group and ask that they demonstrate the learning task. Keep track using a checklist
- during time set aside for individual work, visit specific students individually at their desk and conduct the assessment
- ask the children to submit that which demonstrates mastery of the content and/or skills you have been teaching (e.g. models, written essays, drawings, diagrams).

---

5 Collect data

In order to show that a student has demonstrated learning you will need to collect data. This data is essentially the results of any tests or observations you conduct in order to evaluate the performance of the student. Examples of the types of data you can collect include:

- observational data based on the results of structured, randomly timed observations
- observational data based on anecdotal observations
- written, oral or practical classroom tests
- 'task analysed' checklists (see Chapter 7 for a more detailed account of the use of task analysis)
- assignments that have been submitted.

According to Deppeler (1998), observation is arguably a teacher's most important tool in planning and implementing curriculum for supporting students with disabilities and impairments. Regardless of whether background information is current and detailed, teachers should still undertake their own observations and/or assessment. An intervention program based on background information alone or information collected by others will not provide adequate information for planning curriculum. Assessment can be completely or partially based on a range of observational data.

Collecting and recording observations:

- prevents forgetting
- is not affected by previous expectations
- is useful for analysing the relationship between the learning environment and the behaviour
- is useful for recognising changes in the type or frequency of behaviour
- evaluates the effectiveness of any strategies and programs
- provides a basis for setting and modifying short-term goals.

Observing a student's behaviour closely as he or she is involved in an activity and 'best guessing' gives a good indication of modifications that need to be made, or provides a clearer basis for further observation. The collection of observational data is necessary for program development and implementation, and for ongoing evaluation. It assists in identifying realistic goals that suit the learning needs of the student.

In order to facilitate the observation process, Deppeler (1998) has developed the 'Data Collection Coding Sheet', which can be used to collect a sample of behaviour of a student or a group of students (see Box 4.5 and Form 1 in the Useful forms section). The sample of behaviour should contain a minimum of three observation sessions. If appropriate to the behaviour, it may be observed across several settings or times of day. Other behaviours may be best observed in the same setting over several sessions.

Behaviours can be tabulated and reported as percentages along with a brief summary of:

- the context in which behaviours occurred
- interpretation of the data
- modification for subsequent observation
- (and/or) next steps to be taken based on interpretation.

Box 4.4: Using the Data Collection Coding Sheet

1 Select a 4-, 8- or 16-minute variable interval schedule based on the behaviour and the time available for observation. The following examples illustrate schedules that might be selected for various behaviours:

- **4-minute schedule:** for observing the pattern of on-task behaviour in a 40-minute classroom or work-related activity, or for observing the frequency and type of social interactions that occur during a lunch break.
- **8-minute schedule:** for observing the frequency of self-stimulatory behaviours of a student who is with the same teacher all day or for observing the proportion of on-task behaviour during a four-hour work-shift.
- **16-minute schedule:** observing less frequent behaviours over a day or several shorter sessions during a week, for example, aggressive behaviour, swearing, confrontations or initiations of social interactions, questioning, or for observing the proportion of on-task behaviour during an eight-hour work-shift.

2 You might need another person (such as another staff member or classroom volunteer) to assist you with observations. You can show these people how to conduct the observations and record them on the sheet, or you may conduct them yourself. Use some sort of timing device (stopwatch, wrist watch, computer, kitchen timer). Set it for the number of minutes indicated in the column of the appropriate schedule. When the timer beeps, identify visually what the student is doing, and immediately set the timer for the next interval. Then record what you observed using symbols, for example:

T	on task
P	off task, passive
D	off task, disruptive or destructive
N	no social interaction, isolated from others
W	no social interaction, but watching others
P	not directly involved in social interaction with others but physically apart of group
I	initiates social interaction, conversation
R	responds to social interaction, conversation
S	engaged in conversation or activity with another/others

Or make up your own symbols for other behaviours. Some behaviours may also be used in a yes/no format (for example, tantrums, or independently initiating work activity).

Data Collection Coding Sheet

Student: Martin	Date: April 25, 2004
Observer Name: Mr Smith	Starting Time: 8:15 am
Setting: Japanese language room	Activity: Japanese culture – tea ceremony

Comments	4 Minute		8 Minute		16 Minute	
Listening to teacher reading	2	T	12		12	
Watch demonstration of tea ceremony	5	T	3		8	
Not participating in student tea ceremony (sitting at desk at back of room)	7	P	9		28	
Throwing paper balls at group of children	1	D	4		2	
Sitting at desk not participating	3	P	6		24	
Watching 'tea ceremony' video	6	T	14		6	

Adapted from: Kubany, E.S. and Sloggett, B.B. (1973), 'Coding procedure for teachers' in *Journal of Applied Behaviour Analysis 6*, pp. 339–44.

3   Record details regarding changes in events, activities, etc. in the 'comments' section, ie what happened during or immediately before or after each type of activity etc.
4   Count up the number of observations for each category of behaviour recorded and divide by the total number of observations to get a percentage for each behaviour.

Some behaviours are best observed across several settings or times of day, while others may be best observed in the same setting over several sessions. Another excellent source of data you can collect can come from student learning portfolios. Portfolio assessment is addressed in some detail later in this chapter.

---

6   Summarise data

Once you have collected your data it is important to summarise it so that you can begin to make sense of it. Sometimes checklists may run into a number of pages (especially if they have been used for an entire class) and individual results will need to be extracted. Summarising the data involves the construction of very brief summaries of any observations you have conducted (expressed in percentage terms if you have conducted structured observations) and statements reflecting overall performance against the curriculum criteria you have set for individual students. Some teachers use data summaries as the basis for written reporting of student progress to parents.

7   Display data

If you have collected and summarised data that can be quantified in terms of numbers or percentages (such as test scores, assignment marks, or structured observation results), and which have occurred over a period of time, you may consider constructing graphs to demonstrate progress, such as this one:

Example: Data display for spelling-test results

Martin takes a spelling test each week based on lists of ten words he has made errors with in his own writing. His scores for correctly spelled words can be summarised as follows:

Week 1: 3/10	Week 4: 5/10	Week 7: 9/10
Week 2: 3/10	Week 5: 7/10	Week 8: 4/10
Week 3: 4/10	Week 6: 6/10	Week 9: 8/10

Martin's results might be more easily interpreted if expressed on a graph as follows. This graph clearly demonstrates an improving trend in Martin's spelling-test results over the nine-week period.

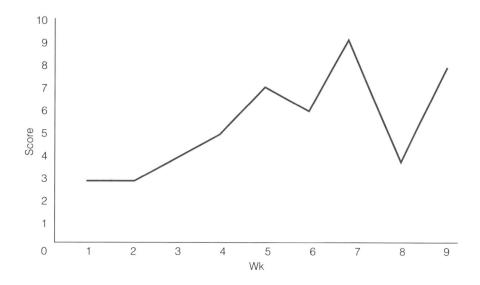

8   Interpret data and make decisions

The final stage in the process is to interpret the data and make decisions based on that interpretation. For example, if a teacher were to interpret the above spelling-test results in isolation from other factors, it might be determined that Martin is making good progress on his spelling and whatever teaching methods are being used are effective. If the improvements were sustained over time it might be determined that Martin no longer requires the extra supports provided to him in order to continue to achieve the same results. Probes into Martin's spelling throughout the year, which might also include checking to see if there is a general spelling improvement in his writing, would assist a teacher to determine if spelling continued to be a problem or strength area for Martin.

Portfolio assessments

Portfolio assessments are sometimes described as a different or 'stand alone' approach to teacher-based assessments. We believe, however, that portfolios do not constitute an assessment in their own right, but rather are an excellent tool for assisting a teacher to conduct the most useful type of classroom assessment—curriculum-based assessment.

Student portfolios are a simple concept and are commonly used in classrooms, especially primary-level classrooms. They are, however, also an excellent means of demonstrating student performance and achievement at the secondary-school level. A student portfolio is simply a collection of key pieces of a student's work that demonstrate progress against defined curriculum objectives.

Portfolios are useful for two main purposes. Firstly, they provide concrete evidence for curriculum-based assessments. When, as a teacher you are providing written reports of student progress to parents, you may cite evidence for your assessments as being present in the portfolio. They are also useful for times when you meet with parents and children to discuss progress. You can use the portfolio contents as a basis for discussion, and the student can show his or her parents examples of their 'best work'.

Box 4.5: Organising a student portfolio

Student portfolios can be organised according to:

- chronological order
- subject or theme
- specific, pre-determined curriculum objectives
- a combination of the above.

Some teachers dislike using portfolios for assessment purposes because they view their compilation as extra work. This need not be the case. Most children, even very young children, can take responsibility for the upkeep and maintenance of their own learning portfolios under the direction of the teacher. Exactly how much direction is required from the teacher will depend on the children, but in many cases the maintenance of portfolios requires very little input from the teacher. Student portfolios should be treated with some reverence by the teacher as receptacles of a child's 'best work'. Students will then be more likely to treat them with respect and keep them in good order. Strategies teachers can use to ensure that portfolios are appropriately maintained include:

- helping students identify items for inclusion in their portfolio, then making the student responsible for ensuring these items are included
- having students record the contents of their portfolio on the front cover
- conducting brief sessions with the entire class (five to ten minutes) on a regular basis, during which students must update and organise their own portfolios
- conducting brief sessions with the entire class (five to ten minutes) on a regular basis during which students have their portfolios checked for organisation by peers

- using any teaching 'down time' (such as periods when students are completing individual or group activities that do not require significant teacher input) to check up on individual portfolios.

There are many different formats a portfolio can take. Student portfolios can be stored in file folders in a central classroom location, or they might be stacked boxes (one per student) containing the child's work. The 'look' of a portfolio is only limited by what is appropriate to meet the needs of children in the classroom. One element common to all portfolios should be an index. This can feature on the cover or on a separate sheet within the portfolio. The index should list:

- the date each item in the portfolio was included
- a descriptive title of each item
- a reference to the curriculum objective the item relates.

Although there are no limits to what type of format you can choose for portfolios in your classroom, we recommend that you stick to a single, standard format for all the children in your class. This makes maintenance of the portfolios easier (as students can peer-review portfolios) and also produces a more standard format for you to evaluate and base decisions on.

Gardner's 'Multiple Intelligences'

Gardner's (1983) 'Multiple Intelligences' theory is well known to most educators in schools today and, while useful, is a rather lengthy topic in its own right and not addressed in any great detail here. The theory does, however, present teachers with new and important ways of thinking about classroom-based assessment as an aid to guiding instruction and tracking achievement. The multiple intelligences are a set of capacities that have traditionally been outside the scope of definitions of intelligence. Originally they included visual/spatial intelligence; logical/mathematical intelligence; verbal/linguistic intelligence; musical/rhythmic intelligence; bodily/kinesthetic intelligence; intrapersonal intelligence; and interpersonal/social intelligence. Gardner (1999) later added naturalistic, existential, and spiritual intelligences to this set, although these are yet to receive the same levels of attention as the original seven intelligences.

Gardner suggests that for the purposes of teaching we do not need a highly structured assessment based on the multiple intelligences, and questions the validity of many formalised, structured tests that have been devised to assess multiple intelligences. He argues that:

> For most children, unfettered exploration in a Spectrum classroom or in a children's museum is enough to give a rough-and-ready picture of their intelligences at a given moment in their lives. Nothing more is needed, and as

their intelligences are likely to evolve, it is important not to place too much weight on a single profile obtained at a single moment (Gardner 1999).

With Gardner's recommended 'rough-and-ready' approach in mind, how is a teacher to structure an assessment for multiple intelligences? According to Gardner, an experiment in setting up a preschool 'Spectrum classroom' produced a viable model for useful classroom-based assessment. This classroom was an area in which children were encouraged to play in centres of their choosing. Each centre was designed to encourage the children to use one or another of the multiple intelligences in order to play games, complete activities and solve problems. For example, their musical intelligence was sampled at one centre by inviting them to play with simple musical instruments and learn songs (Gardner 1993). These assessments were all carried out in their natural context (the classroom) where the children felt comfortable and at ease.

The suggestion that multiple-intelligences assessments can be informal in nature gives teachers who wish to conduct them significant latitude. Obviously, teachers must first be quite familiar with what exactly the multiple intelligences are and what they look like in terms of performance. Teachers who wish to conduct an evaluation of children's strengths with respect to the various multiple intelligences could set up a variety of centres, each targeting a different intelligence. For example, a centre measuring bodily/kinesthetic intelligence may require children to perform some kinds of sporting or dance activities needing coordination and physical skill. A centre measuring logical/mathematical intelligence may require children to solve problems using a variety of algorithms. What is important is that each centre contains activities that relate almost solely to a single type of intelligence so that the performance of a child is not confused with his or her capacities in the other intelligence areas.

More structured, 'authentic' assessments for the multiple intelligences have been suggested by others (Bellanca et al. 1994, see Box 4.6). Authentic assessments are those that replicate as closely as possible situations encountered by children in the 'real world' outside of school. Authentic assessment is seen as a hands-on and dynamic way to evaluate a child using a variety of traditional and non-traditional assessment approaches.

Box 4.6: Authentic assessments

Bellanca et al. (1994) suggest the following types of assessment under the umbrella of 'authentic assessment':

Exhibits   Using exhibits, children would research a topic then develop some kind of exhibit to demonstrate what they have learned. The most obvious of these would be a poster presentation; however, other types of exhibit can include models, artwork, computer presentations, brochures and advertisements.

Performances   Children demonstrate their learning through some type of performance. They might be expected to write and perform a play, do a poetry reading, participate in a musical presentation, read a short story, produce a short film, put together a mock (or real) radio show, or do a creative dance. The audience might be small groups, the entire class, or groups outside of the immediate class.

Journals and logs   Children keep a reflective journal that represents their learning journey. This is an excellent way for children not only to document some of the 'hard facts' about what they have learned, but also to be metacognitive and reflect on times they learned effectively and times they did not and how they might improve their learning in the future. Logs and journals do not need to rely solely on the written word. They can also include pictures, audio and video recordings, and presentations on a computer.

Demonstrations   Demonstrations are a particularly powerful way for children to show their learning, and can be an excellent teaching and learning tool as well as an assessment tool. A demonstration can include one child teaching another, or a whole group or class, how to do something.

Products   Teachers have traditionally assessed children based on products. These products have often included essays, or objects that have been produced to demonstrate learning. Products are still a valid form of assessing, especially when used in combination with other approaches. Products can include models, art work, books produced by children, charts, videos, audio products, textile products such as costumes, maps, or computer presentations.

Problem-solving process   This involves having children either solve problems or invent problems for others to solve. When assessing problem solving it is important to watch children as they work through the process rather than simply evaluating the finished product. Examples of problem-based assessments include having children write mystery or detective stories for others to solve, solving mathematical problems, solving problems in which they are given a scenario or historical context, or coming up with a different application for a tool.

Graphic organisers   Graphic organisers can assist children to become more metacognitive about their learning. They physically, with pen and paper, map out the process their learning has taken, while outlining points where they have produced a product or developed a particular demonstrable skill. Graphic organisers not only help you to evaluate the pathways a student takes in his or her learning, but also help them to see how they learn and how they might improve their learning.

Projects Projects include the familiar teacher-set papers and tasks, but can also include stu-
dent-developed research projects into a particular topic. Engaging children in projects
assists you to evaluate their research skills and the ways in which they gather, select and
use information. Children may engage in Internet research, sharing information with other
groups of children, preparing and using surveys, or creating a community group, structure or event.

Anecdotal assessments

When used judiciously along with other forms of assessment, anecdotal
information can be an important component in the development of an overall
picture of a child's needs, strengths, interests and motivations. Anecdotal
information, in the context in which it is referred to here, includes information
gained from informal discussions with the child, his or her peers, past teachers,
family members, and other school staff. It also includes any notes you take
down in class on an ad hoc basis, informal rating scales and checklists.

Interviewing parents

As discussed previously, parents are an essential source of information when
conducting assessments, and much of the information teachers gather from
parents falls in the 'anecdotal' category. This includes comments made by
parents, either verbally or through notes sent into school.

It is important that you develop a good relationship with parents as they
can be an excellent source of both information and support at the school.
Collaboration is the key. The flow of information needs to be two-way. Not
only can parents provide you with valuable information, but you can do the
same for them, offering them an insight into their child's progress at school.
Your relationship with parents should begin as early as possible in the school
year (or before) and ideally will be friendly, empathetic and productive.

The following list of questions, which may be helpful to you in gaining a
deeper understanding of a child when interviewing parents, have been selected
and modified from a list suggested by Spinelli (2002).

- What are your child's strengths and need areas?
- What are your child's special talents?
- What motivates your child? What are his/her interests?
- Does your child like school?
- Does your child have any particular fears or worries?
- Does your child have many friends? What are they like?
- How does your child relate to teachers?

- Does your child become involved in group activities or does he/she prefer to work alone?
- Does your child take responsibility for completing tasks?
- What is your child's educational background (schools attended, contexts etc.)?
- What are your goals for your child this year?
- Is there anything else I should know or any other information I should have?
- What information can I provide to you both now and on an ongoing basis? How can I help you this year?

While these questions can be used as a guide, do not feel limited to them, and omit those that have little value in your own learning context. You want an interview that stays on topic and concentrates on as little extraneous information as possible. This does not mean, however, that parents should not be permitted to digress from the topics you have listed for discussion. There may be more important topics the parents wish to discuss that you have not thought of. Any digressions should be focused on the purpose of the meeting, which is to share information about the child. All information from parents, however informal, should be treated with the utmost confidentiality, even amongst other school staff you work with. If you wish to share some of this anecdotal information with others you must first seek permission from the parents to do so.

When interviewing parents be sure to do so in a place in which they feel comfortable. This may be a welcoming area at the school, or even in the child's home if this is suggested by the parent. (School administrators should always be kept informed of any school-related meetings that take place away from the school campus.) Provide refreshments such as coffee and tea and make every effort to keep the atmosphere light and informal. Fostering this type of atmosphere should help to elicit better responses to your questions, and it also shows parents that they are regarded as important members of the school, and your classroom, community.

Interviewing children

Eliciting helpful responses from children in interviews can require significant skill. Most good teachers have already developed this skill through their past interactions with children, and if a child has attended your school in previous years you are likely to already have developed some form of relationship (even if it is only a face and name recognition), which will assist in making the child feel comfortable in an interview situation.

Interviews with children of any age are best kept informal. You are after candid and honest responses, not the responses children think you want to hear, and the best environment for producing these responses is a casual and relaxed one in which children feel free to speak their mind. With this in mind, any interviews should take place in areas familiar to the child, such as the classroom, school library, gymnasium, or outside on a sporting field or playground. Places that are generally 'out of bounds', such as staff rooms, staff offices and parent rooms, are best avoided. Interviews should be held privately, but all teachers need to be aware of the possible ramifications of being alone in a room with a child.

You may wish to use similar questions to those you used when interviewing the child's parent, but rephrased so as to be appropriate. The following list could serve as a useful starting point.

- What are your strengths? What areas do you sometimes need help with?
- What are your special talents?
- What helps you to want to get your work done at school? What are your interests?
- Do you like school?
- Do you have any particular fears or worries?
- Do you have many friends? What sorts of things do you do with them?
- Do you generally get along with teachers?
- Do you like to work alone or in groups?
- Whose job is it to make sure you get your school work done?
- Tell me about your last school.
- What do you want to learn this year?
- Is there anything else you want to say?
- How can I help you this year?

Interviewing school staff

In many respects interviewing your colleagues at school should be one of the easiest assessment tasks to conduct. As you probably already know the staff you want to interview, an informal and comfortable situation can be set up in a neutral area in the school, such as the staff lounge or work room. The following chapter is devoted to collaborating with your colleagues; the basic principles of collaboration need not be repeated here. It is enough to say that in most cases your relationship with your colleagues should be warm and professional, and if this is the case then conducting an interview should be a simple matter of taking the time to have a chat.

You will probably want to interview key members of staff, such as previous teachers or support staff. Other staff who have spent more limited time with the child may also be interviewed at your discretion if you think the information you gain will justify the time you spend.

School staff will doubtless be able to provide you with some 'hard data' such as test results or work samples. This is useful information to have. In addition you may want to conduct an interview using similar questions to the ones used for the parents and child.

- What are the child's strengths and need areas?
- What are the child's special talents?
- What motivates the child? What are his/her interests?
- Does the child seem to like school?
- Does the child seem to have any particular fears or worries?
- Does the child have many friends? What are they like?
- How does the child relate to teachers/school staff?
- Does the child become involved in group activities or does he/she prefer to work alone?
- Does the child take responsibility for completing tasks?
- What is your understanding of the child's educational background (schools attended, contexts etc.)?
- What goals could we continue with this year?
- Is there anything else I should know or any other information I should have?

Analysis of your interviews

Once you have conducted your interviews you can compare the responses using a qualitative-research technique known as triangulation (Lincoln and Guba 1985). Triangulation involves comparing multiple sources of information and analysing the similarities and differences to give you a more comprehensive view of the subject. Interview data of the nature described above can be most easily triangulated using Form 2 in Useful forms. It can be copied and modified to record and analyse your own interview responses.

This chapter has examined psychological and teacher-based types of assessment. We hope that the section on psychological assessments has helped you to better understand and interpret any of these formal reports that you might come across. We also hope that the section on teacher-based assessment has given you some ideas on which to base your own assessments and educational decisions. The following chapter deals with collaboration—an essential element of good inclusive practice.

KEY TERMS FROM THIS CHAPTER

Assessment The determination of whether learning has taken place or whether further instruction is required.

IQ A statistical device for identifying where, on a continuum that works in

two directions from a midpoint defined as 100, an individual compares
with his or her same-age peers on a cognitive ability test.

Percentile rank   A way of showing how well an individual has performed on
the test compared to others of the same age.

Portfolio assessment   A collection of key pieces of a student's work that
demonstrate progress against defined curriculum objectives.

Curriculum-based assessment   Using curriculum objectives as a basis for
measuring what a child is able to do.

FURTHER READING

Gardner, H. (1999), *Intelligence reframed: Multiple Intelligences for the 21st
Century*, New York: Basic Books.

Taylor, R.L. (2000), *Assessment of Exceptional Students: Educational and
Psychological Procedures* (5th edn), Needham Heights, MA: Allyn &
Bacon.

5

Collaborating with colleagues

Collaboration is essential for meaningful inclusion to occur. This chapter suggests ways in which you may make your classroom more inclusive through collaboration with colleagues. We use the term 'colleagues' here in the broadest sense, to include not only other teachers, paraprofessionals and other professionals, but also parents. Your relationship with each of these colleagues will differ as a consequence of the roles each person may play. At times you will be a leader, sometimes an equal partner, and at other times you will follow the lead of others. This chapter includes some strategies we hope will maximise the results of the work you do with colleagues in order to benefit not only children with diverse needs, but all children in your classroom.

KEY IDEAS IN THIS CHAPTER
- communication with colleagues
- conditions for optimum collaboration
- problem solving
- working with paraprofessionals
- collaboration with other teachers
- collaboration with health and allied health professionals
- collaboration with parents

Communication

Collaboration and communication go hand in hand. Collaboration is essentially a process whereby participants develop shared meanings and/or a shared agenda and then, in a cooperative way, set out to implement that agenda. This can be achieved through positive interactions and communication. High-quality communication is extremely important and is related to the success of any collaboration (Foreman 2001).

Box 5.1: Hints for making communication more effective

The following advice for making communication more effective when working in a collaborative situation has been provided by Deppeler (1998). It is important to develop and keep these competencies in mind during any collaborative interaction.

- Arrange seating in a circle so that all members can see each other and no one person is seated in a position of 'authority'.
- Welcome all team members and ensure that everyone has been introduced to each other. Have first-name tags ready.
- Emphasise that decisions are to be made collaboratively by the team and that the ongoing and continually evolving process is as important as any of the decisions taken as a part of that process. There are no 'right' or 'wrong' decisions, only those that the team makes through the collaborative and ongoing process of planning.
- Promote contributions from all team members by using a variety of questioning techniques.
- Ensure that all team members have heard and interpreted the same meaning from what has been stated by asking for clarification and/or restating information.
- Focus on one question/issue at a time.
- Do not evaluate or judge ideas, comments or suggestions—restate for clarification.
- Create a visual display on a large chart paper or a white board to summarise and capture the information generated during the meeting.
- Review with team members at the end of each discussion question to check that the information accurately represents what has been said.
- Conclude each session with a plan. Make sure each team member has checked the plan.
- Send a follow-up note to all participants outlining the meeting discussion and decisions.

Good collaboration with colleagues does not occur automatically. Friend and Cook (1996) identified a number of prerequisites for collaboration to occur. These include:

- **Collaboration should be voluntary**   People can be forced to meet but they cannot be forced to truly collaborate. Collaboration involves willing parties coming together to achieve a common goal.

- **Collaboration requires parity between participants** All members of a collaborative team must be seen as equal. This promotes a freedom for all members of the team to provide, process and evaluate ideas and information. This does not preclude members of a team taking leadership roles in different areas, but rather means that all contributions are considered equal regardless of whom they come from.
- **Collaboration presumes mutually agreed-on goals** Members of a collaborative team must work towards a clearly articulated common goal or goals.
- **Collaboration requires shared responsibility and shared resources** All members of the group must be a part of the process of arriving at and agreeing on decisions. In this way the decisions will be supported. Resources to achieve team goals should be available to all members of a collaborative team as required.
- **Team members must be collectively responsible for the outcomes of their decisions** This means that all team members share the success or failure of any collaborative effort. No single individual should be singled out for credit or blame. This helps collaborative teams to work together.

One of the main advantages of working in a collaborative team relates to problem solving. The process of inclusion often throws up specific problems for which there are no easy or single solutions. Often these problems are unique to your classroom or a particular child, when general blanket advice on inclusion is not helpful. In these instances the only way to proceed is to solve the problem and move forward. Often we can solve problems ourselves, but occasionally it is helpful to consult colleagues who are aware of our specific circumstances and can assist in solving the problem. This sharing of ideas and solutions is encouraged by most progressive school administrators and makes good sense.

Box 5.2: Five steps for solving inclusive problems

Hobbs and Westling (1998) identified a structured five-step collaborative problem-solving process useful for application to problems with inclusion:

1 **Defining the problem** This involves establishing a shared recognition of the existence of a problem as well as a shared understanding of exactly what the problem is.

2   **Identifying causes**   The collaborative team needs to consider the antecedents of the problem. Teams can ask themselves what the most likely explanation for the occurrence of a problem is and what variables influence the cause or causes.

3   **Setting objectives**   At this stage the collaborative team looks to where it wants to be when the problem is solved. Teams need to consider at what point the problem will be considered 'solved'. Setting objectives allows collaborators to plan a sequence of interventions aimed at solving the problem.

4   **Identifying solution activities**   Having examined causes and set objectives, the collaborative team should now be in a position to develop a plan for solving the problem. Hobbs and Westling (1998) suggest that 'brainstorming' ideas is a good place to begin before prioritising and planning the implementation of activities designed to solve the problem.

5   **Monitoring for success**   Evaluating and monitoring the process is important in order to see if the plan is actually solving the problem or if the collaborative team needs to revisit some of the stages.

In your role as an inclusive teacher, true collaboration will not always be possible. There will be times when you will need to exercise your authority as a classroom leader or respect the authority of others in order to achieve a smooth-running inclusive classroom. The concept of collaboration is, however, important to keep in mind and to put into practice as often as is practically possible in your dealings with colleagues. In this sense collaboration is a matter of attitude, not adherence to a set of rules or guidelines.

Collaborating with other professionals in the inclusive classroom

Often teachers who have children with diverse abilities in their classes will be required to work with other professionals. These include specialist teachers, doctors, psychologists, occupational therapists, speech/language therapists, physiotherapists and a wide variety of other professionals. Sometimes this grouping of professionals working for the benefit of a child works well, but at other times there is considerable tension that results from different philosophies and approaches, and the treatment requirements of different disciplines. Teachers must respect the professional autonomy of these other professionals while at the same time ensuring that a sound inclusive educational program is not disrupted but rather is enhanced by their presence in the school.

Collaborating with other teachers

There are a number of ways in which you can collaborate with other teachers. Some of these depend on the nature of the staff available at your school, while others can be adopted at almost every school. Working with other teaching staff is important because of the extra assistance, experience and ideas this can bring to your classroom (Jakupcak et al. 1996). Collaborations with other teaching staff can occur in almost every area of teaching. This includes assessment, planning, emotional support, problem solving and even instructional support face to face with children. This is possible not only with school special-education or integration teachers, but also with other regular classroom teachers.

Teaching colleagues can often be very helpful in your assessment of the learning needs and strengths of individual children in a number of ways. Firstly, they can provide advice and ideas on the most appropriate types of assessments to carry out for particular children. This is especially true of teachers who have taught your child in the past and who can also provide you with important background information. Other teachers can also assist you in conducting assessments. In some ways it is even better to have a teaching colleague conduct some assessments than to do them yourself when your knowledge and relationship with a particular child might compromise your objectivity (Taylor 2000). If your school has employed a special-education teacher with few other teaching duties then it is often easier to schedule sessions when you can collaborate on assessments. If you choose to collaborate with a teacher who has a full load of classroom teaching, then you might have to negotiate a time for collaboration during that teacher's 'preparation time' during the week. Giving up this time is a significant sacrifice for many teachers but if you can work out a reciprocal arrangement the burden may be reduced.

Planning is another area in which you can collaborate with other teachers. Special-education teachers can often offer you practical advice and support when it comes to planning in terms of how to be more inclusive, and how to fit everything you want into your plans. The advice of regular teachers can also be invaluable. As with assessment, co-planning times with specialist teachers are probably easier to schedule than with regular teachers, but forming planning partnerships with normal teachers is rewarding and worth the effort. When choosing a teacher (or teachers) to plan with we suggest you choose those with whom you have something in common. In many cases this will be a teacher who teaches the same age group as you. In other cases it may be a teacher who teaches the same subject area. The benefits of co-planning with other teachers are many and may include, but are not limited to, those listed in Box 5.3.

Box 5.3: Benefits of planning with other teachers

The benefits of co-planning with other teachers are many and may include, but are not limited to:

- the development of ideas you might not have thought of
- using limited resources so that demand is not placed on them at the same time
- a critique of your teaching plans resulting in a more 'robust' program
- reduced work—you can use ideas from the unit/lesson plans of others (as appropriate) and they can use yours
- greater consistency in the curriculum across a subject area/grade level
- a more enjoyable, social planning experience. Development of a support network
- a greater awareness of what is occurring in other classes, especially helpful if your co-teacher is absent and the replacement needs advice
- assistance with context-dependent problem solving.

Collaboration with other teachers need not stop at assessment, problem solving and planning. There are a number of ways you can collaborate with other teachers on instruction. This is beneficial because it can bring together the expertise of two teachers in one classroom. Collaborating on instruction generally requires support from school administration as your teaching schedule will need to have points of contact with the teacher with whom you are collaborating. Collaboration on instruction is a non-traditional approach to teaching, but these days few school administrators should have doubts about its worth. As with all other forms of collaboration, it may be easier to schedule collaboration time with a special-education teacher than a classroom teacher, but both types of instructional collaboration can be rewarding.

Models of instructional collaboration outlined by Cook and Friend (1995) include the following:

- **One teaches, one supports**   One teacher leads the lesson while the other assists in providing individual assistance and child monitoring. This type of session is more appropriate when two teachers are available to teach a single class of children, but may also work in specific instances when two classes are combined into one large group. Instances where this would be an effective teaching approach with two combined classes would be reasonably uncommon.
- **Station teaching**   Children are divided into two or more groups to work at different 'stations' around the room. Both teachers visit from group to group (or groups rotate to the teachers) and teach either different concepts or different parts of the same idea, depending on expertise. This model

can be effective with combined classes of children in a large room or with a single class with two teachers.

- **Parallel teaching**   Suitable only for single classes where two teachers are available. Parallel teaching involves dividing a class into heterogeneous halves and having each teacher teach the same lesson to one of the groups. Advantages of this are that groups are smaller, enabling more child participation, and that some children may prefer the instructional style of a particular staff member. Teachers may also teach in ways (for example, more visual, or more text based) that better suit particular child groups.

- **Alternative teaching**   The class is divided into a larger group and a smaller group. One teacher works with the large group while the other teaches the small group. This smaller group can be used for a variety of purposes. Remediation is the obvious one, but it can also be used to enrich instruction for children achieving at a higher level or for those who have specific interests in special areas of the curriculum. The important thing is not to make participation in the smaller group seem like a punishment or a place only for those having difficulty with work. This model is best suited to single classes where two teachers are available, but in some circumstances may be appropriate for combined classes.

- **Team teaching**   Two teachers share the instructional role equally. Team teaching is particularly effective when teaching a topic that involves a lot of interaction, and possibly role-play. It also helps present a topic in more depth because both teachers contribute information. This style of teaching is probably best suited to an expository approach where a presentation of information is important. It can work well with single or combined classes.

Another model of instructional collaboration not directly touched on by Cook and Friend (1995) is one of individual consultation. Individual consultation can occur when children are working on individual projects. Children can work on their own projects (possibly in the school library), using available staff members for advice and assistance. Combining classes for sessions such as these can be effective because children can get different points of view from other teachers on their particular projects.

You should not limit your collaborations with other teachers to the situations and contexts described above. The collaborative models and tips provided in the remainder of this chapter, for use with parents, paraprofessionals and other professionals, can also easily be adapted to your work with other teachers. The key is to choose and adapt which strategies work best for you in your own school context.

Collaborating with health and allied health professionals

When working with children with diverse educational needs it is inevitable that you will need to work with other professionals with particular training and expertise in specific areas. In an inclusive classroom these are known as 'integrated therapies' (O'Toole and Switlick 1997). These professionals might include doctors and nurses as well as allied health professionals such as psychologists, physiotherapists, occupational therapists, speech/language therapists, audiologists, and other therapists such as music therapists. Each profession has its own way of working that sometimes does not fit well with the ways schools and inclusive classrooms work. Your job as an inclusive teacher is to negotiate how you work with other professionals in your classroom to get the most out of them while still retaining an inclusive atmosphere.

Differences in approach

Some professions emphasise a medical-style 'treatment' approach to children with diverse abilities (O'Toole and Switlick 1997). This generally involves medical-style assessments followed by a prescribed course of treatment. This style of treatment is entirely appropriate in many cases, and teachers must work with the other professionals to ensure that it is implemented in the most inclusive way possible. In instances where an inclusive approach is not appropriate, steps should be taken to ensure as little disruption to the classroom routine as is possible.

An example of a therapy discipline which has elements that lend themselves to inclusion and also elements which do not is physiotherapy. Many of the assessments conducted by physiotherapists need to be conducted one on one and in private. Treatment, however, while sometimes needing to be done in a one-on-one environment, can at times be designed so that it occurs as part of the classroom program. Warming up and stretching prior to a physical-education class, for example, might be seen as one opportunity to implement some physiotherapy treatment in a more inclusive setting. Children can be encouraged to engage in other types of treatment activity at different times during the day that fit in, or almost fit in, with what they are doing with the rest of the class.

It is inevitable, however, that times will need to be made during the school day for individual sessions with therapists. We are aware of instances where children with diverse abilities have been so embarrassed by being withdrawn to see other professionals that they have willingly given up lunch-hours and recess times to see them (Loreman 2000). This practice is probably best avoided: it is unfair to expect a child to miss out on break times, which are often valuable social interaction times with their peers.

Ways other professionals work: service delivery options
There are several modes of service delivery commonly in use by other professionals working in schools. These range from practices that are not inclusive to practices that are highly inclusive. Many therapists will need to employ a range of service-delivery modes in order to do their job, but in planning for treatment it is helpful to be aware of the available options.

While it will not always be possible, it is important to try and work as close to the collaborative end of the scale as possible.

Scheduling with other professionals
Scheduling child appointments with other professionals is a complicated matter. Not only do you need to reconcile their schedules with yours, but you also need to take into account the child's need for adequate break times and the need to cause the least amount of disruption to the regular school day as is possible. At times withdrawal from class to attend therapy sessions is unavoidable if the therapy provided during school hours is to be effective and appropriate. What needs to be considered, however, is when to schedule these withdrawals. There might be times of the week, for example, where children are permitted to work on a variety of individual projects related to their own identified goals. This is more common with older children who can take more responsibility for their own work, which can easily be spread throughout different areas of the school (library, music area, etc.) in any given lesson, especially when they are working on individual projects. Times such as these might be the best occasions to schedule sessions with other professionals. It is less noticeable that the child requiring consultation has been withdrawn, and in doing this during individual work time the child does not miss 'group lessons' that other children have the benefit of attending.

As has been mentioned, withdrawal from class can be significantly reduced if the other professional is willing to work with the classroom teacher and other staff to come up with ways that any therapy can be built in to the daily routine. In many cases teachers and paraprofessionals will be required to implement daily therapy due to the impracticalities and prohibitive cost of having other professionals visit the school on a daily basis for brief sessions. This implementation can include administering medication, implementing a physical, speech or occupational therapy program, or taking steps to include techniques in the classroom that arise from psychological intervention. As all of the above falls outside the area of expertise of most teachers, implementation of programs devised by other professionals should be approached with extreme caution. A teacher's agreement to implement the programs of other professionals should be conditional on the following:

- the other professional has conducted a thorough assessment and has explained the results to the teacher
- the other professional trains the teacher in the correct implementation of the therapy, outlining any risk areas to avoid
- the other professional provides the teacher with a plain-language written description of the required therapy, with pictures/diagrams where appropriate
- the other professional has explained the assessment and therapy to the parents of the child and a permission form (see Form 3 in Useful forms) has been signed
- the other professional agrees to regular monitoring (set firm dates) of the progress of the child and reviews of the therapy to ensure it is still appropriate
- the other professional agrees to be available to the teacher for advice or consultation as required.

Linking therapy goals to classroom activities

Ideally, therapy goals should be linked to activities already occurring in the classroom (Dettmer et al. 1999). This will not always be possible, but should be viewed as the best option for therapy provision. As a teacher you will need to work closely with other professionals to identify areas of your regular classroom program that are conducive to therapy implementation. In a perfect world, the other professionals would be on hand for input during your planning sessions. This method of integrating therapy into regular classrooms is commonly supported in the literature in this area, but in our opinion is patently unrealistic in the real world of teaching. Time is hard to find for people working with children, and getting a number of varied professionals together on a regular basis for classroom planning sessions is near impossible. Instead, we recommend what we view as being the next best option. It is not as comprehensive a process as actually formulating plans with other professionals at their inception, but it is more realistic and achievable.

As with most of the suggestions in this book, the idea is straightforward. We suggest that you plan your regular teaching activities in the same way that you always do. Once you have done this you should then consult with the other professionals and identify areas where therapy can be built into the existing program. A form such as the one provided in the example opposite can be developed by you for this purpose.

This daily therapy plan provides a model that can be used by teachers in both primary and secondary-school settings. When meeting with another professional, you should have your daily (or weekly, if you prefer) classroom activities already listed so that the person you are working with has some idea

Daily therapy plan

For ___James Green_____ Date __14 February__

Daily classroom activity	Therapy opportunity?	Person to implement therapy	Brief description of therapy
Arrival from bus. Hangs up coat, etc.	Yes. O.T. goal 1 —fine motor	Teacher	James will unzip his own jacket using his thumb and index finger to grasp zip.
English class— responsive writing to a news article	Yes. O.T. goal 1 —fine motor	Teacher	Instead of using his computer, James will use a pen for his response using the O.T. designed grip.
Physical Ed.— Athletics. Long jump.	Yes. Physio goal 1 —flexibility	Physiotherapist	Therapist will integrate stretching during warm up & warm down. Will assist with jumping activities.
Recess	No		
Science—Video (cells)	No		

of what you are working on and can make suggestions. The first column allows you to do this. The description need not be detailed; you can discuss what you have planned during your meeting. In the second column you should identify if integrating therapy is even possible, and if so exactly what type of therapy and what specific goal is being addressed. In the third column you identify who is responsible for the implementation of the therapy. You may list yourself, the child, a paraprofessional, parent, classroom helper or the actual therapist (if they will be available at that time) in this section. This person is responsible for ensuring the therapy is properly carried out. The last column allows for a very brief description of the therapy to be carried out and how it will be integrated into the regular program. This straightforward way of integrating the work of other professionals into your daily classroom routine represents a realistic option for classroom planning in this area. We have also provided a blank form in the Useful forms section (Form 4).

Working with paraprofessionals in the inclusive classroom

Paraprofessionals are people who help schools and teachers provide services to children with diverse abilities. Although in some areas measures are underway to provide some formal training (Leighton et al. 1997), they are generally non-certified staff who operate under the guidance and supervision of a designated certified school staff member (a teacher or teachers) or other professionals. Paraprofessionals are known by a number of titles including teacher assistant, teaching assistant, paraeducator, teacher aide and instructional assistant (Riggs 2001). They are most commonly used to support either single children or small groups of children requiring additional assistance (Friend and Bursuck 1999).

Box 5.4: Roles for paraprofessionals

In the course of providing support, the paraprofessional fills a number of roles, described by Frey (2001) as falling into five areas:

1 providing instruction—implementing teacher plans, providing personal assistance, re-teaching skills
2 assisting with assessment under teacher direction
3 maintaining effective communication between children, staff and families, including maintaining confidentiality
4 providing leadership for children and staff in areas including the facilitation of *child social relationships*, and modelling effective instructional strategies for staff
5 record keeping as required.

The employment of paraprofessionals should be based on school and classroom need. Schools should be careful to ensure that the employment of a paraprofessional will actually lead to a more effective educational program (Leighton et al. 1997; Giangreco et al. 1999). Schools and teachers need to examine their practices and decide how best an extra staff member might fit in to enhance these practices. There are a number of common pitfalls of which to be aware.

Some teachers are tempted to delegate the responsibility for the education of children with diverse abilities to paraprofessionals (Giangreco et al. 1991; Giangreco et al. 1999). This practice is both unethical and unprofessional. While not disparaging the work of paraprofessionals in classrooms (many are well trained, experienced and good at their jobs), the onus is on the classroom teacher to construct, implement and evaluate educational programs for all children. It must be remembered that in most countries paraprofessionals need have no training or experience to be employed (Hadadian and Yssel 1998; OECD 1999; Riggs 2001). The paraprofessional is there to assist and work with the classroom teacher, and it is the classroom teacher who must use this help in ways that best promote the learning and inclusion of children with diverse abilities and their peers (Lamont and Hill 1991).

Collaboration is the key, and thus those who work together towards common goals are often the most effective. Pickett et al. (1993) describe teachers and paraprofessionals as working as differentiated teams, that is, they perform different tasks that complement each other. Teachers provide leadership and define the daily classroom roles of paraprofessionals, while paraprofessionals assist teachers in meeting instructional objectives, managing children and maintaining the instructional environment.

Box 5.5: Do you need paraprofessional help?

Giangreco et al. (1999) outline ten guidelines for deciding whether paraprofessional supports is needed:

1 make your decisions in collaboration with students, parents, other teachers, school administration and therapists
2 if you build on the capacity within the school to support all children, drawing on the knowledge, skills and abilities of existing staff members, you may reduce the need for a paraprofessional
3 consider paraprofessional support on a case-by-case basis and be judicious in making decisions
4 clarify any reasons why paraprofessional supports are being considered
5 match child support needs with the skills of the paraprofessional being considered
6 explore opportunities for natural supports (which, as the term implies, occur in the context of the day) from others such as staff, classmates and parent volunteers etc. who would be in the school even if the child with diverse abilities were not
7 consider school and classroom characteristics such as access, adaptive equipment, class sizes and groupings, attitudes etc—sometimes changes to these characteristics can eliminate the need for a paraprofessional

8   consider workloads and available support from special-education teachers and related services

9   explore administrative and organisational changes that may reduce the need for a paraprofessional by allowing the child more independence

10 consider if paraprofessional support can be a temporary measure.

Regardless of how your particular school views paraprofessionals, it is important to realise that the roles of paraprofessionals working with you need to be negotiated and clearly defined in advance. The multiple roles paraprofessionals can now play in a school mean that clearly defined responsibilities for these staff members are essential. In defining the role of paraprofessionals in your classroom you are essentially ensuring that you are able to work better as a team because both parties know what is expected of them and what is not (Pickett et al. 1993; Doyle and Lee 1997; Leighton et al. 1997; Goessling 1998). You may like to formalise this negotiation of roles by producing a brief written document with your paraprofessional. This written document is not a 'job description' in the industrial sense, but rather a joint understanding of paraprofessional responsibilities that best meet the needs of children in your classroom. An example is provided below.

Example: Paraprofessional role and responsibilities

One particular paraprofessional in a Year 6 class in 2003 was responsible for assisting the teacher in:

*   preparing and modifying instructional materials for all children
*   assisting children with disabilities to be organised and ready on time for lessons
*   one-to-one or small group instruction/therapy sessions as required
*   toileting and feeding children with disabilities. Documenting this
*   ensuring children with disabilities get out to and return from outside breaks
*   communication—informing the teacher of unusual/significant child progress or specific difficulties
*   writing daily communication book home after teacher consultation
*   ensuring classroom rules/behaviour expectations are consistently applied
*   assisting children with disabilities on and off school bus
*   acting as a resource/help for all children in the class
*   assisting children with disabilities only when genuinely required
*   facilitating child friendships and fostering a caring classroom.

As a part of your leadership role it is generally your job as the teacher to act as supervisor of the paraprofessional, even if this is limited to the times when the paraprofessional is actually working in your class (Lamont and Hill 1991; Giangreco et al. 1999). Supervising other staff involves skills that many teachers already have—it is just a matter of applying them to a new situation.

A set of seven competencies for teachers supervising paraprofessional staff was identified by Wallace et al. (2001). You will already have many of these competencies, but you may need to develop some as you work with paraprofessionals. They are:

- **Communicating with paraprofessionals** Sharing information about children as well as identifying roles of classroom staff.
- **Planning and scheduling** This includes not only scheduling and the establishment of instructional plans, but also linking the skills and interests of paraprofessionals to tasks.
- **Instructional support** Supporting paraprofessionals in the instructional process and providing feedback on performance.
- **Modelling** Modelling a caring and respectful manner in interactions with children.
- **Public relations** Involving the paraprofessional in decision making, and advocating on behalf of the paraprofessional to those in authority. Keeping members of the school community informed of the roles and responsibilities of paraprofessionals.
- **Training** Providing on-the-job training in order to foster more effective instructional or other classroom skills.
- **Management of paraprofessionals** Maintaining regular supportive interactions with paraprofessionals and contributing to their development.

Inclusive instructional approaches with paraprofessionals

How is an inclusive instructional approach with paraprofessionals best achieved? The reality is that some children require a significant amount of assistance in order to complete classroom tasks. How we provide children with this assistance, while at the same time not using paraprofessionals in ways that impede progress in other areas, is a matter requiring creative thinking and good organisational planning and teaching. As with everything, situations vary from context to context, but we hope you are able to adapt some of the following ideas to your situation:

- use paraprofessionals to work with the rest of the class
- attach paraprofessionals to extra need, not to individual children
- use paraprofessionals as a resource for children not experiencing difficulties

- paraprofessionals can be asked to prepare and develop instructional materials
- paraprofessionals can help you gather data on children
- paraprofessionals can be your partners.

Using paraprofessionals with the rest of the class

Research suggests that in some classrooms paraprofessionals are not used in ways that enhance either learning or social acceptance for children with diverse abilities. Indeed, paraprofessionals have been found to either dramatically accelerate or impede the progress of a child depending on their approach (Hill and Whiteley 1985; Gormley and McDermott 1994; Giangreco et al. 1999). For example, it is not uncommon for paraprofessionals to sit directly next to the child they are supposed to assist, even if their help is not required. There are many reasons to avoid this practice. These include a negative impact on peer interactions due to a separation from classmates, fostering a dependence on adults, and putting limitations on receiving competent instruction or instruction with the peer group (Hill and Whiteley 1985; Gormley and McDermott 1994; Giangreco et al. 1997; Giangreco et al. 1999; Loreman 2000).

Many teachers are concerned about the ethical and legal implications of using paraprofessionals to work with children other than the identified (and often funded) child with diverse abilities. They are concerned that money targeted to specific children should be used solely for that child (Loreman 2001). In many situations, however, having paraprofessionals work with other children is a practice that legitimately supports the learning of the child with diverse abilities while being of benefit to the others at the same time. One way of viewing paraprofessionals is as assistants for all children in a class (Giangreco et al. 1997). This then gives the classroom teacher more time in which to work with the child with diverse abilities, which results in better supported learning for that child. Children with diverse abilities need not always be placed individually or in small groups with paraprofessionals. There are many times when the paraprofessional can, and should, be used to free up the teacher to work with individuals or small groups of children.

Attaching paraprofessionals to extra need, not to individual children

It is important that no stigma is attached to children who receive assistance from the paraprofessional, or at least that any stigma is reduced. Inclusive classes may function best when spending time with the paraprofessional is seen by the class as being for all who need help, instead of only for specific children who frequently have difficulty with class work (Giangreco et al. 1997). Given this, paraprofessionals can be assigned to areas of extra need rather than to individual children. In doing this the extra needs of many children, including but not limited to just those with extra funding, can be met. For example, a group of children completing a military obstacle course as part of a high school outdoor education or physical education class may be placed in situations where they need help. They might, for instance, need to cross a muddy ditch in which some of the children will get stuck. The teacher might place a willing paraprofessional at this point on the course to help the children get out. The paraprofessional will have been assigned to the class due to the presence of a child with a physical and intellectual disability, who will almost certainly need to be helped out of the mud *along with a number of others*. The paraprofessional is therefore assisting in the area of greatest need for the child with diverse abilities, and is also assisting a variety of other children in the process.

Using paraprofessionals as a resource for children not experiencing difficulties

In order to even further reduce any stigma attached to working with a paraprofessional, it is worthwhile having children not experiencing any difficulties spend time with the paraprofessional. Far from being a waste of valuable paraprofessional time, this can help in building relationships between all children and the paraprofessional so that that staff member is seen as more than someone solely attached to children having difficulties. It can also help these children to work on improving their strengths while at the same time giving the classroom teacher greater scope to work with the child with diverse abilities.

Using paraprofessionals to prepare materials

In some cases paraprofessionals may best support the learning of children with diverse abilities when they are not in the classroom at all. Sometimes the most inclusive and effective use of a paraprofessional's time is in the preparation of materials for use in the classroom where the development of these materials directly assists and supports the learning of children with diverse abilities, or in carrying out clerical duties to allow the teacher to spend more time with children (Giangreco et al. 2001). An example of this is a child with a visual impairment but no other disabilities. This child may only need items translated into braille or larger print to be able to function effectively in a well-run and supportive classroom. A child such as this may not need direct assistance from a paraprofessional, whose time would be best spent developing appropriate classroom materials for the child's use. There are many situations in which using a paraprofessional to develop materials or to carry out clerical tasks is the best way to support inclusive learning.

Using paraprofessionals to gather child data

In order to make decisions about educational programs we need to thoroughly assess and evaluate current child achievement. Ways of doing this were outlined in Chapter 4. Paraprofessionals can be of significant help to teachers when evaluations are being conducted, in many cases being able to conduct parts of the assessment under the instruction and supervision of the teacher (Frey 2001). An example of this would be the collecting of structured child observation data. While the teacher is busy instructing the class, the paraprofessional could be taking timed observations that can be collated and analysed with the teacher at a later time. Involving paraprofessionals in this process not only helps them to get to know the children they work with better, but also involves them as partners in the educational process.

Paraprofessionals as partners

Teachers and paraprofessionals should ideally both be working towards a shared vision or goals for child learning. When teachers and other classroom staff can develop a shared vision and shared expectations for the children in the class, children are then faced with less inconsistency in their dealings and instruction from the classroom team (Doyle and Lee 1997). Teachers should also make good use of the skills and experience many paraprofessionals have. These can often be used most effectively when there are problems to be solved. Both the solving of problems and the development of a shared vision can be achieved through meetings. Regular, scheduled, sit-down meetings with paraprofessionals are important, but some research suggests that teachers do not often do this (French 2001). We believe that these teachers do themselves a disservice. While we recognise that school staff are busy people who are often already involved in a large number of meetings, we believe that regular meetings between staff who work closely together are amongst the most important meetings to have in a school. This is especially so if you work with a number of different paraprofessionals. Having all staff in the one place at the one time to discuss issues can lead to not only greater continuity of approaches in the classroom, but can also act as a forum for sharing ideas, and in so doing lead to more effective child learning (Doyle and Lee 1997). Furthermore, meeting on a regular basis might actually save time, as the need to communicate the same information on an individual basis will be reduced. An example of how a teacher might work with a paraprofessional in an inclusive way during instruction comes from Mrs Jones' mathematics class.

Case study: Mrs Jones and her paraprofessional partner

Mrs Jones teaches mathematics to a Year 8 class of 26 children. The class includes one child with a significant intellectual disability and two children with learning disabilities. These three children, along with two others in the class, are having difficulty with some of the concepts in a graphing unit being taught. Mrs Jones has a paraprofessional in the classroom and decides to use a mid-unit review session to work with children experiencing difficulties. As Mrs Jones does not want to single these children out in front of their peer group, she plans an inclusive approach to the session.

At the beginning of the session Mrs Jones reviews the types of graphs they have covered in the unit to date in front of the class. These include pictographs, circle (or 'pie') graphs, bar graphs and line graphs. This review takes about ten minutes before the class is divided up into six groups. Mrs Jones ensures that groups are mixed-ability and that the three children with identified disabilities are placed in different groups. The other two children having difficulties with the unit are placed one each in the groups that include the children with learning disabilities. In grouping the children in this way Mrs Jones has ensured that all children experiencing difficulties are not in the same group (this avoids stigmatising them) and that the children experiencing difficulties have been limited to three groups. Mrs Jones is certain she can spend time with each of the three groups. If the children experiencing difficulties were spread across all six groups this would not be possible.

Mrs Jones has developed six activity stations for the session. Each group works on the graphing activity at a station for a set amount of time before all groups rotate to the next activity. Mrs Jones spends the entire 'activity station' time working with the three groups that include children with disabilities. She visits them at their stations and teaches and emphasises the basic concepts to these groups. In doing this in small group settings she is able to help the children having difficulties come to terms with the concepts. While Mrs Jones is doing this the paraprofessional supervises the other groups as they work through the activities. The activities are well designed so that each group can work independently on them.

At the end of the session Mrs Jones facilitates a class reflection and discussion on the activities, and reinforces the concepts under review. Each child leaves the class with their individual needs met. It should be noted that Mrs Jones doesn't always teach in this way—she divides her time fairly between all children as best she can—but with the extra flexibility a paraprofessional provides she is better able to spend meaningful time with children she might not otherwise be able to.

Scheduling paraprofessionals

It is the job of the classroom teacher to schedule the activities of the paraprofessional for the time they are working in their classroom. Teachers who work well with paraprofessionals plan for their presence in the classroom well in advance of the class. Good written schedules can provide both security and guidance to a paraprofessional (Pickett et al. 1993). Many teachers do not provide their paraprofessionals with written plans or schedules, opting for oral communication (French 2001), but this is a mistake. People like to know what they are doing in advance in order to be able to best prepare themselves.

There are as many different ways of timetabling paraprofessionals as there are ways of planning classes in general. Many teachers, especially experienced teachers, have developed their own individual ways of planning that best suit their style. We have prepared an example of a schedule for a single day in a primary-school class with a full-time paraprofessional. The idea is simple, and as such we believe it is easy to implement and adapt to your existing planning format. We have also provided a blank form in the Useful forms section (Form 5) for you to work with.

The method of daily planning demonstrated here can work equally well in a primary- or secondary-school setting. In both cases, the principle is the same. The advantages of using this method are that it is simple, can be done relatively quickly as part of normal planning, and the format forces you, as the teacher, to think about not only your role in the classroom but the role of the paraprofessional. This planning format has the flexibility to allow you to include assignments for the paraprofessional you work with that are outside of the common one-on-one work with children with diverse abilities. In classes where other professionals work, the format can be extended to include them as well.

The 'Daily plan schedule' opposite is only a summary plan for a single day in a primary-school classroom. Obviously, there is frequent need when teaching for more detailed plans for specific lessons. A more detailed 'Single lesson plan', using the same principle, is demonstrated after the 'Daily plan schedule'. We have also provided a blank forms in the Useful forms section (Forms 5 and 6).

Paraprofessionals during break times

There are two issues connected with the use of paraprofessionals during break times such as recesses and lunch times. The first is an industrial issue and the second relates to children. The industrial issue relates to the right of the paraprofessional to take breaks as outlined in any industrial agreement they might have. If no industrial agreement is in place, then school principals and teachers should take into account the allocation of fair and reasonable times for breaks away from children and other forms of work. This can be difficult to implement, especially where some children require supervision during break times. Sometimes paraprofessionals may need to be absent from class for short periods of time to make up for time spent feeding or toileting children with significant physical disabilities.

Direct one-on-one supervision of individual children during break times is a practice that should be avoided providing it is safe to do so. Like all children, children with diverse abilities need to spend time away from adults in order to develop friendships and become involved in age-appropriate social relationships. The presence of a paraprofessional following a child at close range can seriously inhibit the formation of these social relationships (Loreman 2001). In instances where constant, close supervision is required it should be

Daily plan schedule

Teacher ___Mr Smith_____ Class ___Year 5_____ Date ___April 17_____

Time	Lesson	What teacher does	What paraprofessional does
8.45–9.00	Children enter: roll-call, admin tasks, etc.	Marks roll, completes admin tasks.	Supervises children hanging up coats, bags etc. Reminds child with disability to use toilet and helps if required.
9.00–9.15	Review of homework task (children were asked to watch news as part of a unit of work on the media).	Guides class discussion on topic.	Joins in class discussion.
9.15–10.00	**English** Class continues to work on media topic. 10-minute video 'Behind the News' followed by 15-minute mixed-ability group discussion on the issues raised. Discussion questions are set in advance and a group response must be recorded. 10 minutes spent on individual written responses. 10 minutes at end of class to review group and individual responses.	Supervises video. Rotates around mixed-ability groups, providing input where required. Supervises individual written tasks, providing help as required.	Supervises video. Provides extra assistance to mixed-ability groups who require it. During individual task ensures that child with a disability is using the modified materials. Provides help to all children as required.
10.00–10.30	**Physical Education** (with specialist teacher). Soccer skills session. In small groups, the children are to practise taking shots for goal both with and without an active defender.	Demonstrates method. Instructs individuals throughout activities.	During transition to outside, paraprofessional reminds and assists child with disability with toileting. Remains on hand to assist in supervising small groups during session.
10.30–10.50	Recess.	Briefly assists with feeding child with disability then takes break.	Takes break.
10.50–11.00	Children enter. Daily 'quick quiz'.	Teacher conducts quiz. Children attempt to better their own score from yesterday.	Immediately on entering building, reminder and assistance with toileting.

Daily plan schedule   (continued)

Teacher <u>Mr Smith</u>   Class <u>Year 5</u>   Date <u>April 17</u>

Time	Lesson	What teacher does	What paraprofessional does
11.00–12.00	**Mathematics** Problem solving. Whole class attempts to solve two 'real life' problems demonstrated by teacher on board. Small mixed-ability groups solve three more, then individual 'bookwork' on problem solving.	Leads class discussion, supervises mixed-ability groups, monitors individual work providing assistance as required.	Ensures child with disability is provided with a meaningful role in the small group. Ensures that this child locates and can cope with modified individual work.
12.00–1.00	Lunch.	Has lunch break.	Assists with feeding and toileting until 12.15 then takes break.
1.00–1.15	**Silent reading.**	Ensures all children have appropriate reading material. Reads himself to set example.	Continues with remainder of lunch break.
1.15–2.00	**Science** Bats. Children continue with their research projects on bats. Project formats have been left to the discretion of children and include models, posters, essays, illustrated 'books', and in one case a CD-ROM.	Provides individual consultation to children according to need.	At 1.15, reminds and assists with toileting. Provides individual consultation to children according to need.
2.00–2.20	Recess.	Takes break.	Briefly assists feeding child with disability then takes break.
2.20–3.10	**Art** (in art room). Clay sculpture. Some techniques of clay sculpture are demonstrated including the use of tools and water. Children work on their own sculptures.	Demonstrates techniques. Supervises and provides feedback on sculptures.	On entering school building from recess, reminds and assists with toileting. Uses rest of time to prepare modified materials (as directed earlier by teacher) for tomorrow.
3.10–3.15	Prepare for home. Announcements.	Makes announcements.	Assists child with disability to prepare for home. Final toilet reminder and assist.
3.15	Class dismissed.	Available for brief parent consultation.	Supervises all children travelling home by bus.

Single lesson plan

Subject area/grade English—Year 10 _____ Date and time April 21, 9.30–10.20

Lesson topic	Literature study—Macbeth

Lesson goal:	For the children to develop an understanding of the way women are represented in Macbeth, and the social and cultural reasons for this.
Materials:	Plays (class set); poster paper, felt markers and stands (six sets).

Procedure:	Teacher introduces lesson topic and how it relates to a deeper understanding of the play as a whole.
	    Class is divided into six mixed-ability groups. Each group moves to a space in the room where there is a chart stand and blank poster paper.
	    The first task of each group is to list ways in which women are portrayed in the play. Examples of this might include 'evil', 'mysterious', 'sneaky', 'lead to the downfall of men', 'irrational', etc. A group 'recorder' then writes these up on the poster paper.
	    The next task of each group is to find passages in the text that support their conclusions on the way women are represented.
	    The six groups then share their findings.
	    Teacher then leads a brief discussion with the whole class on the historical background to society's view of women in England at that time. Differences and similarities between then and now are highlighted. A homework task is then set.

Homework task:	Research the treatment and views society had of women in Shakespeare's time. Write a two-page report on this.
Teacher does:	Introduces topic; divides class into groups; sets task; engages with each group and provides input as required; facilitates groups sharing; leads discussion on women in the 1600s; sets homework.
Paraprofessional does:	During activities moves from group to group encouraging input from all children. Ensures that child with visual impairment is able to contribute. Ensures that braille version of play is available. While groups share findings and teacher leads final discussion, paraprofessional leaves class and uses time to locate appropriate
Assessment:	Success of this session will be judged on the quality of group responses and the homework tasks.

done discreetly. Staff can usually stand a reasonable distance away and still supervise effectively. They can also pretend to be watching other children or doing a different activity. The less time a staff member spends with a child during break times the better.

Box 5.6: Paraprofessional supervision checklist

- ❐ Have I assessed my classroom and identified areas in which a paraprofessional can be most effectively used?
- ❐ Have I negotiated and communicated clearly defined roles with my paraprofessional?
- ❐ Have I ensured that my paraprofessional has the skills to perform well in these roles?
- ❐ Is my paraprofessional aware of the need for confidentiality, discretion, and the general philosophy behind the practice of inclusion?
- ❐ Have I provided my paraprofessional with adequate background information on the children he/she will be working with?
- ❐ Is my paraprofessional aware of how I plan and are they able to use my plans for guidance?
- ❐ Is my paraprofessional aware of my classroom routines and policies?
- ❐ Has my paraprofessional been introduced to the class in such a way as to communicate that his/her authority over children is the same as any staff member?
- ❐ Have I taken steps to ensure that my paraprofessional feels comfortable working with me and can work as a collaborator in the classroom with me?

Collaboration with parents in the inclusive classroom

It has become increasingly evident that partnerships between the home and the school are particularly beneficial for children with diverse abilities, and the notion that family involvement is important to the success of these children in regular schools is now widely accepted (Strickland and Turnbull 1990; Lewis 1992; Hayes 1998). Parents can bring a wealth of knowledge about their child that the school might not have previously been aware of (Lipsky 1989). A parent's in-depth knowledge of their child's needs and abilities can help schools and teachers to decide appropriate learning tasks, environments and teaching styles (Hayes 1998). School professionals can use this knowledge to construct programs that better address the needs and interests of the children they teach. Indeed, parent participation and cooperation is regarded as essential to good school programming. Goals being pursued at school can also be pursued in the home where the context of the learning is often more comfortable and secure for a child. The chances that skills learned both at home and school will be generalised are greater in these instances (Ashman and Elkins 1998; Hayes 1998).

Despite this, parents as a resource are often undervalued by schools and educational professionals in general. Indeed, Sommerstein and Wessels (1996), frustrated in their roles as parents, remark that, 'We have analyzed, organized, scrutinized, and even successfully litigated, and yet we are still affecting children only on a case-by-case, limited basis. What else do we need to do?' (p. 367). Parental relationships with schools cover the spectrum from productive and cordial to outright hostile and combative. Schools may view parents who are intent on being involved in their child's education as intrusive and overbearing, especially those parents who have resorted to the media or the courts in order to have their children included in a particular school (Erwin and Soodak 1995). On the other hand, parents may lack the confidence to become involved in schools staffed by professionals who seemingly know 'what is right' for their child educationally (Sommerstein and Wessels 1996). Open and mutually supportive parent–school partnerships can help to address the 'us and them' mentality that exists in many of today's schools. More involvement of parents as partners can help to reduce misunderstandings and so help to produce a more harmonious experience for all involved, including the child (Sommerstein and Wessels 1996).

So how might a collaborative relationship with parents be best achieved? Firstly, as is the case with other people with whom you work, it is important to have clearly defined roles. Parents already perform a number of roles, many of which can translate directly to teaching and learning situations. More than 20 years ago Turnbull and Turnbull (1982) conceptualised the roles of parents of children with diverse abilities as they relate to education. They described a variety of roles that are still valid today (see Box 5.7).

Box 5.7: Parent roles

Parents as decision makers   Parents can make decisions about child placement and school issues such as curriculum, instruction, resourcing and personal care.

Parents as advocates for the rights of their child   Parents have a role to play in ensuring that their child receives appropriate educational services and care. Parents are usually the most motivated of all the stakeholders to ensure that the rights of their children are not infringed on, given that they love their child and that the general responsibility, both legally and morally, for the well-being of their child rests with them.

Parents as teachers Parents are well placed to act as teachers of their own children as they have the most contact with the child and usually know their interests and abilities better than anyone else.

Turnbull and Turnbull (1982) argue that the level of participation in these roles should be based on the preferences of the parents, which are then respected by professionals. We suggest that all parents of children with diverse abilities be given the opportunity to collaborate with schools in each of these areas.

Parents as decision makers

The obvious way for parents to collaborate in decision making is through participation in their child's 'Program Support Group'. In some parts of the world parent involvement in this group is mandated, but the quality and quantity of their contributions relies on both their willingness to participate and their acceptance by the rest of the group and the larger school community. Parents need to be empowered. They need to feel that their contributions to the decision-making process are both respected and acted upon. Teachers need to make parents feel like the equal partners they are if this is to be achieved. Dettmer et al. (1999) suggest the participation of willing parents in the Program Support Group can be enhanced through good communication by:

- being aware of tone of voice and body language
- welcoming parents with a cup of coffee and a smile
- being honest and specific. Do not avoid difficult issues
- giving one's point of view as information, not necessarily the absolute truth
- listening at least as much as talking
- checking to ensure your messages are understood
- avoiding educational jargon
- distinguishing between problems and people
- focusing on positive or informative aspects of a problem
- making a few positive contributions for every negative one
- incorporating good ideas and suggestions from parents into the final plan.

Following these guidelines will help to produce an honest and professional relationship with parents while at the same time encouraging them to participate in decision making in a meaningful way.

Parents as advocates for their child

Parents are usually the best advocates for their child. As a teacher you should be aware of this and make some provision for parents to exercise this role. Probably the best way you can ensure that parents are good advocates for their child is for you to form an open and trusting relationship with them. In doing this, parents are probably more likely to address their concerns with you before any problems get out of hand. Any problem requiring parental advocacy can be viewed as a problem to be solved in partnership with the parents. Having said this, parents should also be made aware of their options for action if they feel a concern is too large to be dealt with at the classroom level, or if they feel their concern has not been adequately addressed. These options might include speaking with the school principal, administrators and officials outside the school, or government-run advocacy bodies.

The more active parents are in an educational program, the better advocates they can be. Parent involvement in the classroom and in program planning is to be encouraged. Parents who are an integral component in the day-to-day activities in a classroom are best placed to make suggestions about how education might be improved for their child.

Parents as teachers

Involving willing parents as teachers can be of enormous benefit to any child. The insight that parents can provide into the strengths, needs and interests of their child makes them well placed to act as teachers. Furthermore, most parents have already been teaching their children for years. Speaking, dressing, manners, washing and a whole host of other skills are usually taught to children by parents before they even arrive at school. As an educator you can assist parents by providing them with a framework and strategies to help them better teach their child once they have reached school age.

There are two settings in which parents can teach their children, the home and the school. Education at home can be both formal (through assistance with homework tasks) or more commonly, and often with greater effect, informal. Homework tasks should usually be set so that children need minimal assistance from parents. At times when assistance is required, a parent can be called on by the child. As a teacher you may also find it helpful to flag to parents which homework tasks in particular their child might need assistance with. If the parent you work with is involved in planning or in working on activities in the classroom then he/she will be better placed to provide appropriate assistance. These parents will probably be aware in advance of the instructional goals of the particular task.

One of the best ways parents can be involved in providing instruction at home is through their involvement in the decision making and planning process. Depending on the child and the context of the home, learning objectives can be set that can be worked on in multiple environments. Parents can reinforce at home what is being taught at school. An example of this might be to assist a child in gaining more meaning from the printed word. The objective might be for the child to examine a book and try to gather information about what the book might be about from the illustrations etc. before tackling the print. This objective can be worked on in reading sessions at school, but it can also be addressed in the home if the child has stories before bedtime. In this situation the parents can encourage the child to examine the book before it is read in the same way it is done at school.

Objectives that can be taught in this way both at home and at school should be clearly identified in advance with the parent and a loose plan that respects the informality of the home setting should be developed for when and where instruction will occur in the home. A planning sheet might look something like the planning sheet opposite (see also Form 7 in Useful forms).

Parent involvement in a classroom can also be extremely helpful. It can create a bond between teacher and parents and can produce an atmosphere of shared responsibility for the education of children. Parents can work in a variety of ways in a classroom, but teachers must take care to ensure that they do not take the place of a paid member of staff (such as a paraprofessional) and are not expected to undertake tasks that would normally be assigned to a member of staff or for which they are not trained and qualified. Given this, tasks such as toileting other children, for example, are probably best left to trained school staff.

In order for the work parents do in a classroom to be productive, parental classroom roles must be clearly defined in advance and adhered to. A shared understanding must be negotiated, similar to the shared understanding you must develop with paraprofessionals, as to what a parent will and will not do in the classroom. By taking the time to do this a lot of problems that result from misunderstandings may be solved in advance.

Box 5.8: Classroom tasks for parents

The types of tasks parents can assist with in the classroom include, but are not limited to the following:

- assisting in supervising and facilitating activities with small groups of children
- teaching workshops in areas in which they have talents (e.g. drama, art, writing)
- assisting in non-instructional tasks such as administration (word processing, etc.) or class bulletin boards
- assisting individual children during individual project/work time

Learning at home planning sheet

For Jim

Objective	What happens at school	What can happen at home
1. To examine a book and try to gather information about what the book might be about from the illustrations etc. before tackling the print.	During small group reading time Jim is encouraged, along with the group, to predict what will happen in a story based on non-print information.	During bedtime stories encourage Jim to predict what will happen in the story based on the title, cover, and the illustrations. Jim may need to be guided to examine the book in a logical order (i.e. front to back).
2. To re-tell a story in his own words, covering all the major content points.	At the end of a story Jim is encouraged to re-tell the plot to another child and ask questions about parts he does not understand.	After his bedtime story Jim can re-tell the story to Dad and ask any questions he has about the story.
3. To write his own story based on the themes found in a book he has read.	After reading a story Jim is encouraged to think of a new context for the themes of the story and to write a new story.	Jim can be encouraged to tell his own story based on the themes/moral encountered in his bedtime story.

- assisting children to research assignments
- assisting with child clubs
- giving talks to the class in areas of expertise
- organising a class parent group
- assisting on community outings and school special events
- reading to children

Collaborating with colleagues requires some effort on the part of teachers, but the reward for students can be a program that better meets individual needs within the context of an inclusive environment. Your role as a collaborator will vary from context to context, but we hope that the information contained in this chapter can easily be adapted to suit your situation and make your collaborations more productive. The next chapter examines inclusive development and management of an individual student program. We hope that what you know about collaborations with colleagues will inform your reading of this chapter, and that you are able to see areas in which such collaborations are possible as you develop and manage your own student programs.

KEY TERMS FROM THIS CHAPTER

Colleagues Teachers, paraprofessionals, other professionals and parents.

Collaboration A process whereby participants develop shared meanings and/or a shared agenda and then, in a cooperative way, set out to implement that agenda.

Paraprofessionals People who help schools and teachers provide services to children with diverse abilities.

Allied health professionals Psychologists, physiotherapists, occupational therapists, speech/language therapists, audiologists and other therapists such as music therapists.

FURTHER READING

Cook, L. and Friend, M. (1995), 'Co-teaching guidelines for effective practice' in *Focus on Exceptional Children*, 28(2), pp. 1–12.

Dettmer, P., Dyck, N. and Thurston, L.P. (1999), *Consultation, Collaboration, and Teamwork for Students with Special Needs*, Needham Heights, MA: Allyn & Bacon.

Giangreco, M., Broer, S.M. and Edelman, S. (1999), 'The tip of the iceberg: Determining whether paraprofessional support is needed for students with disabilities in general education settings' in *Journal of the Association for Persons with Severe Handicaps*, 24(4), pp. 281–91.

Giangreco, M.F., Edelman, S.W., Evans Luiselli, T. and MacFarland, S.Z.C. (1997), 'Helping or hovering? Effects of instructional assistant proximity on students with disabilities' in *Exceptional Children*, 64(1), pp. 7–18.

Turnbull, A.P. and Turnbull, H.R. (1982), 'Parent involvement in the education of handicapped children: A critique' in *Mental Retardation*, 20(3), pp. 115–22.

6

How to develop and manage an individual program

Individual programs for diverse learners help educators to ensure that these children are making progress at school. Well-written individual programs also help a teacher to systematically structure and sequence learning in specifically targeted areas. This is not to say that everything a child learns at school will or should be included in an individual plan. Rather, individual programs provide a focus point for the main emphasis of a child's learning over a specified period of time. Used properly, they can be an excellent aid to teaching on a daily basis. This chapter explores ways in which useful individual program plans for diverse learners can be developed and documented. It discusses how relevant goals can be devised and written so as to make them easy to evaluate during, and at the conclusion of, a teaching sequence.

KEY IDEAS IN THIS CHAPTER
- individual programming
- the role of the Program Support Group in developing a program
- developing a long-term vision
- linking assessment to program development
- establishing long-term goals and learning priorities
- establishing short-term behavioural objectives
- indicators of achievement
- a template for individual planning

The individual program plan

Issues surrounding curriculum provision to children with diverse abilities and their peers in inclusive settings are central to successful inclusion (Margolis and Truesdell 1987; Clough 1988; Gormley and McDermott 1994; Carpenter 1997; Cole and McLeskey 1997). The idea that children with diverse abilities should be provided with individual programming has now also been incorporated into the legislation or policy of almost every Western country (OECD 1994). Classrooms are expected to provide instruction in well-defined learning problems related to the specific needs of the child with diverse abilities, while also ensuring that they are included in the regular program as much as possible (Madden and Slavin 1983; Strickland and Turnbull 1990). The paradigm of modification of the regular curriculum is based on a number of assumptions about children with diverse abilities. These include that children with diverse abilities often learn at different rates, may be unable to perform standard assessment tasks, and often may require more practice and repetition to consolidate learning (Ryndak and Alper 1996).

Supporters of individual education argue that a child's specific educational goals can be targeted and met through the effective use of an individual educational program (Alter and Goldstein 1986; Strickland and Turnbull 1990; Cheney and Demchak 1996). The careful and systematic structuring of appropriate educational goals for a child with a diverse ability through adaptation and modification of the regular curriculum is viewed by supporters as an excellent method of providing an appropriate education, while also allowing for inclusion in a regular class (Strickland and Turnbull 1990; Cheney and Demchak 1996).

Box 6.1: Advantages of individual program plans

There are many advantages to planning programs for individuals as they tend to:

- help to ensure accountability—the person responsible for providing instruction has clear curricular expectations that must be addressed and which are monitored (Goodman and Bond 1993)
- help compensate for lack of attention in curriculum—often the regular curriculum is not comprehensive enough to target areas relevant to the lives of children with diverse abilities (Clough 1988)
- give parents the opportunity to have input into what their children learn (Strickland and Turnbull 1990)
- provide a structure that assists educational collaborators in focusing on important areas of learning for a child (Goodman and Bond 1993)

- provide information on how certain aspects of curriculum will be taught to a child (Ryndak and Alper 1996)
- outline in advance additional resources and support services a child may require (Ryndak and Alper 1996)
- provide a framework for assessment (Goodman and Bond 1993)
- are useful records at times of transition (Deppeler 1998).

Modification of curriculum to suit an individual child does, however, have its critics. Some view this type of process as a means of singling out as 'other' and marginalising people with disabilities in order to exercise control over them through special programs (Corbett 1993; Danforth 1997; Evans and Vincent 1997). Individual plans are also criticised for presenting children with disabilities with too prescriptive a curriculum. Such a tightly constructed plan of learning is seen by critics as leaving little opportunity for a child to direct his or her own learning and, as a result, the instruction becomes teacher centred (Goodman and Bond 1993). Individual goals also frequently focus on specific skills rather than cognitive aspects of learning (Weisenfeld 1987; Collet-Klingenberg and Chadsey-Rusch 1991; Goodman and Bond 1993). Often these skills are applicable to only a limited number of situations. There is some evidence to suggest that narrow skill development such as this is the overriding focus of the curriculum for children without disabilities (Collet-Klingenberg and Chadsey-Rusch 1991; Goodman and Bond 1993).

Box 6.2: Disadvantages of individual program plans

The negative aspects of individual program plans are that they:

- are often not linked to the regular curriculum and can isolate a child within a class-room (Ryndak and Alper 1996)
- represent additional paperwork for teachers (Gerardi et al. 1984)
- are not used by many teachers to guide instruction (Margolis and Truesdell 1987)
- perpetuate the notion that children with disabilities are inherently different to other children (Ryndak and Alper 1996)
- often involve narrow, mundane learning tasks (Collet-Klingenberg and Chadsey-Rusch 1991)
- often focus on 'training' rather than 'education' (Goodman and Bond 1993)
- are not child centred, rather, they are prescriptive and provide little opportunity to follow up a child's incidental interests (Goodman and Bond 1993).

While there are many disadvantages associated with the use of individual program plans, most of these can be overcome if the plan is viewed as a fluid document that operates within the context of the regular class curriculum. Individual program plans can assist you to include a child with diverse abilities into your classroom if care is put into the development and implementation of these plans.

Role of the Program Support Group in individual program planning

Involvement of a Program Support Group is fundamental in the process of developing an individual program plan for a child. Indeed, it is the primary task of the Program Support Group to not only ensure that adequate assessment is carried out, but also to develop, assist and monitor the implementation of the curriculum for a child with diverse learning needs (Strickland and Turnbull 1990; Friend and Bursuck 1999; Mastropieri and Scruggs 2000). Program Support Groups have different names from region to region, but in this context the term refers to the committee of important people involved, including the child. The membership should include parents, the child (if possible), teachers, a school administrator, and other professionals and paraprofessionals.

Regular Program Support Group meetings should be scheduled and held, along with additional meetings called on the basis of need. This will enable you to monitor the implementation and evaluation of the plan, and to respond by making changes to any elements of the plan that require these changes. Program Support Group meetings should be run as formal meetings with an agenda set beforehand and minutes taken and later distributed to all members of the group. An example of an agenda for a Program Support Group meeting (adapted from Strickland and Turnbull 1990) is on page 116 (see also Form 8 in the Useful forms section).

Another important role of the Program Support Group is to ensure any medical and physical needs are provided during lessons. An example of the way this can be provided is through the use of forms which are signed by each member of the group so that everyone is aware of the children's needs (see Form 9 in Useful forms as an example). See also Chapter 9 for further medical requirement needs.

Compiling an individual program plan

It is often helpful to think of individual program plans as being hierarchical in nature. They begin with broad visions and goals that are gradually broken down into more manageable segments for teaching. The style of the individual program plan we recommend is structured as a flow-chart.

Agenda for meeting of Program Support Group

Child: Jeremy X   Date of meeting: April 1

Place: West Wing, White House School   Time: 2:00pm – 4:30pm

PSG Members:
Mr and Mrs X, Parents
Jeremy X, Child
Mr Smith, Classroom Teacher
Mrs Jones, Curriculum Coordinator
Mrs Williams, Program Aide
Mr Consultant, Programming for Child Differences
Mrs Hunt, Probation Officer

Purpose: To begin the process of developing an individual program plan for Jeremy

Status   First Meeting

Time	Activity	Program Support Group members responsible
2:00 – 2:05	Introduction of committee members.	Mrs Jones
2:05 – 2:10	Review and approval of agenda, and explanation of procedures to be followed during meeting.	Mrs Jones
2:10 – 2:15	Discussion and agreement as to chairperson and 'case manager'. Recommendation of Mrs Jones to the position.	Mr Smith Mr Consultant
2:15 – 2:45	Review of evaluation information and current levels of performance. • Jeremy, insight into own levels of performance in all six subject areas. • Mr Smith, identification of strengths and needs. Data gathered through tests and informal observations. Presentation of work samples. • Mr Consultant, presentation of data from standardised testing. Mr & Mrs X, observations of Jeremy's level of functioning.	Jeremy Mr Consultant Mr Smith Mr & Mrs X
2:45 – 3:30	Identification and agreement of the areas in which specifically designed instruction is required.	All members
3:30 – 4:20	Development of goals, objectives and evaluation criteria and schedules in each designated area. Identification of and agreement on necessary related services. (Another meeting may be required to complete this.)	All members
4:20 – 4:21	Determine placement. Likely that Jeremy will continue at the White House School.	Mrs Jones
4:21 – 4:30	Summary of meeting. Clarification of areas requiring further work at a future meeting. Date set and agreed to by all members for next meeting.	Mrs Jones
4:30	Adjournment of meeting.	Mrs Jones

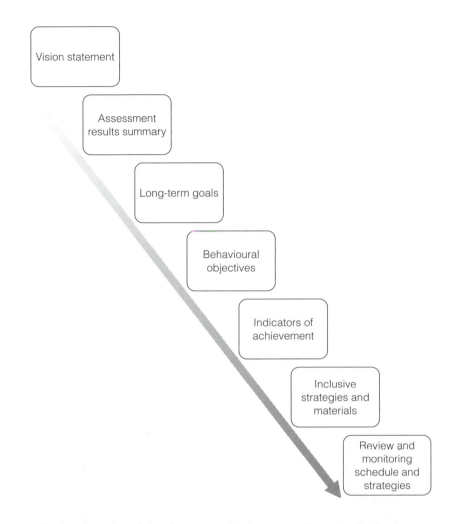

Blank examples of the forms required to compile an individual program plan can be found in the Useful forms section. The examples here were completed following the steps in the flow-chart above. We shall now go through these steps, one by one, to clarify the elements they comprise.

Vision statement

Very few individual program plans in the past have included a vision statement, however, this can be an important part of the process of developing a useful plan. The vision statement is a brief message at the beginning of an individual program plan that, in a very general sense, attempts to convey the 'big picture' of where those involved with the child hope he/she is headed. The statement should be positive and may involve the hopes and dreams of the child, family and school staff. A good vision statement can help provide direction for the long-term goals being set. An example of a vision statement would be:

> Our hope for the future is that Jeremy will be able to live as independently as possible, with minimal assistance from others in daily living activities, shoppingand personal care. We hope he will hold down a job he enjoys with an employer who values his contributions. We would like Jeremy to enjoy an active social life and develop close friendships and life-long relationships with people he loves and values, and whose company he enjoys.

This statement, while brief and very general, does provide some direction for the setting of long-term goals. It expresses future hopes in three main areas: independent living, employment and social life. Jeremy's goals, then, can be written to reflect these dreams for his life as an adult. This statement should be placed in the space provided on the 'Individual program plan' (see opposite and Form 10 in Useful forms).

Developing a vision statement may take some time and effort as the views of all members of the Program Support Group should be taken into account. In developing the vision statement the following questions might be asked:

- What does the child enjoy doing now? Does this activity have any long-term implications?
- What are the child's dreams for the future?
- What are the parents' dreams for the future?
- What would you like to see the child do on leaving school?
- What would you like to see the child doing when he/she becomes an adult?
- What are the components of a happy and fulfilled life? What do you think will lead to the child having a happy and fulfilled life as an adult?
- Is there any reason why the child may not attain his/her dreams? How can these be overcome?

Assessment results summary

If you have followed the procedures outlined in previous chapters you should, by now, have gathered a range of information about the child with diverse abilities. This information should tell you a lot about his or her background, interests, strengths, needs, and progress in terms of the curriculum. This information is vital to the successful development of an appropriate education plan.

Prior to the Program Support Group meeting, each member of the group should be given adequate time to thoroughly read and understand the reports

Individual program plan

Child name:	Jeremy	Age:		Grade/Year
Coordinating Teacher	Mr Smith	Date:	April 15	

Vision Statement: Our hope for the future is that Jeremy will be able to live as independently as possible, with minimal assistance from others in daily living activities, shopping, and personal care. We hope he will hold down a job he enjoys with an employer who values his contributions. We would like Jeremy to enjoy an active social life and develop close friendships and life-long relationships with people he loves and values, and whose company he enjoys.

Assessment Results summary:

Assessment Type	Description of Results
WISC-III (psychologist)	• Full-scale IQ of 58. • Global difficulties across each subset but particularly in reading comprehension, spelling and written expression.
Vineland ABS – Expanded form: Interview and Classroom Editions (psychologist analysed)	• Below-average performance in all domains. • Difficulties particularly acute in socialisation and motor skills domains. • Socialisation: does not interact well with others, tends to play alone. • Motor skills: gross motor particularly acute. Slow, difficulty with obstacles, tends to lose balance.
Structured observations at school (teacher and aide conducted)	• Difficulty maintaining positive social relationships: plays alone or argues/fights. • Does not respect 'personal space' during social interactions.
Anecdotal information (teachers, parents, aide, Jeremy)	• Does not recognise opportunities for positive social interactions. • 'Personal space' an issue.
Curriculum-based assessment (teacher)	• Counts to 1000, adds, subtracts, multiplies, simple division. Simple graphing OK. Basic understanding of fractions. Uses concrete aids. • Reads phonetically. Comprehension poor on books over about Grade 3 level. Frequent spelling errors. Difficulties with written expression. • Excels in art. Primarily interested in painting. Has mastered advanced techniques including shading and use of oils & canvas. Aptitude is emerging in other areas such as sculpture.

of each assessment. This should not take place immediately before the meeting, as some members of the group may need time to consider the reports in detail. If some members do not understand particular aspects of the assessment reports, these should be explained to them at the Program Support Group meeting by the person who wrote the report, or by someone who understands the type of assessment that has been undertaken.

The assessment results summary is exactly that. It is a summary of the results of all assessments carried out prior to the Program Support Group meeting. The purpose of the assessment results summary is to remind members of the Program Support Group about the most significant findings from each of the assessments. It is not supposed to be a comprehensive description of every aspect of each assessment. By the time the Program Support Group meeting is held it can be assumed that each member of the group is familiar with the original reports. It is the task of the person responsible for the coordination of the individual program to complete the assessment results summary prior to the first Program Support Group meeting. An assessment results summary should be no longer than one page, and where possible should be written in point form. An example of an assessment results summary for Jeremy follows. It comprises the bottom half of the 'Individual program plan' (see Form 10 in Useful forms) You will note that it contains a variety of assessments, including formal psychological assessments, observation, work samples and curriculum-based assessments.

Long-term goals

Long-term goals are an important part of any program. They should describe what is to be achieved with a child over an extended period of time. The length of time a long-term goal should cover varies from context to context, but generally speaking a long-term goal should cover no longer than a one-year period. This one-year timeline is very common in schools today. In some cases long-term goals have been known to cover periods as brief as six or even three months where the teaching sequence has been intensive.

Long-term goals should result from elements of the vision statement along with the information that is included in the assessment results summary. Long-term goals can be quite general in nature. They paint a broad picture of areas in which the child is to develop over an extended period. It is important to keep them simple and clear when writing them so that anyone involved can understand them.

Indeed, simplicity is the key to effective individual program plans. Not only should goals be simply stated, but they should also be few in number. Each long-term goal will eventually be accompanied by a number of behavioural objectives, and those developing the plan need to keep in mind what is realistic to achieve in a regular classroom over the specified time period given levels of staffing and resources. Remember that the purpose of an individual program plan is not to cover everything a child will learn at school, but rather to create a focus on some of the most important areas of learning for that child. Generally speaking, there is rarely any need to go beyond three long-term goals for any one child.

Example: Poor practice

Sally was a dedicated and hard-working teacher. She wanted Albert, a child with a disability in her class, to develop and grow in a wide variety of areas. The Program Support Group agreed, and together they set seven long-term goals for Albert. To each of these goals they attached five specific behavioural objectives to be achieved. This made a total of 35 objectives for the year.

Being a diligent teacher, Sally ensured that she reflected each of these objectives for Albert in her regular classroom program. She soon found, however, that there were so many objectives she couldn't keep track of them all. She also found that there was never enough time during the week to adequately address each of these objectives with Albert. She kept up with the paperwork involved in monitoring each of the objectives by working late into the night.

At the end of the year Sally's assessments demonstrated that none of the goals for Albert had been fully achieved, although partial progress had been made towards some. The failure to achieve Albert's goals was the result of too many goals. Instead of focusing on a few important areas, Sally was 'spread too thin' by trying to achieve too much. Despite her hard work, by trying to accomplish everything she succeeded in accomplishing nothing.

After the careful examination of the vision statement and the assessment results summary, each member of the Program Support Group should, individually, list what they consider to be important areas where goals could be set in order of priority. When each member of the group has done this, the Program Support Group should then discuss and agree on what they consider to be the main priorities as a group. This may involve some debate as to which learning areas are more important that others. These priorities should then be written up on a separate form and used as the basis for writing the goals. An example of a filled out form for Jeremy follows (see also Form 11 in Useful forms). The first form is an example of what an individual member of the Program Support Group might list, based on Jeremy's vision statement and assessment results summary. The group list is an example of what priorities

Long-term goals

(Individual list)   Group list   (please circle whichever applies)

Child name: Jeremy X	Date: April 15

Learning Priorities
(in order of most important to least important)

1)	Learning social skills
2)	Employment-related skills
3)	Foster artistic talents
4)	Improve mobility
5)	Improve academic performance

Long-term goals

Individual list   (Group list)   (please circle whichever applies)

Child name: Jeremy X	Date: April 15

Learning Priorities
(in order of most important to least important)

1)	Developing social skills
2)	Fostering artistic talents
3)	Improving mobility/motor skills
4)	Improve academic performance
5)	

might have been agreed on for Jeremy after some discussion by all members of the Program Support Group.

Once priorities have been established, the Program Support Group can begin the task of wording the long-term goals. In devising long-term goals it is important to remember the points in Box 6.3.

Box 6.3: Hints for establishing long-term goals

In devising long-term goals it is important to remember that:

- there should be a focus on the strengths as well as the needs of a child—it is unfair to expect a child to always work in areas that he or she is not good in
- goals should be based on the Program Support Group's priorities
- goals should be written in terms of learning outcomes and they need to be child-centred—a long-term goal stating something like 'To include Jill in all art classes' is based on what school staff intend to do with Jill, not on what Jill will actually accomplish; a better goal in this instance might be 'For Jill to improve her level of participation in art classes', which outlines what Jill needs to do in order to accomplish her long-term goal
- goals need not be too specific—the behavioural objectives that follow this section will deal with this
- a time should be provided as to when it is expected each goal will be accomplished.

Examples of goals for Jeremy are shown in the example below. Because his Program Support Group wanted to avoid crowding his program with too many long-term goals, they chose to focus on the three highest priorities only. His goals are as follows:

Example: Long-term goals for Jeremy

1 *For Jeremy to improve his social skills and to increase his level of social interactions, both at home and in the community. Timeline: End of year.*
2 *For Jeremy to extend and further develop his artistic talents and skills. Timeline: End of year.*
3 *For Jeremy to improve on his current level of mobility and general motor skills. Timeline: End of Term two.*

Notice that Jeremy's goals relate to his top three priorities established by the Program Support Group. They are also limited to a realistically achievable number, are written in terms of what Jeremy needs to do, are brief and clear, and a timeline for completion is provided. One of the goals is clearly focused on a strength while the others are worded positively.

The final thing to do in relation to goals is to check if they live up to what is hoped for in the vision statement. When we compare Jeremy's goals to the 'vision statement' we can see that the social-skills goal addresses the vision for an active social life in the future. The goal of developing his art skills relates to a possible future career as an artist given his talent and love of art. It also focuses on one of his strengths. The mobility goal addresses the future desire for a more independent lifestyle. Each of these goals is a step closer to achieving the overall vision for Jeremy.

Behavioural objectives

Behavioural objectives are statements, based on the long-term goals, that say what needs to be done in order to achieve these goals. Behavioural objectives are based on the theories of behaviourists such as Watson and Skinner. Behavioural objectives are short-term in nature. They may take anywhere from a few days to some months to accomplish, depending on the child and the educational context. The term 'behavioural' refers to the fact that a child must clearly demonstrate that he/she can do something in order to be said to have achieved the objective. The objective must be precise and measurable. As with the long-term goals, they must be written in terms of what the child must do.

To devise behavioural objectives, individual long-term goals must be examined one at a time. Members of the Program Support Group must ask themselves, 'What sorts of things does the child need to do to demonstrate that he/she has achieved this long-term goal?' As is the case with long-term goals, Program Support Groups should be careful not to select so many behavioural objectives that it is impossible to fit them all into a year. As a general rule, we recommend no more than four behavioural objectives per goal and if it is possible to achieve the goal with less than four objectives, then this should be done. For Jeremy, the behavioural objectives for one of his goals could be as follows.

Example: Establishing behavioural objectives for Jeremy

Child name: Jeremy X
Goal for examination:
For Jeremy to improve his social skills and to increase his level of social interactions both at home and in the community.
Timeline: End of year

What needs to happen to achieve this goal?

1 Jeremy needs to learn to respect the 'personal space' of others.
2 Jeremy needs to better identify instances where he could participate socially with other kids.
3 Jeremy needs to become more involved in community activities with his peers.

Once the Program Support Group has established what needs to be done in order to achieve the goal, some further assessment must take place to ensure these priority areas are relevant to the student. We believe this is best done using a task analysis.

Using task analysis to identify behavioural objectives

Task analysis is a simple process whereby broad learning tasks are broken down into simple components that can be learned one at a time until the broader task is mastered. Task analysis has been around for many years and is based on behavioural–psychological principles. Linear and tightly constructed approaches to teaching, like task analysis, have been criticised by many for being teacher centred and too narrow in focus, resulting in training rather than education (Weisenfeld 1987; Collet-Klingenberg and Chadsey-Rusch 1991; Goodman and Bond 1993). This criticism is valid, and we certainly do not suggest that task analysis is an appropriate basis for an entire educational program. Rather, it is presented here as a valuable tool that can be used to assess and teach specific skills where the normal teaching sequence has proved inadequate for a particular child. It is a good means of assessing a child's progress against a set of criteria from which you can derive some short-term objectives.

There are two types of task analysis: general task analysis and specific task analysis. The principles behind each type are essentially the same. The difference is in the level of detail. A specific task analysis, often used more as a teaching tool, is discussed in Chapter 7. A general task analysis determines the major components or steps that would usually occur in performing a task, and is often used more for assessment purposes. It enables identification of the basic steps to be taught, and helps you to identify what skills a student needs to focus on as part of short-term objectives. In order to construct a general task analysis you need to record the steps by performing the activity or task (a) yourself and (b) while watching someone else performing it. Be sure to include the social and communicative components as well as the physical components of your task in the analysis.

An example of a general task analysis for the task of asking for information is as follows.

Example: General task analysis—asking for information

1 Wait until the person is free to attend to you.
2 Greet the person.
3 Wait for the person's attention.
4 Make request for information.
5 Answer any questions or requests for further details that may be required.
6 Wait for reply.
7 Listen to reply.
8 If the person cannot help, thank them and leave.
9 If the person can help, check the information given by:
   • repeating back main points, or
   • asking them to please repeat the information.
10 If the information given is not clear ask for clarification and then repeat back main points.
11 Thank the person for the assistance and leave.

This example may seem a fairly detailed breakdown of the components involved in asking for information, however, there is room to break each of the components down even further if required. We recommend that when using a task-analysis approach to teaching you should first develop the general task analysis and then measure the child's progress against the components you have outlined for the task. This process enables you to identify areas requiring further attention, which can then be included as short-term behavioural objectives.

An example form (see opposite) has been set up to record Sarah's progress on the task of asking for information. As can be seen, in the initial assessment Sarah was able to complete each of the components of the task (as indicated by a ✔) up to the step requiring her to ask for clarification (as indicated by a ✗). It is these areas marked with an ✗ that can form some of your behavioural objectives for a particular goal. (See Form 12 in Useful forms for blank).

Once you have identified what the short-term behavioural objectives should be, the process of formally writing them up can begin. One format that is useful in writing many behavioural objectives is:

By the end of . . . *[put date here]*, . . . *[child name]* . . . will be able to . . .

For Sarah, this might read: 'By 19 September, Sarah will be able to ask for clarification and then repeat back main points if the information is not clear.' This format is useful because it not only provides a timeframe for accomplishing the behavioural objective, but also sets the objective in terms of what the child needs to do.

Imagine that, based on the 'Establishing behavioural objectives' example discussed earlier, a general task analysis was conducted on Jeremy's social

General task analysis

Child: _Sarah_

Task: Asking for information	Progress (Date)						
Step	09/9	10/9	12/9	13/9	15/9	18/9	19/9
Wait until the person is free to attend to you	✓	✓	✓				
Greet the person	✓	✓	✓				
Wait for the person's attention	✓	✓	✓				
Make request for information	✓	✓	✓				
Answer any questions or requests for further details that may be required	✓	✓	✓				
Wait for reply	✕	✓	✓				
Listen to reply	✕	✕	✓				
If the person cannot help, thank them and leave	✕	✕	✓				
If the person can help, check the information given by: •repeating back main points, or •asking them to please repeat the information	✕	✕	✓				
If the information given is not clear ask for clarification and then repeat back main points	✕	✕	✕				
Regardless of the answer given, say 'Thank-you' and leave.	✕	✕	✕				

Note: ✔ means 'achieved'
✕ means 'not yet achieved'

skills goal, which found that Jeremy had difficulties respecting personal space, initiating contact and responding to others. An example of his behavioural objectives follows.

Example: Jeremy's behavioural objectives

Goal: *For Jeremy to improve his social skills and to increase his level of social interactions both at home and in the community.*
Timeline: *End of year.*
Objective 1: *By the end of term two Jeremy will stand no closer than approximately 50 cm from other people during conversations without prompting 60 per cent of the time when under observation.*
Objective 2: *By the end of term three Jeremy will increase his initiation of positive social contact with other children at lunch and recess by 60 per cent when under observation.*
Objective 3: *By the end of term three Jeremy will increase the amount of time he responds in a positive manner to social interactions initiated by other children by 50 per cent when under observation.*
Objective 4: *By the end of the year Jeremy will select two community activities (such as sport clubs, Scouts, hobby clubs) and will choose to participate in at least 70 per cent of the activities run by these community bodies.*

Note that objectives 2 and 3 both relate to the same priority (point 2) on the 'Establishing behavioural objectives' example. Given the two-way nature of social interactions, Jeremy's Program Support Group decided that two objectives were required. Note also that the behavioural objectives are written in fairly precise terms, including a percentage amount of improvement or attainment required in each area. A percentage is not essential, but there needs to be some way of measuring progress, and expressing progress in terms of a number is often helpful. In Jeremy's case his Program Support Group thought that a 50 to 60 per cent improvement or attainment in each area was a realistic target.

In some instances terms used in behavioural objectives will need to be defined in advance. In Jeremy's case the term 'positive' is used in relation to social interactions. It may be necessary to define this term so that all members of the team and, most importantly, Jeremy know what is expected. Defining terms such as this can be done in a footnote at the end of the list of objectives. For example:

A 'positive' social interaction is one that is conducted in a friendly manner involving smiles, reciprocal conversation and polite social conventions such as greetings and the use of phrases such as 'please' and 'thank you'. Aggressive physical contact, name-calling, swearing and yelling should not be present in a 'positive social interaction'.

Well-written behavioural objectives spell out what is required in order to achieve the long-term goal. While they mention targets, exactly how these targets are to be measured is not spelled out. This is the job of the indicators of achievement.

Indicators of achievement

Indicators of achievement are written to assist in guiding the measurement of the objectives. They explain what measurement tools will be used, what level of performance is required with respect to these tools, and the times and methods for use of these tools. There may be one or more indicator of achievement for each objective depending on the context. Indicators of achievement are useful because they require Program Support Groups to think through their measurement strategy before the individual program plan is implemented. They also serve as an extremely helpful guide for teachers once the teaching sequence and busy everyday classroom activity has begun. Instead of having to devise measurement methods during this busy time, previously developed indicators of achievement put them at the fingertips of the teacher whenever they are required.

Box 6.4: Devising indicators of achievement

In devising your indicators of achievement you need to consider:

- whether the measurement tool already exists (such as a commercially available standardised test) or needs to be developed by the Program Support Group and whether the observations are going to form the basis of the measurement data
- how often will progress be measured
- who will be responsible for implementing the assessment
- the times during the day when progress measurement will take place
- where the measurement of the objective will take place.

When devising indicators of achievement (see Box 6.4) it is important to take note of assessment techniques such as those discussed in Chapter 4. If baseline data has not been taken already as part of the initial assessment process, it will need to be gathered before the teaching sequence begins. This allows you to compare the data gathered during and after the teaching sequence with data recorded before the teaching sequence to see if progress has been made. Indicators of achievement for one of Jeremy's behavioural objectives, discussed previously, might be as follows.

Example: Jeremy's indicators of achievement

Goal: *For Jeremy to improve his social skills and to increase his level of social interactions both at home and in the community.*
Timeline: *End of year.*
Behavioural objective 4: *By the end of the year Jeremy will select two community activities (such as sport clubs, Scouts, hobby clubs) and will choose to participate in at least 70 per cent of the activities run by these community bodies.*
Indicators of achievement: *Jeremy will have chosen and joined two community clubs by the end of term one. A calendar of activities for each of these clubs will be acquired and Jeremy (under supervision of his parents) will record which ones he attends or does not attend. In order to achieve this objective Jeremy will attend 70 per cent of the activities for each group. Jeremy will keep a brief weekly diary (3–4 lines) describing his participation in the groups for that week. This will support the data from the calendar.*

Notice that a variety of measurement techniques will be used to measure Jeremy's progress on the objective outlined here. The indicators of achievement delineate what sort of data will be gathered, by whom, when and where. A variety of data sources is used, including a diary and self-monitoring.

Inclusive strategies and materials

If you have followed the steps we have outlined, you should now have a fairly comprehensive individual set of goals and objectives for a single child. The checklist in Box 6.5 should ensure all bases have been covered. The key now is to begin to decide how each objective might be addressed in an inclusive way so that the child is not withdrawn from regular classroom activities in order to work on his goals. This section of the plan looks at how the goal will be taught. It includes information on settings, groupings, modes of teaching, and links to the curriculum. This subject will be addressed in greater detail in Chapter 7, and the plans you make should be noted on the individual program plan. To link the long-term goal with the behavioural objectives, indicators of achievements and the inclusive teaching strategies for the objective, you can use Form 13 in Useful forms when you get to Chapter 7.

Box 6.5: Individual program checklist

Outside meetings

- ❏ Gather assessment data/reports
- ❏ Complete the assessment results summary
- ❏ Conduct general task analysis after long-term goals are met

During meetings

- ❏ Prepare a vision statement
- ❏ Examine the assessment results summary
- ❏ Establish learning priorities as individuals
- ❏ Establish learning priorities as a group
- ❏ Devise long-term goals
- ❏ Establish behavioural objectives
- ❏ Write up behavioural objectives
- ❏ Devise indicators of achievement
- ❏ Gather baseline data as required
- ❏ Consider inclusive strategies and materials
- ❏ Set review schedule

Review and monitoring schedule and strategies

The final section of an individual program plan relates to review and monitoring. It is important that an individual program plan is regarded at all times as a working document to be changed and modified by the Program Support Group as required. It is for this reason we suggest they be drawn up on a computer to allow for easy modification. As the individual program plan is an active document it should be reviewed as often as possible. As a minimum we suggest once every school term, but the more often you review the plan the more effective it will be. Your proposed schedule for review should be set out in the document in advance, but should not preclude the calling of extra review meetings as required.

Prior to each formal review session any ongoing assessment data should be gathered and prepared for presentation to the Program Support Group. If behavioural objectives and goals are met earlier than expected, then new ones should be set by the group to replace them.

The final question to be asked is, 'What changes need to be made?' In some instances modifications to some of the areas mentioned above can result in successful achievement of the goal or behavioural objective by the child. In other instances, however, the goal or behavioural objective may need to be abandoned in favour of another, more attainable target. Continuing to work at an unmodified goal or behavioural objective on which a child is making no progress over a significant amount of time is not only pointless but is often counter-productive. Continued work in areas in which no progress is made is both boring and potentially damaging to the child's self-esteem.

Box 6.6: Poor progress?

If no (or little) progress is made on goals during the designated time, the Program Support Group should consider whether:

- the goal or behavioural objective was inappropriate in the first place
- the expected level of achievement was overestimated
- enough time for practice and teaching had been allowed
- there was a problem with assessing progress
- the teaching strategies had been appropriate
- the materials were appropriate
- the goal or behavioural objective was important to the child.

This chapter has discussed how to construct an individual plan of learning for a child. While this type of plan can be an important tool to assist you to focus on the needs of the child with diverse abilities, it should not be used in isolation from the rest of the class and curriculum. How to infuse your individual plan into your classroom program forms the basis of discussion in the following chapter.

KEY TERMS FROM THIS CHAPTER

Individual program plans   A written plan that provides a focus point for the main emphasis of a child's learning over a specified period of time.

Program Support Group   A committee of important people involved in the planning including a child. They ensure that adequate assessment is carried out and also develop, assist and monitor the implementation of curriculum for a child with diverse learning needs.

Vision statement   A brief message at the beginning of an individual program plan that, in a very general sense, attempts to convey the 'big picture' of where those involved with the child hope he/she is headed.

Assessment results summary   A summary of the results of all assessments carried out prior to the Program Support Group meeting.

Behavioural objective   An objective that requires that a child must clearly demonstrate that he/she can do something in order to be said to have achieved the objective.

Task analysis   A simple process whereby broad learning tasks are broken down into simple components that can then be learned one at a time until the broader task is mastered.

FURTHER READING

Goodman, J.F. and Bond, L. (1993), 'The individualized educational program: A retrospective critique' in *Journal of Special Education*, 26(4), pp. 408–22.

Ryndak, D. and Alper, S. (1996), *Curriculum Content for Students with Moderate and Severe Disabilities in Inclusive Settings*, Needham Heights, MA: Allyn & Bacon.

Strickland, B. and Turnbull, A. (1990), *Developing and Implementing Individualized Education Programs*, Colombus, Ohio: Merrill.

7

Inclusive instructional design

In the previous chapter we discussed how to plan and monitor an individual program plan for a specific child. While this is a good way to stay accountable and to ensure that progress is being made, these programs will not assist you to run an inclusive classroom unless they are infused into the regular classroom curriculum. Individual program plans should never be taught in isolation. This chapter discusses how to link individual program goals and objectives to the regular classroom curriculum. It examines modification of materials as well as some frames to assist you in structuring your teaching and curriculum planning for all students.

KEY IDEAS IN THIS CHAPTER
- defining a curriculum
- identifying curriculum adaptations
- linking individual objectives and the classroom curriculum through:
    - unit planning
    - individual lesson planning
- modifying the educational environment:
    - the materials
    - the resources
    - instructional strategies
    - learning outcomes
- using task analysis as a teaching tool

Defining curriculum

Central to the teaching and learning that occurs in schools is the curriculum. Curriculum is an umbrella concept that is comprehensive in scope and complex in practice. In broad terms it has to do with the teaching and learning of knowledge, skills and attitudes. It embraces issues such as subject matter, pedagogy, assessments/evaluation and related resources involved in the organisation, delivery and articulation of education programs (National Board of Employment Education and Training 1992; Deppeler 1998). This book discusses each of the elements included in this definition of curriculum throughout the various chapters. This chapter deals largely with the subject matter and related resources involved in the delivery and articulation of education programs, that is: What is to be taught and how?

When teaching learners with diverse abilities, curriculum can be divided into two broad areas. These are 'core curriculum' and what we call 'elaborative curriculum'. Core curriculum consists of areas judged to be basic and essential for all students: basic in that they provide both a foundation on which subsequent learning may be built and also the conceptual and methodological tools to continue their own learning. They are essential as their intention is to equip students for a satisfying and effective participation in social and cultural life. A vital aspect of the core curriculum is its affinities with democratic ideology and its assumption that constructive and active participation is the right and responsibility of every person (OECD 1994b; Deppeler 1998).

The term 'elaborative curriculum' relates to all other aspects of curriculum that could be considered 'non-core'. The elaborative curriculum is important as it adds richness, depth, scope and variety to the core curriculum. What constitutes core curriculum and what constitutes elaborative curriculum is context dependent and depends on the views, attitudes and values of everyone involved in the educational process. For some, learning in school subject areas such as fine art or music would be seen as non-essential, and therefore could be classified as elaborative curriculum. For others with strong views on the importance of art and music in society, learning in these subject areas might be seen as essential and they would be included as part of the core curriculum. Most teachers already have an idea as to what they consider core curriculum and elaborative curriculum, ideas which vary from teacher to teacher. Much of what you emphasise in your teaching of all children, including diverse learners, will be based on these ideas.

We believe that the learning of children with diverse abilities should be based on a mixture of both the core and elaborative curriculum. The proportion of time you spend on each of these divisions of curriculum will depend on the individual child and the learning context. Often children with disabilities will require a greater focus on aspects of the core curriculum. Children who are gifted and talented may need a greater focus on the elaborative curriculum so that they can advance on swiftly attained learning in core-curriculum areas. It is important to ensure, however, that no matter who the child is, elements of both curriculum divisions are included to allow for a rich educational experience based on solid foundations.

Questions for identifying curriculum adaptations

We know of no country in the world in which the regular curriculum is appropriate for all students. While most education systems claim that their curriculum is appropriate for all, this is never the case unless some form of curriculum adaptation takes place. Few education systems include learning goals as basic as toilet training or self-feeding in their regular curriculum. Similarly, educational outcomes relevant to those children who are extremely academically advanced often fall outside of what is planned for in the regular curriculum for students up to the end of secondary school. While good instructional design for the entire class can minimise the need for adaptations, sometimes the only way to cater for children with these diverse needs is to adapt the curriculum in order to accommodate their learning goals.

Box 7.1: Questions identifying curriculum adaptations

Deppeler (1998) posed these questions as those that teachers should ask in identifying curriculum adaptations:

1   Can the learner take part in the curriculum in the same way as others? If not …

   (a)   can the learner take part in the curriculum in the same way as other students if the environment is modified?

   (b)   can the learner take part in the curriculum in the same way as other students if instructional strategies are modified?

   (c)   can the learner take part in the curriculum in the same way as other students but with different learning outcomes?

2   What adaptations are needed to maximise learning and participation?

Deppeler's (1998) questions in Box 7.1 are based on the premise that children with diverse abilities should be participating in the curriculum in the same way that other children do in the first instance. Teachers can sometimes be guilty of automatically making modifications to the curriculum for students with diverse abilities when this may not be necessary. It is easier for the teacher and more inclusive for students with diverse abilities if they can take part in classroom activities with no modifications at all. In instances where children are unable to participate in the curriculum without modifications being made, then the least obtrusive modifications should first be considered. For example, modifications are often less obtrusive in a classroom if they involve modification of materials rather than direct assistance from an additional staff member.

Identifying links between individual objectives and the classroom curriculum

If you have been following the advice in this book you should, by now, have developed an individual program plan for your student with diverse learning needs. For this plan to assist in the process of inclusion it must be infused into your class curriculum. Many teachers have difficulty reconciling individual plans with the common curriculum, and as a result many individual programs have been taught in isolation (Goodman and Bond 1993). This has had the effect of isolating students with diverse abilities, even though they are physically present in the classroom. What follows is some advice on how you can teach the classroom curriculum while also addressing the individual goals of your diverse learners.

Unit planning

It is important to begin thinking about how you might address individual learning goals for diverse learners when you are at the stage of planning a unit of work. A unit of work is a sequence of lessons or sessions on a particular topic (or topics) designed with the aim of achieving an identified curricular outcome or number of outcomes. An example of a unit of work might be a series of physical-education lessons on hockey. One lesson might address learning the rules, another lesson might address skill development, another might teach about teamwork in hockey, while other sessions might be allowed for practice and consolidation of skills and knowledge through brief games. At the end of the unit of work it would be hoped that students would know how to play hockey according to the rules, and would have developed the skills to do so.

As you are mapping out your units of work you should also be aware of aspects of the unit in which the opportunity to address individualised goals is present. You can do this in a structured way. Box 7.2 lists eight essential elements of inclusive unit design as proposed by Onosko and Jorgensen (1998).

Box 7.2: Eight essential elements of inclusive unit design

1 a central unit issue or problem
2 an opening grabber or motivator
3 lessons that are linked to a central issue or problem
4 richly detailed source material
5 culminating projects
6 varied lesson formats
7 multiple assessments
8 varied modes of student expression.

These eight essential elements, while well suited for use with children with diverse abilities, are also appropriate for children who do not have significantly different learning needs. Units designed in this way do not differ greatly, if at all, from the traditional view of units of work. In essence, Onosko and Jorgensen (1998) are suggesting that units be built around problems or issues rather than the more traditional approach of basing units around topics. This does not mean that units can no longer teach about certain topics, but rather that emphasis is given to specific problems and issues within those topics as a basis for teaching and learning. For example, rather than basing a unit of work in science on the topic of genetics, the subject matter may be explored better through a central question or problem such as, 'Is cloning animals ethical?'

In using a problem-based approach such as this, students are able to explore the science of genetics from different perspectives and in different ways in order to answer the central question. The role of the teacher in this situation is to provide an appropriate resource environment for children to explore the question or questions, while using their own knowledge to guide the children and provide appropriately focused teaching. Individual, even traditional, lessons could still occur within this framework in order to provide all children with the information and skills they require to answer the central unit question.

The advantage of using a problem or issue-based approach in inclusive unit design is that each student can produce results that reflect his or her ability. There is no 'one size fits all' curriculum, with general criteria set in advance that may either never be reached by some children with diverse abilities, or that may restrict children who may be gifted to a narrow focus. In investigating a problem or issue, children are free to work at a level appropriate to them, and are judged only against their own past performances. Having students complete units of work based on issues or problems results in a more individualised approach for all students and, due to this, infusing elements of a child's individual program plan into the regular curriculum becomes much easier. We suggest, however, that you first plan your unit for the class prior to identifying common links between the whole-class program and your individual child program. The 'Unit planner' sheet presented over (see also Form 14 in Useful forms) is based on the eight essential elements of inclusive unit design discussed previously.

The unit planner incorporates the major elements of inclusive unit design. It states the central problems or issues, provides information on lesson sequence and culminating projects, and outlines an ongoing assessment schedule. You will notice that under 'ongoing assessments' there is scope to schedule a range of different assessment topics and activities that can be implemented according to the different ways in which students can express their learning. This is so that teachers can check to see if students are coping with the content of the unit, and so that adjustments can be made if they are not. This planner is flexible enough to suit most planning contexts, being largely open-ended in nature, while also providing a reasonably structured framework into which you can infuse individual learning priorities for children with diverse abilities.

In order to infuse individual goals and objectives into your unit plans you should first compare your unit plan to your individual program plan (as discussed in Chapter 6) to see if there are any points of 'contact' where individual goals could easily addressed in the course of teaching the unit. The completed form on page 141, based on a World War I unit example, might help you to do this (see also Form 15 in Useful forms).

You will notice in the example that the relevant long-term goals are listed beside the questions serve as 'goals' for the unit in general. The relevant behavioural objectives derived from these goals are then listed beside the planned sequence of lessons. In doing this the teacher can keep these specific objectives in mind when planning the individual lessons, and ensure that opportunities to work towards these objectives are provided. Not every lesson has an objective listed beside it. This is because there is no requirement for each and every lesson taught in a unit to address the goals listed in the individual program plan. It is enough that goals are addressed adequately throughout the year. This can be done by focusing on them during selected 'key lessons' in a unit.

Unit planner

Dates: March 1–25	Class: Year 9C

Subject area:
History – World War I

Central issues/problems
Could World War I have been avoided?
What was life like for soldiers?
What influence did this war have on the lives of people today?

Opening grabber/motivator:
Documentary on WWI followed by class discussion.

Summary of series of linked lessons:

1. Introduction to WWI. Causes, human cost, geographical orientation.	2. Avoiding WWI – was it possible? Class debate.	3. Internet research in computer lab – What was life like for soldiers?
4. Library research – What was life like for soldiers?	5. Group presentations – what was life like for soldiers?	6. Field trip to war memorial.
7. 'Chalk & Talk' and video on life during wartime.	8. WWII veterans and civilians visit and discuss their lives during wartime.	9. Brainstorming: What influence did WWI have on our world today?

Culminating projects:
Individual projects answering central questions.

Ongoing assessments (additional to culminating projects):

When?	What content/skills?	What form will it take?	How did student/s demonstrate learning?
Lesson 2	Knowledge of WW1 causes.	Class debate.	Submission of written arguments. Verbal presentation of ideas. Partic. in devel. of arguments.
Lesson 5	Understanding of human cost of war. Conditions for soldiers.	Small-group class presentations (5 mins/group).	Groups to provide class handouts. Develop materials for pres. Ability to answer questions.
Lesson 9	Understanding of impact WWI has on us today.	Brainstorming session.	Contributions to brainstorming. Expanding on ideas of others.

Unit planner—Infusing individual targets

Dates: March 1–25	Child: Sandra D	Class: 9C

Subject area: History—WWI

Central issues/problems	Relevant goals:
• Could World War I have been avoided? • What was life like for soldiers? • What influence did this war have on the lives of people today?	• To improve verbal communication skills. • To develop fine motor skills. • To develop computer skills.

Summary of series of linked lessons:	Relevant linked individual objectives:
1. Introduction to WWI. Causes, human cost, geographical orientation	Malablah
2. Avoiding WWI: Was it possible? Class debate.	By the end of March Sandra will be able to verbally present information to the class as part of a group. (Goal 1, Objective 3)
3. Internet research in computer lab: What was life like for soldiers?	By the end of March Sandra will be able to effectively 'point and click' a 'mouse' on the computer to access the internet. (Goal 3, Objective 1)
4. Library research: What was life like for soldiers?	By the end of March Sandra will be able to turn the pages of a book unassisted. (Goal 2, Objective 3)
5. Group presentations: What was life like for soldiers?	By the end of March Sandra will be able to verbally present information to the class as part of a group. (Goal 1, Objective 3)
6. Field trip to war memorial.	
7. 'Chalk and Talk' and video on life during wartime	
8. WWII veterans and civilians visit and discuss their lives during wartime.	
9. Brainstorming: What influence did WWI have on our world today?	

Suggested culminating project:

Taped 'radio broadcast' news report from the era.

Individual lesson plans

Once you have planned your unit you can move on to planning the individual lessons that make up that unit. Teachers have different ways of planning lessons, and often use formats adapted to suit their own individual planning style. The planning format we are using as an example is an expanded version of the 'Single lesson plan' (Form 6) demonstrated in Chapter 5; it will also assist you to plan lessons for any paraprofessional who might work with you. We used this format because we believe it is straightforward and can be adapted to suit the planning preferences of most teachers. Depending on your planning style you might write less or more detailed plans. This is up to the individual teacher, but by addressing the categories set out below you are helping to ensure that individual goals are infused into the regular curriculum in a meaningful way.

This lesson planning form takes into account the individual objectives of learners with diverse abilities and provides teachers with an opportunity to briefly outline how those objectives will be addressed in the context of the lesson. It should be noted that the section for diverse learners should not just be used when an individual objective is being pursued. This section can also be used to plan for modifications that occur in the course of lessons where no individual objectives are being pursued. This leads us to the question: What curriculum modifications can be made in an inclusive classroom? The following section addresses this.

Modifying the educational environment

As discussed, whether modifications of a learning situation need to be made at all for children with diverse abilities should always be the first consideration. In most situations, however, modifications to the educational environment will need to be made at some point in order to maintain an appropriate education for all children in a class. Deppeler (1998) has identified five main areas in which modifications can take place: the physical environment, the materials environment, the resources environment, instructional strategies and learning outcomes. Modifications to the physical environment are dealt with in detail in Chapter 9; the other four aspects of modifying the education environment are outlined below.

Modifying the materials environment

Deppeler's (1998) suggested materials modifications relate mostly to written materials. This recognises the predominance of language, and particularly reading- and writing-based tasks, in the modern classroom, and the difficulty some children with disabilities have in this area. The first suggestion is to increase the

Individual lesson planning form

Subject area/grade _Science—Grade 3_ _____   Date and time _____

Lesson topic	Pond study—Tadpoles to frogs. Lesson 3 in unit series of 6.

Lesson goal:	To introduce children to the 'tadpole to frog' life cycle.
Central problem:	What happens when tadpoles turn into frogs?
Materials:	Class fish-tank and tadpoles collected last week. 'Life cycle of a frog' chart. Relevant books.
Procedure:	Teacher introduces lesson topic. Children are asked the question 'What happens when tadpoles turn into frogs?' They are asked to investigate this problem using the Internet, books, their own observations from the fish tank, and discussion with one another in small groups. Resulting from their research the children are asked to draw in the correct sequence what happens to tadpoles as they become frogs.
Homework task:	None for this lesson.
Diverse learner objectives for this lesson:	Katie By the end of Term Three Katie will be able to visually track an item as large as a coin against a white background for a period of 45 seconds. (Goal 2, Objective 3)
Inclusive materials and procedures:	When her group is observing tadpoles at the tank, one will be removed to the smaller fishbowl, set against a piece of white paper, and Katie will be encouraged to 'track' the movements of the tadpole with her eyes. Other students will also examine this individual tadpole to see if any changes have taken place.
Alternative assessment:	Visual tracking timed and documented.
Teacher does:	Introduces topic; divides class into groups; sets task; engages with each group and provides input as required; facilitates groups sharing; leads concluding discussion on frogs using chart.
Paraprofessional does:	During activities moves from group to group encouraging input from all children. When Katie's group is at the tadpole tank, provide direct assistance to ensure that an individual tadpole is moved to the smaller tank. Encourage Katie to visually 'track' the tadpole—time & document this. Encourage other children to study this tadpole. Encourage Katie to study larger tank.
Assessment:	Resulting from their research the children are asked to draw what happens to tadpoles in the correct sequence as they become frogs.

'readability' of written passages. For some children this will entail enlarging the print, for others it will mean double spacing or using a particular font. Measures such as these can make the decoding and comprehension process easier as the print becomes more 'user friendly' and students with disabilities do not need to expend energy on coming to terms with the printed format.

Box 7.3: Ways to modify the material

Deppeler (1998) outlines the following materials modifications:

- increase the readability
- highlight critical features
- reduce extraneous details and simplify the layout
- supplement with visual cues (pictures, diagrams, mind maps, illustrations)
- supplement with written cues and prompts
- reduce the amount of material selected
- simplify the language (use shorter sentences and simpler vocabulary)
- include selected content (essential content, experience-based or interest-based)
- use alternative materials (do not rely solely on print—use models, videos etc.)
- create new materials
- use student work folders for daily assignments.

Highlighting critical features is another strategy that can assist in comprehension. This enables students to concentrate on key features of a text, producing a core understanding of the main events or issues in a passage of text. One way of highlighting critical features, besides under-lining or colour coding sections within a text, is to reduce extraneous details, leaving only what is absolutely essential behind. This can involve removing words, sentences, paragraphs, or even entire pages of a text. While these approaches usually do not allow for an appreciation of the aesthetics of a written piece, they will help to get the main points across to the reader. Similarly, simplifying the layout of a written piece can also be useful. This may involve eliminating any distracting and non-essential footnotes, diagrams or pictures.

While eliminating extraneous information is one way to enhance understanding of print for children with disabilities, taking the opposite approach can also work well for some children. Supplementing print with visual cues can assist some children to gain meaning from print (Phinney 1988). This is a strategy commonly used with young children who use non-text clues to assist them in reading stories (Higgins 1985), and is appropriate for use with children at the early and pre-reading stage. Similarly, supplementing difficult passages of text with written notes simplifying the concepts can be effective for more advanced readers.

Teachers also need to consider content when modifying the materials environment. To meet the needs of some children it may be necessary to present only the most essential elements of content, or the core curriculum. Deppeler (1998) suggests that there are three types of knowledge:

- 'must know' knowledge, which is pre-requisite or essential
- 'should know' knowledge, which is important but not essential
- 'could know' knowledge, which is neither essential nor particularly important.

The focus should first be on 'must know' knowledge. 'Should know' and 'could know' knowledge may not be useful until after key knowledge has been mastered, and may also confuse or overload the memory of a child with a disability. Not only can teachers reduce the amount of content selected in materials, but they can also ensure that what is selected is based on the past experience or interest of the individual student. An example of this might be a piece of creative writing where a child with difficulties in this area is asked to outline a sequence of events (instead of writing a full story) based on an experience they have had in the past. Expanding this into a full story (which might come under 'should know' skills) might then follow.

It is important to cater for a range of learning styles in the classroom, and in order to do this a variety of alternative materials should be provided to students. While many schools are striving to improve literacy acquisition in children, an overemphasis on print should be avoided as some children may learn better in some content areas from alternatives like videos, discussion, models or movement. This can be especially true for children who have experienced difficulties with print in the past and whose lack of confidence in this area gets in the way of learning important concepts. New materials may need to be created to provide alternatives to print. This can be time consuming for teachers, but the benefits can go beyond the children with diverse abilities and benefit others in the class as well.

Modifying the resources environment

Aspects of modifying the resources environment, such as the provision of additional support from colleagues, were discussed in Chapter 5. In addition to the provision of these resources, however, the coordination of a range of community and other support services needs to be given some thought.

Box 7.4: Modifying the resources environment

Deppeler (1998) outlines the following modifications to the resources environment:

- provide additional instructional support (paraprofessionals, volunteers, peer tutors, parents, other professionals)
- coordinate a range of community and other support services
- utilise additional technological resources (computers, augmented communication devices, video, audio)
- collaborate with other teachers.

Schools can benefit in many ways from maintaining a close relationship with the wider community, and teachers in inclusive classrooms can also draw on community resources to assist them in their work. Sometimes beginning this process is as easy as opening up the phone book and locating associations formed to support people with various disabilities. Often specific associations have been set up to support children with particular disabilities including autism, Down syndrome, cerebral palsy, visual impairments and hearing impairments (to name just a few).

More general organisations, some specifically targeted at supporting inclusive practice, are also becoming more prominent. These organisations can often provide you with advice and support to assist you in running an inclusive classroom. Depending on their levels of resources, other more tangible forms of support such as the loan of specialised equipment may also be provided by these community agencies. Some community agencies not specifically set up to support children with diverse abilities might also be helpful. Philanthropic agencies such as Rotary may engage in fund-raising activities on behalf of a school to provide specific resources if there is a request and demonstrated need. These organisations are often run by volunteers. The involvement of non-volunteer agencies should also be investigated by schools working towards the provision of inclusive schooling.

Non-volunteer agencies that support people with disabilities are often funded and run by the government. Depending on where you are located, services for children with diverse abilities and particular disabilities may be the responsibility of the national or local government health department, education department, justice department or department concerned with social services and welfare. Regardless of where your relevant government agencies are located, they should be investigated as a possible resource to assist you in including your diverse learners. Different levels of support are naturally provided by different governments, but what is available should be used to its full extent, providing the support is relevant and helpful. This extra support can come in the form of advice, program coordination and, in some cases, the direct provision of material resources to the school.

The use of technology in schools to support all learners is becoming increasingly common. Computers in classrooms are now the norm in many Western societies, and other technological aids have been specifically developed to support children with disabilities. Technology has assisted some children to communicate, meet academic targets and even develop friendships in online environments. This is known as 'assistive technology' (see Box 7.5 for examples) because its prime purpose is to assist children in completing other tasks. This technology, however, is often expensive, and in purchasing items to assist children to learn, schools and teachers need to exercise caution. You should ensure that any technological items purchased are required to meet a specific need. Secondly (and this seems obvious), you should ensure that the students can actually operate the technology in a meaningful way. We have seen some schools fall victim to the lure of assistive technology only to discover that the students it has been purchased to assist are unable to operate it.

Box 7.5: Examples of assistive technology

Assistive technology currently in use in schools includes the following:

Switches These are more or less an on/off button that children, even those with extremely poor motor control, can use. Switches come in different sizes and can be used to activate prerecorded messages, toys, appliances or anything else that can be controlled with an on/off switch. Some computer software has been designed that allows navigation through different programs using only a switch. The applications of switch technology are almost limitless.

Alternative keyboards A wide range of adapted keyboards are now available on the market. Some have overlays that change the context and layout of the keys, and some have enlarged keys or are designed to suit differing ergonomic situations.

Mouse alternatives Most commonly these can include a trackball, touchpad or finger-tip controller. Touch-sensitive screen overlays can also be useful for children trying to come to terms with cause and effect at a basic level. Ultrasound or infrared beams mounted on a headset can also guide the mouse by using small head movements.

Speech recognition software Still very much in its infancy in terms of precision, this software can be useful for those who can speak clearly and can enable a child to type simply by speaking into a microphone. Currently, this software does not adapt well to a variety of users and the resulting transcripts need to be carefully checked for frequent errors.

Text to speech software This software can essentially read documents to a child. Very useful for developing readers or students with visual impairments.

Other software A wide range of educational software has been developed to assist students with a wide variety of disabilities. Much of this is suitable for all children as concepts are frequently reinforced through games and repetition.

(Ryba et al. 2002)

Technology is a rapidly changing field, and advancements and improvements are being made so frequently as to outdate any information in a book that addresses technology almost immediately. It is for this reason that we do not dwell on the topic in any great detail. One of the best sources of information about the latest in assistive technology is the Internet. A large number of commerical websites can be located by entering the keywords 'assistive technology' into a web search engine.

Modifying instructional strategies

Deppeler (1998) provides a good overview of research-supported inclusive instructional strategies (see Box 7.6) but it is by no means exhaustive. Many of these strategies are discussed in greater detail in Chapter 8.

Box 7.6: Inclusive instructional strategies

Deppeler (1998) outlines the following modifications to instructional strategies:

- use modelling and direct instruction
- provide additional demonstrations using a step-by-step approach
- pre-teach vocabulary and concepts using concrete experiences
- use role-play and simulations
- interact more frequently—set more practice items and provide guided practice with frequent feedback
- use a variety of positive feedback (points, certificates, and other reward systems, and graph or chart progress)
- use more frequent and more specific praise
- use cooperative and partnered learning strategies

- use a variety of modes for learning activities—do not rely on passive listening—use hands-on activities, 'active learning' (models, video recordings, computer-assisted instruction etc.)
- change the pace of instruction—increase wait time for oral responses, shorten instructions, and repeat key elements
- give additional time to complete set work
- ask more questions and use different levels of complexity
- provide hints or clues to facilitate student responses
- use a variety of modes for responses (do not rely solely on written responses, use diagrams, tape recordings, construction of posters, models, videos etc.)
- incorporate personal interests, special talents
- integrate social skills, life skills and applied academics in the curriculum
- incorporate metacognitive learning and problem-solving strategies wherever possible (e.g. How can I help myself? How else can I solve this problem?)
- incorporate self-management strategies wherever possible (self-monitoring, self-correcting, self-reinforcement)
- use criterion and performance-based assessment activities (portfolio presentations, demonstrations, exhibitions, etc.)
- integrate direct observation and evaluation into the design of instructional strategies.

Modifying learning outcomes

When modifying learning outcomes it should be remembered that students with diverse abilities can participate in the same general activity as other students but with an expectation for different learning outcomes using the long-term goals and short-term objectives established for the individual. Deppeler (1998) outlines modifications to learning outcomes as in Box 7.7.

Box 7.7: Ways to modify learning outcomes

Deppeler (1998) outlines the following ways to modify learning outcomes:

- select a similar task, but one that is at an easier level within the same curriculum (check behavioural objectives for the same curriculum area)
- select an appropriate task directed towards a behavioural objective from an alternate curriculum area (social skills, life skills or pre-employment).

It is also possible to teach the same activity to all students but to expect a different result from a child with diverse learning abilities based on individual objectives. For example, in a science lesson on flowers the rest of the class might be expected to name all of the parts of the flower as a learning outcome by comparing real flowers to diagrams in a book, while the learning outcome for the diverse learner might be to name the colours of the flowers under examination. Both the diverse learner and the rest of the class are doing the same activity, but for very different reasons.

The most inclusive of these modifications to learning outcomes identified by Deppeler (1998) is the selection of a similar but easier task within the same curriculum area. For example, some children might be expected to write a one-page story reacting to a picture they are shown, while the diverse learner is only expected to write two sentences. This is essentially the same curriculum outcome of 'writing about a picture' but is assessed on very different levels with different expectations and definitions of success.

Selecting tasks from alternative curriculum areas based on individual objectives should be viewed as a last resort in the inclusive classroom, because it essentially entails a child working in isolation. The use of this type of modification to learning outcomes should be primarily reserved for times when all children are working alone or on individual tasks so that the differences between what the diverse learner and the rest of the class are doing are not obvious.

Task analysis as a teaching tool

Task analysis was discussed in Chapter 6 and an example was provided. Task analysis is a way of assessing students to establish relevant short-term behavioural goals. It is a simple process whereby broad learning tasks are broken down into simple components that can then be learned one at a time until the broader task is mastered. Besides being an excellent tool for assessment, task analysis can also be useful for helping you to structure your teaching, particularly where direct instruction is involved. A word of caution, however, is required at this stage. Task analysis is just one of many teaching tools that can be used for all children, not just those with disabilities. Furthermore, not all children with disabilities will benefit from task-analysed behavioural teaching methods. A task-analysis approach needs to be used judiciously and sensitively to ensure that it does not become inflexible and inappropriate to the needs of a student.

As mentioned previously, there are two types of task analysis, general task analysis and specific task analysis. The principles behind each type are essentially the same, but a general task analysis is usually more appropriate for initial assessments while a specific task analysis can be helpful in planning teaching sequences.

Specific task analysis

Child: Sarah

Task: Asking for repeat & clarification	Progress (Date)						
Step	12/9	13/9	15/9	18/9	19/9	20/9	21/9
Say 'Could you please repeat that for me?'	✔	✔	✔	✔	✔	✔	✔
Say aloud the most important points in single words or short phrases.	✔	✔	✔	✔	✔	✔	✔
Ask 'Is that correct?'	✗	✗	✔	✔	✔	✔	✔
If yes, say 'Thank-you' and leave.	✗	✗	✔	✔	✔	✔	✔
If no, say 'I had better write down this information.'	✗	✗	✗	✗	✗	✔	✔
Get pencil and paper ready.	✗	✗	✗	✗	✗	✔	✔
Say 'Would you please repeat that once more for me, so I can write it down?'	✗	✗	✗	✗	✔	✔	✔
Write down the key words.	✗	✗	✗	✗	✔	✔	✔
Read the key words aloud.	✗	✗	✗	✔	✔	✔	✔
Ask 'Is that correct?'	✗	✗	✗	✔	✔	✔	✔
Regardless of the answer given, say 'Thank-you' and leave.	✗	✗	✗	✗	✗	✗	✔

In the general task analysis example in Chapter 6 Sarah was able to complete each of the components of the task (as indicated by ✔) up to the step requiring her to ask for clarification (as indicated by ✗). A specific task analysis, which breaks this step down into smaller components, can then be devised and used as a structure for teaching the subskills which will enable Sarah to complete the tasks listed in her general task analysis, and as a result achieve her goal listed in her individual plan.

In devising a specific task analysis you follow the same procedure for devising a general task analysis. The only difference is that you are now dealing with a smaller task. The specific task analysis can be written up using the same form as for the general task analysis, and progress can be recorded as the child masters each of the components as follows. Once all the components of the task are checked off, the child can be said to have mastered the entire task. In the example you can see that on 21/9 Sarah mastered each of the components of the specific task analysis.

While concentrating on specific individual targets, the use of task analysis in the inclusive classroom on a day-to-day basis is also possible. In order to use task analysis in an inclusive way, teachers need to avoid doing too much direct teaching and rely on peers and creative learning opportunities that arise in a dynamic classroom. For example, the task analysis given could be tackled through drama and role play, or could be integrated into an inclusive unit that focuses on gathering information for any number of reasons. The way you teach will depend very much on the type of task analysis you devise, and in the end it is the role of the teacher to find creative ways in which to reach all students.

This chapter has examined ways of infusing the regular curriculum with a more individualised approach to meet the needs of all students. The next chapter follows on from this and examines some more teaching strategies to promote effective inclusion in your classroom.

KEY TERMS FOUND THIS CHAPTER

Curriculum   Has to do with the teaching and learning of knowledge, skills and attitudes. It embraces issues such as subject matter, pedagogy, assessments/evaluation and related resources involved in the organisation, delivery and articulation of education programs.

Core curriculum   Curriculum areas judged to be basic and essential for all students.

Assistive technology   Technological aids that have been specifically developed to support children with disabilities.

FURTHER READING

Goodman, J.F. and Bond, L. (1993), 'The individualized educational program: A retrospecive critique' in *Journal of Special Education,* 26(4), pp. 408–22.

Onosko, J.J. and Jorgenson, C.M. (1998), 'Unit and lesson planning in the inclusive classroom: Maximising learning opportunities for all students' in

Restructuring High Schools for All Students: Taking Inclusion to the Next Level, C.M. Jorgensen ed., Baltimore: Paul H. Brookes, p. 273.

Ryba, K., Curzon, J. and Selby, L. (2002), 'Learning partnerships through information and communication technology' in *Educating Children with Diverse Abilities,* A. Ashman and J. Elkins eds, Frenchs Forest, NSW: Pearson Education, pp. 500–29.

Collaborative instruction to promote inclusion

Collaboration is fundamental to creating an inclusive learning environment in which responsibility for successfully educating a diversity of learners is shared amongst the members of the school community. Collaborative organisational structures support a school climate of teamwork, cohesion, shared responsibility and sense of purpose. In order for diversity to enrich student learning, educators must create positive social environments that avoid isolation, rejection and stereotyping, and structure instruction to promote high levels of interaction that is supportive, respectful and accepting of all students (see Chapter 10). This chapter outlines the key features of collaborative learning for both professionals and students and suggests some practical guidelines for enhancing success.

KEY IDEAS IN THIS CHAPTER
- collaborative organisational structures
- cooperative learning strategies
- instruction and interventions through peer-tutoring
- reciprocal teaching activites

Collaboration

In order for inclusion to be successful, collaboration should occur at all levels including collaboration with teachers and other professionals, and with families and members of the broader school community. Collaborative organisational structures support a school climate of teamwork, cohesion, shared responsibility and sense of purpose. A variety of collaborative structures have emerged that support and enhance professional collaboration, including peer collaboration, collaborative consultation and cooperative teaching. Some of these structures were presented in Chapter 5.

The question about how instruction might be provided effectively and flexibly to the diverse range of students in our classrooms has generated a number of alternative instructional strategies. Schools can be structured competitively, individualistically or collaboratively. In competitive and individualistic structure, students typically compete with each other for letter grades awarded for submitted work or performance on exams. Under this structure a limited number of students achieve high grades, students tend to work independently and collaboration amongst students is not encouraged. There has been substantive research over the past 90 years that has compared achievement in collaborative arrangements with achievement in competitive and individualistic learning. These studies have provided strong support for the effectiveness of collaborative instruction for improving social and academic competence for students of diverse abilities. Collaborative learning benefits students in many ways, including higher academic achievement (Johnson and Johnson 1989; Webb et al. 1995; Slavin 1995, 1990; Tomlinson et al. 1997; Putnam 1998), self-esteem (Johnson and Johnson 1989) and peer relationships (Johnson et al. 1986), and positive relationships between students and teachers (Tomlinson et al. 1997). Meta-analyses and other reviews of research (Slavin 1983; Educational Research Service 1989; Natasi and Clements 1991; Wade et al. 1995; Johnson and Johnson 1989) have provided positive support for the effectiveness of collaborative learning. Furthermore, these studies demonstrated that, compared with competitive or individualistic learning, students who learned in a collaborative environment were more actively and fully engaged in their learning, demonstrated better critical thinking and reasoning skills, generated more novel ideas when presented with problems and transferred more of what they learned to new contexts.

Active involvement in learning has been shown to be especially important for students with disabilities and others who tend to be passive in academic settings. Collaborative learning also reduced students' levels of stress and anxiety when compared with competitive methods, and promoted more positive attitudes toward the content matter and to the learning experience itself, and increased retention. Collaborative instruction also enables students to develop important peer relationships that contribute to social development. The benefits of collaborative instruction are particularly important in influencing the engagement of students who are at risk of being marginalised.

Box 8.1: Advantages of using collaborative instruction

There are many advantages of collaborative instruction and they can be summarised as:

- interactive and cooperative rather than competitive and individualistic
- individualised learning goals and individual accountability
- structured and positive learning in heterogeneous groups
- active participation and higher levels of engaged time compared with teacher-mediated instruction
- improvement in self-esteem and attitude towards academic tasks
- increased participation of all students in classroom learning
- higher academic achievement and retention
- ideal learning context for teaching, practising and reinforcing pro-social behaviours
- improvement in peer and student–teacher relationships
- increased respect for diversity
- collaborative skills are valued by society for work and leisure.

A number of collaborative instructional strategies that are simple to implement can increase a teacher's effectiveness in teaching the diverse range of students in their classroom. Cooperative learning, peer tutoring and reciprocal teaching are examples of collaborative instructional strategies that structure student interaction in heterogeneous groups, encourage mutual interdependence and provide for individual accountability.

Cooperative learning

Cooperative learning encourages collaboration through structured interaction in small groups. As the name implies it involves students in cooperation for a shared outcome. One of the goals of a cooperative learning is to enhance individual student understanding and retention of whatever is being taught through group work. Another is to develop positive attitudes toward subject matter and toward learning in general. Cooperative learning also helps develop interpersonal and social problem-solving skills.

The characteristics of cooperative learning include:

- face-to-face interaction
- positive group interdependence

- individual accountability
- emphasis on tasks
- responsibility, appropriate use of interpersonal and small-group skills
- group processing.

Setting up cooperative learning and making it successful

Using cooperative-learning groups as an instructional strategy requires some modification to more traditional instructional procedures and planning. Teachers have not always implemented cooperative learning effectively. Further, not all cooperative learning groups lead to collaboration (Cohen and Lotan; Hollins et al. 1994, 1995) or demonstrate positive outcomes for all students (Blumenfeld et al. 1997). So what makes a cooperative-learning group successful? Research has identified several strategies that teachers can use to enhance the effectiveness of cooperative-learning groups. These have been listed in Box 8.2 and some are discussed in the pages ahead. In Chapter 5 we emphasised the importance of effective communication for successful collaboration. You may wish to refer to this chapter again for hints on how to make your communication more effective.

Box 8.2: Twenty strategies to enhance effectiveness of cooperative-learning groups

1 Assign students to heterogeneous groups.
2 Assign students to small groups of optimal size (4–6 students).
3 Decide on a group composition that will result in a high level of participation and cohesiveness in the group.
4 Review and modify group composition regularly.
5 Arrange seating in a circle so that all students can see each other and no one person is seated in a position of 'authority'.
6 Select a task that students are willing to do and that is effective in engaging students in the content to be learned.
7 Incorporate manipulative materials to encourage involvement and to provide a focus for group activities.
8 Specify both the academic and collaborative objectives.
9 Establish rules for peer involvement in groups.
10 Determine the role assignments (e.g. encourager, observer, recorder, research runner, includer, checker etc.).
11 Teach students group-interaction skills e.g. how to question, listen, share, paraphrase and participate.

12 Monitor student interactions.

13 Practice acting in the role of facilitator.

14 Provide adequate spacing between groups to minimise distraction.

15 Promote interdependence along with individual responsibility.

16 Use some form of individual and group accountability.

17 Individualise the criteria and task requirements so all students have an opportunity for success.

18 Provide feedback to students on both the task and the process.

19 Include student evaluation and reflection of group performance.

20 Recognise outstanding group performance.

Assigning students to cooperative learning groups

The first issue for teachers planning a cooperative-learning (CL) activity is how to constitute the groups. First, what is an appropriate size? The optimum size suggested for CL groups is between four and six students. Fewer students may not provide sufficient differing points of view. More students may prevent group cohesion or cause some students to withdraw completely from active participation. A larger group requires more time to develop productive collaborative relationships.

Heterogeneous groups composed of students of different ethnic backgrounds, genders and races, and with varying learning styles and achievement levels, are preferable. Students of different abilities should be equally distributed in each group. Students at higher levels of competence may be better at explaining concepts to others in the group and may do so more frequently. The process of explaining will improve these students' understanding while other students can benefit from the explanations provided by these peers. Further, the development of intellectual argument and acceptance of a variety of perspectives promotes mutual construction of meaning and is vital for the social interaction and development of all students. Grouping students of varying abilities and achievement levels typically leads to a greater variety of ideas and more frequent giving and receiving of explanations in discussion.

It is important to remember that forming heterogeneous groups does not mean randomly selecting students and assigning them to groups. Therefore, when thinking about assigning your students to groups, try to view them along a continuum of a number of characteristics. Some characteristics may be important for particular groups or tasks. For example, some students may be particularly proficient at hands-on construction or dramatic performance or music. Others may be more or less socially skilled or verbal in a group context. Grouping students who can stay focused on a task with those who find it more difficult to do so may be an effective way to create a group with complementary styles. By observing groups and changing their composition regularly you can take advantage of individual students' strengths and capabilities and ensure that the same students are not always the most skilled in the group. Assigning each person in the group a specific role and changing the roles is also very important to ensure that one or two students do not dominate or take over the role of leader in the group and that everyone has the opportunity to function in each of the differing roles.

The manner in which the teacher establishes the CL experience is also important for promoting positive outcomes. Teaching students how to work in groups, and clearly outlining the learning task and expectations of students can have a positive effect on the quality of the group interaction. Students with disabilities should be placed in groups and monitored to ensure that participation is successful.

Selecting the task

Teachers should attempt to construct or select tasks that will engage all students in the content to be learned. Tasks that lend themselves to collaboration are those that have more than one solution, that can be expressed in a variety of formats and, most importantly, that require discussion and explanations in order to demonstrate student thinking. Stein et al. (1996) found that a teacher's choice of task could influence students' thinking and learning. Emmer and Gerwels (2002) found that the use of manipulative materials that are shared by group members was an important characteristic of more successful CL activities. The manipulative materials encouraged student involvement and helped provide a focus for the group activities. Finally, the CL task must be clearly defined so students understand what is expected from them in the assignment.

Promoting positive interdependence

Successful CL activity creates positive interdependence amongst group members who support, assist and encourage each other. This happens when the group's goal or product outcome *depends upon all* of the group members' actions. No single student should feel successful until every member of their group is successful—in achieving both their individual learning task as well as their group learning task. Interdependence builds group cohesion and improves performance.

Example: Group interdependence

In this example, the group's task is complete when every member of the group can give one rule for 'good listening'. Achieving this group goal depends on the performance of every member of the team. Each member of the group will be a specialist for a different part of the narrative—for instance, one person will specialise on the characters, another on the plot, another on the setting. The group must cooperate on how to put the narrative together.

Group participation: Doing this task depends on the participation of every member of the team. Each member of the group will have a different role. Your group will be credited on how well each of you performs in that role. One of you will be the encourager and will be responsible for getting everyone to state their ideas, another will be the checker and will need to check that everyone can say how your group solved the problem.

Reward for this group's achievement depends on the performance and the participation of every member of the team in different roles.

It is not always easy to design activities with task or role interdependence. Emmer and Gerwels (2002) suggest that interdependence may not be needed in every lesson. When interdependence is absent from a lesson, 'teachers can use other compensatory features to encourage group interaction and involvement' (p. 87).

Individual accountability: Individual goals
Interdependence ensures that each student's contribution to the task is important for the group's success. Additionally, it is vital that each student is individually responsible for his or her own success. In an observational field-based study of 18 school teachers experienced in the use of CL, Emmer and Gerwels (2002) found that the use of individual or group accountability (or both) was associated with lesson success. Accountability can vary with each student. Each student will be responsible for learning something but not every student will be expected to have learned the same thing. Individual evaluations are vital for determining what each student has learned. Teachers can also encourage students to evaluate their own learning and performance in the group.

Box 8.3: Increasing individual accountability

Some ways a teacher can increase individual accountability is to require each student to:

- perform an identifiable part of the group task
- record his or her observations in individual notebooks (to be collected and read)
- record individual work contribution (daily) in a notebook
- report individually on group work

- evaluate their individual performance—the achievement of their goals and how well they functioned within the group.

Procedures for accountability should be balanced to maintain individual responsibility along with collaborative processes but without increasing teacher preparation and assessment time.

Monitoring the group functioning
The close monitoring of CL groups is essential for their success (Emmer and Gerwels 2002). The teacher must take an active role in monitoring the task progress of the groups and group interaction. Emmer and Gerwels (2002) suggest monitoring is needed at the beginning of a CL session to ensure students understand their task, and during the activity to identify any academic or group interaction difficulties. It is also an opportunity to clarify instructions, remind students about effective collaborative and communication strategies and to answer questions. Teachers should observe individual participation as well as group performance and the quality of the interaction among the students. Who is participating and who, if anyone, is not? Are the behaviours necessary for successful CL (listening, encouraging, volunteering ideas, negotiating) in the students' repertoires? To what extent do students provide explanations and demonstrations, paraphrase and question each other?

Teachers can also have one or more students act as an observer for the group—monitoring encouragement, interruptions and participation. The 'Observation wheel' (see Box 8.4) is an excellent tool for structuring these activites. This information, when used constructively, not punitively, can serve as a basis for enhancing students' reflection, evaluation and social skills development.

Box 8.4: Observation wheel

1   Use one observation wheel for each five-minute interval.
2   Place the names of the students on the wheel, exactly as they are sitting in the group.
3   Indicate when a student speaks to another student with an arrow pointing in the direction of the receiver.
4   Indicate further messages with marks across the shaft of the arrow
5   Place an * against a student's name every time he or she interrupts or talks over another member.

6 Place a ✔ next to a student's name every time he or she encourages another member to participate.

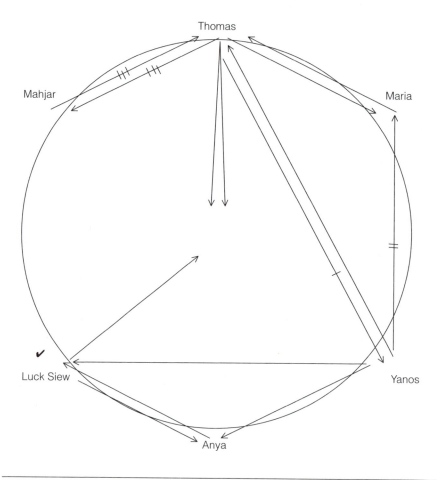

Some of the things students can look out for to help compile the observation wheel include:

- patterns of communication within the group
  - Did members of the group participate equally?
  - Who talked and to whom? Did some students talk more than others?
  - Did some students not talk at all?
  - How often did individual students talk, and for how long?
  - Did some students interrupt others?
  - Did some students encourage others?

- – Was every member of the group listened to? If not, why not?
- – Did the patterns of communication change from the first part of the session to the later stages?

- information sharing
  - – How was information in the group shared?
  - – Was the needed information easily obtained by all group members?
  - – Did students offer their information to other students at appropriate times?
  - – Did students request each other's information?
  - – Did students encourage others to share information?
  - – Did students respond positively to other students' contributions and suggestions?
  - – Did students ask each other questions or paraphrase to clarify their understanding of other students' information?

- decision making and problem solving
  - – Was the information of all group members utilised?
  - – How did the group make decisions?
  - – Was there an obvious leader/organiser?
  - – Was the problem solving of the group effective?
  - – What problems did the group have in working together?
  - – How could problem solving be made more effective in this group?

Feedback to students

Information gained from informal observations and/or using the observation wheel should be used to provide feedback to students. Emmer and Gerwels' (2002) findings that more successful CL lessons were higher in teacher monitoring and feedback emphasises the importance of these activities for identifying difficulties and success in CL groups. Teachers can use this information to modify teaching, redirect group activities and thus help CL groups work effectively. When a teacher or student gives feedback to the group that arises from using the observation wheel, it is essential that the feedback summarises the patterns of communication, but does not name any individual. For example, using the information recorded on the observation wheel the observer could say:

> In this group session some members interrupted several times. More than one member of this group encouraged other members to participate. Some members did not participate at all or only spoke to another member once or twice. As time went on, only a few members of the group actively participated in the decision making.

Group discussion arising from teacher or student observations should also occur without reference to individual students:

> What can we do to increase the participation of all members of this group? Does anyone have suggestions for improving the quality of the communication or the decision-making of this group?

Student evaluation and reflection

Observational information can also be used in conjunction with group reflection and evaluation at the end of a session. Students can be asked:

- How did you feel about the amount of your participation?
- What prompted or prevented your participation?
- What could have been done to gain wider participation?
- To name something each member did that was helpful for the group.
- What is one thing you could do to make the group function better?

Teachers can also have students design their own evaluation form (an example appropriate for lower-grade levels is provided in Box 8.5 for reference).

Box 8.5: CL group-evaluation questions

1	I liked working with the other members of my group.	YES	NO
2	I volunteered information or ideas to my group.	YES	NO
3	I encouraged a member of my group to participate.	YES	NO
4	I listened to others without interrupting.	YES	NO
5	I said something positive about another member's idea.	YES	NO
6	Everyone did something to help get the work done.	YES	NO
7	Everyone helped in making decisions.	YES	NO
8	I asked a question when I did not understand.	YES	NO
9	I thought about how a member felt when they spoke.	YES	NO
10	I learned something from working with my group.	YES	NO

Teaching cooperative learning skills

We have emphasised the importance of monitoring the CL group, particularly through focused observation. After observing students and determining what their various communication and group skills are, teachers can target particular skills for further development. Explicit instruction may be necessary for learning rules (see Box 8.6), expectations for appropriate behaviour and for improving group-interaction skills (how to: question, listen, share, paraphrase and participate). Teaching should always include modelling of good performance of the skill, practice and feedback on performance (see Chapter 10 for resources and teaching social skills).

Teachers sometimes comment that they have tried CL and that it didn't work. The reasons given often include 'The students didn't get along' and/or 'One or two of the students ended up doing the majority of the work—the others just went along for a free ride'. If CL is to be successful, the learning experience needs to be structured to consider the social skills of all the students involved. All students should be encouraged to actively participate by volunteering their ideas and to listen to the ideas of others before selecting a particular solution to a problem. One CL skill that is very important for students is the ability to respond to a number of differing opinions. A range of differing opinions provides students with an opportunity to question their own views and to search for more information. However, in order for this process to be constructive, students must have developed adequate social skills to efficiently communicate their own ideas as well as listen to the ideas of others and to handle praise and criticism. Students' CL skill repertoire should be balanced between behaviours that foster encouragement, sensitivity and friendliness and those that contribute a sense of assertiveness, control and strength (Riches 1996).

Box 8.6: Rules for active listening in a CL group

1   Look directly at the face of the person who is speaking.
2   Stop writing or any other work and be quiet while the other person is speaking.
3   Keep your mind on the content of what the other person is saying (make mental pictures or repeat key words quietly to yourself to help make sense of what they are saying).
4   Listen to how the speaker is feeling as well as to what is being said, and pay attention to his or her facial expressions.
5   Encourage the speaker with head nods and other positives.
6   Do not make a decision until the speaker is fully heard.
7   Ask questions and paraphrase to check and confirm your understanding of both the content and the feeling of what has been said.

Case study: Year 7 studies of society and the environment

Mr Robinson observed various groups in his Year 7 Studies of society and the environment classroom for several weeks. He then made a list of skills needed for further development by all of the students. He also asked students to select from a list of 'good collaborative skills' a personal goal for themselves. Students could decide whether to share their personal goal with others. Mr Robinson then focused on one collaborative skill every week for eight weeks. He began with *participating*, then the following week *accepting* others' ideas at the beginning of group work, then *listening, encouraging, explaining, paraphrasing, asking* clarifying *questions* and finally *giving positive and warm feedback* to other members. Each week Mr Robinson introduced the particular skill with a whole-class discussion of the rationale and purpose of the skill, as well as rules, and modelled good examples of the skill. He then gave his students a five-point scale for rating and reviewing their own performance. Mr Robinson also indicated that he and at least one other student would be using this scale for their observations of group work.

After participating in several activities each week, students engaged in discussion and reviewed their group's performance. Discussion included feedback from Mr Robinson and any student observers. In each subsequent week, Mr Robinson repeated the process, rotating students to observe groups, adding a new five-point scale for each of the collaborative skills, providing feedback about performance and involving students in reflection, evaluation and discussion of their performance. Finally, students reviewed their individual goals for collaborative skills, suggesting particular skills to be included in future class activities.

The following five-point scale of listening could be used in a similar fashion to Mr Robinson: for observing students and as a basis for providing feedback about their listening, and for involving them in evaluation and discussion of their performance.

Five-point scale of listening

1. **Not-listening:**
   - distracted
   - does not look at speaker's face nor acknowledge or respond to speaker in any way
   - fidgets or writes, draws etc. during speaking.

2. **Selective listening:**
   - only listens to one part of the message, e.g. content (what is said) or how it is said, not both
   - wrongly anticipates what is to be said—interrupts

- sometimes looks at speaker, other times tunes out—gazing somewhere else
- rarely acknowledges speaker or responds to what is said.

3 **Learning to listen:**
- maintains good eye contact and looks at speaker's face
- acknowledges with facial expressions and gestures (e.g. head nod) in keeping with message
- listens to content and emotion
- sometimes interrupts and wrongly anticipates what is to be said
- does not ask clarifying questions or repeat back what has been said.

4 **Good listening:**
- waits for key pauses to acknowledge speaker
- appropriate level of eye contact and use of gesture
- repeats main points of speaker without expanding
- does not interrupt
- rarely encourages
- sometimes asks clarifying questions.

5 **Active listening:**
- is very involved and interested
- verbal and non-verbal acknowledgments are often given as speaker pauses
- conveys warmth and interest by positive praise
- repeats key points and volunteers more information
- conveys an understanding of key emotions or their own interpretation of what they understood from speaker
- asks clarifying questions
- encourages speaker to expand and talk further when appropriate
- changes role from listener to speaker only when speaker is fully finished.

Peer-mediated instruction and interventions

Peer-mediated instruction and interventions (PMII) is the collective name given to the various teaching alternatives that involve students working together to support each other's learning. Students' peer-teaching roles vary from providing direct instruction and modelling (peer tutoring) to encouraging and monitoring performance. The focus of these activities is varied and can have interpersonal, cognitive as well as academic objectives and can also be combined with self-management.

Research has consistently demonstrated that PMII has academic and interpersonal and social benefits for a range of students including those with disabilities (Utley et al. 1997; Maheady et al. 2001; Utley 2001). As with the other collaborative instructional alternatives presented in this chapter, there is substantive evidence to support the use of PMII in facilitating the inclusion of students with disabilities, including enhancing academic performance, improving interpersonal relationships and the acceptance of individual differences (Utley 2001). In reviews of PMII, Maheady et al. (1991, 2001) and Utley et al. (1997) have highlighted the positive benefits of exemplary peer-teaching programs such as classwide student tutoring teams (CSTT) (Maheady et al. 1991) and Numbered Heads Together (NHT) (Kagan 1992). As such, the systematic use of PMII provides an effective solution for teachers attempting to meet the instructional challenges of the diverse range of students in their classrooms today.

PMII can be used with individuals and small groups, cross-age or on a classwide basis. PMII includes peer modelling, peer-initiation training, peer networking and peer tutoring (Utley et al. 1997). A special series of remedial and special education (RASE) provides an in-depth analysis of PMII along with a synthesis of research findings and descriptions of good practice (Utley 2001). These authors conclude that PMII components are:

> highly effective for students with special needs because they allow teachers to individualize instruction . . . and the academic and social benefits associated with such programs can be extended to non-disabled pupils in the same setting. (Maheady et al. 2001, p. 70).

Maheady et al.'s (2001) summary of the research on PMII documents the capacity of these instructional arrangements for increasing student achievement, minimising behaviour-management issues and enhancing social skills.

Box 8.7: Advantages of PMII

Among the many advantages of PMII are:

- create learner-friendly instructional environments
- increase student on-task time and response
- reduce teacher–student ratios as students are in effect the tutors for one another
- increase opportunities for students to receive feedback and encouragement
- students prefer peer-teaching instructional alternatives.

Teachers should ensure that peer-mediated instruction and interventions are implemented correctly. Omission of any of the components of a PMII can compromise the effectiveness of the results (Maheady 2001). Frequent monitoring of the progress of all students is also vital to determine whether each and every student is making the intended gains (Vaughn et al. 2001). Like all collaborative arrangements, successful peer collaborations require teachers to engage in careful planning and student training. Teachers will therefore need to employ many of the same strategies suggested earlier in this chapter, for implementing CL groups, if peer collaborations are to be both successful and effective. In short, careful planning, student training, correct implementation and frequent monitoring of student progress are vital for successful peer collaborations.

Peer tutoring

Peer tutoring is a general descriptor for the CL strategies involve pairs of students in teaching and learning on a one-to-one basis. Tutees are the students who receive the instruction or encouragement from the tutors. In cross-age tutoring arrangements an older student acts as a tutor for a younger student. In reciprocal teaching arrangements students alternate between tutor and tutee roles. The effectiveness of peer tutoring is supported by substantial research evidence, and provides teachers with another instructional alternative to cater for the diverse range of students in their classrooms today.

Peer tutoring has been found to have a significant positive influence on:

- students' academic performance (Hedin 1986; Gartner and Lipsky 1990; Topping and Lindsay 1993), particularly for the learning and application of basic skills or factual knowledge
- the social acceptance of students with disabilities and increasing interactions amongst students with disabilities and their non-disabled peers (Garcia-Vasquez and Ehly 1992; Fulton et al. 1994)
- affective and social skills development for both the tutor and tutee (Mastropieri and Scruggs 1987; Foreman 2000)
- self-efficacy and attitudes to learning (Cohen et al. 1990)
- higher-order cognitive-skills development (e.g. Pallincsar and Brown 1984; Davidson 1994; Vaughn et al. 2001; Gersten et al. 2001)
- organisational skills and completion of academic class work (Coenen 2002).

Box 8.8: Advantages of peer tutoring

There are many reasons why peer tutoring should be used including that it:

- allows students to have access to one-on-one assistance
- provides opportunities to learn and interact socially in mutually supportive ways

- creates learning in a supportive context and improves self-efficacy
- assists others in tasks
- heightens engagement of the learner with both the materials and the task
- gives an opportunity for more extended practice on a task than might ordinarily be possible
- is flexibile, cost effective and easily implemented along with existing programs
- allows modelling of academic and social skills by a peer
- improves attitudes about students with disabilities
- enhances social relationships and decreases negative behaviour
- reinforces academic skills
- encourages positive social interaction
- provides an opportunity to experience the value of learning together and helping another
- is time efficient
- is effective with all ability levels
- produces important affective and skills-based improvements for both the tutor and tutee.

Implementing peer tutoring

Implementing peer tutoring in the classroom can involve matching two students for a specific activity or setting up a peer-tutoring program for your whole class or even the entire school. You may wish to develop your own system or implement one of the many well-researched programs that already exist, such as the Class-wide Peer Tutoring Program (Greenwood et al. 1989).

A student of any age can act as a tutor or tutee. Tutors may be approximately the same age or year level as their partner or may be older and, with specific training, may have several roles.

Box 8.9: Successful peer-tutoring programs

As with other collaborative alternatives, the positive benefits can be enhanced by ensuring these elements are included:
- intensive and explicit training of tutors before beginning any program
- 'active' learning activities
- structured and carefully prescribed lesson
- tutoring sessions scheduled to occur frequently but to be of short duration (e.g. four to five times a week for no longer than 30 minutes per session)
- a positive climate in which tutors are made aware of the importance of frequent positive feedback and encouragement for their partners

- high levels of positive feedback and encouragement for both tutors and tutees
- regular monitoring of students' progress, engagement, student interaction and rapport.

There have been many reasons given for the positive effects of peer tutoring, not the least of which is research evidence that states that face-to-face instruction leads to an improvement of two standard deviations over conventional class teaching, with 98 per cent of individually taught learners scoring above the average for group-taught learners (Cohen et al. 1982; Bloom 1984; Wasik and Slavin 1993; Pinnell et al. 1994).

Peer tutoring to support literacy and student reading
Several studies provide support for the use of peer tutoring as an adjunct to support literacy and student reading—often referred to as paired reading. While the specific technique utilised varies, the research literature in support of paired reading is substantial (Devin-Sheehan et al. 1976; Eldridge 1990; Topping and Lindsay 1993; Fuchs et al. 1997) with attainment gains for both tutors and readers widely reported (Topping 1987; Topping and McKnight 1987).

Reciprocal teaching

Reciprocal teaching (RT) was developed as an instructional strategy to improve reading comprehension in small groups of students (Pallinscar and Brown, 1984; Pallinscar et al. 1989). RT activities support students' participation through the practice of specific comprehension strategies with peers. While reading, for example, RT students learn and practise the following comprehension strategies: generating questions, summarising, clarifying word meanings and predicting subsequent content. Initially the teacher models the strategies, then as students become more confident and competent through guided practice, they take increasing responsibility for mediating discussion with their peers. Sessions gradually become dialogues where students prompt each other to use, apply and verbalise a strategy and comment on the application.

The premise of RT is that by engaging in structured and active dialogue with a peer, students with learning difficulties will increase their participation and improve their understanding (Pallincsar and Klenk 1992; Rojewski and Schell 1994). It is expected that the thinking or cognitive processing that is accomplished between learners during RT activities will eventually be accomplished by individual students. This notion that individual cognitive development is constructed through participating in social groups is consistent with the Vygotskian perspective. RT is also said to be effective for students with learning disabilities because it supports self-regulation and motivation and gives student learning a sense of fun (Borkowski 1992). Research has also demonstrated that reciprocal teaching can be effective in a variety of settings (Pallincsar et al. 1989; Fillenworth 1985; Vaughn and Schumm 1995; Lederer 2000).

Teachers wishing to implement RT in their classrooms should consult the excellent resource, *Using Reciprocal Teaching in the Classroom: A Guide for Teachers* by Pallinscar et al. (1989). More recently, Hacker and Tenent's (2002) evaluation of RT in two elementary schools over a three-year period has resulted in guidelines to assist teachers in implementing revised versions of RT in their classrooms, including those that incorporate whole class instruction (see Box 8.10). These suggestions are consistent with those presented earlier in this chapter for enhancing success of CL groups.

As emphasised throughout this chapter, successful implementation of RT, like all collaborative arrangements, depends on careful ongoing monitoring of the learning group. The teacher should pay close attention to student interactions and individual progress and be ready to intervene when necessary. Altering group membership and/or providing explicit teaching or modelling may be required. It is also important for teachers to ensure that the specific academic goals are achieved. For example, in many RT applications little of the activity has encouraged learners to monitor their comprehension, and has focused instead on the generation and answering of literal comprehension questions (Pressley 1998). Slater et al. (2002) suggest that teachers emphasise the importance of this comprehension goal by checking that clarifying questions such as these suggested by Wood et al. (1995) are being used by students:

- Explain why? And how?
- What is the significance of...?
- What would you do if you were...?
- What would have been different if...had happened instead of...?
- What is the similarlity between...and...?
- What caused...? And why...?
- How did...affect...?
- Do you agree with...?
- Why did...happen? Use evidence from the text to support your answer.
- What are the strengths and weakness of two of the characters?

Box 8.10: Starting reciprocal teaching (RT) in your classroom

Step 1   Establish a foundation for RT by reading *Using Reciprocal Teaching in the Classroom: A Guide for Teachers* (Pallinscar et al. 1989).

Step 2 Teach the whole class the four comprehension strategies: predicting, clarifying, questioning and summarising. See pages 7 to 8 of Pallinscar et al. (1989) for suggestions for this instruction.

Step 3 Form groups of approximately six members with a range of reading abilities and within the group form pairs of students with similar reading abilities.

Step 4 Start RT groups with direct and scaffolded instruction. The level of teacher directedness and the amount of scaffolding will depend upon the students' level of skill with each of the four strategies and in working collaboratively in a group. Teachers who have already taught collaborative skills, e.g. active listening (see Box 8.6), may be able to use a less directive approach.

Step 5 Increase RT group independence by reducing level of teacher scaffolding and change teacher role to one of facilitator.

Step 6 Introduce writing into each RT step.

Step 7 Assess students' comprehension by asking higher-level comprehension questions.

(Hacker and Tenent 2002, pp. 716–18)

Modelled Reading (MR)

Modelled Reading (MR) (Deppeler and Gurry 1994) is an example of a paired reading, cross-age peer-tutoring program. MR has typically been used successfully with Grade 5 and 6 students working with students in Grades 1 through 3 or with Year 10 tutors supporting readers in Grades 7 or 8 at the secondary-school level (Bounds 2001; Tonn 2002). MR uses modelling, repeated practice and RT type questions to support the reading of a text. MR (see Box 8.11) provides a number of structured steps that tutors are trained to implement each time they meet with their partner. The steps are designed to scaffold learning, thus allowing students to read at a higher level than they would be capable of if left entirely alone. The structured games: Word Search, Word Practice and Quick Word Check, provide scaffolded opportunities for students to respond accurately to the text, without having to spend cognitive energy on decoding. To ensure that the reader's attention is focused on the appropriate word or words at all times, the reader is engaged by using their finger to track, search or point. MR provides a positive learning environment where tutors are trained to systematically respond with a variety of positive verbal statements about their partner's efforts. Partners meet a minimum of four times per week for approximately 15 minutes.

Box 8.11: Modelled Reading steps

1 Modelling

In this step you are giving your reader an example or model of what good reading is like. You read as the reader points to the words. You must *only* read as fast as your reader can easily point to the words.

2 Word Search

The reader covers the passage with both hands. You say a word aloud. The reader repeats the word, uncovers the page and finds it on the page. Pick up to six words.

3 Word Practice

Point to one of the words that you selected from Word search. Say the word aloud. The reader repeats the word. You can pick up to six words.

4 Quick Word Check

Point to each of the words picked from Word Search and Word Practice. The reader should read each word as you point to it. This step is to check that the reader can easily read the words.

5 Paired Reading

In this step you read along with the reader. Try to read just a little ahead of the reader. Make sure that the reader remembers to point to each of the words. You must only read as fast as the reader can point.

6 Reading Alone

The reader now reads orally while pointing. If the reader hesitates with a word, he or she stops, allowing the reading tutor to provide the word.

You may decide, once your reader improves, not to include the modelling step and instead to begin at Word Search. You should spend no more than 15 minutes with your reader each time.

What does it mean to me?

Together with your partner talk about the following:

- **Who?** Who this page is about?
- **What happened?** What is the most important thing that happened to …?
- **What next?** What do you think will happen next in the story?

Remember to offer words of encouragement and to help your partner if she or he hesitates.

Modelled Reading Bookmark from
Helping You and Your Partner: Modelled Reading Resource Kit (1994), Education
Curriculum and Resources—copied with permission

More PMII examples

Classwide peer tutoring and peer-assisted learning strategies are future PMII approaches. Table 8.1 sets out briefly a description of each and references for further information.

Table 8.1 Two more PMII strategies

Approach	Description	References
Classwide peer tutoring (CWPT)	CWPT is designed to involve students in a particular classroom of the same age in reciprocal peer tutoring. Each student acts as both the tutor and the tutee (10 minutes) during each CWPT session. Students read, provide immediate feedback for errors and correction–answer 'who, what, when, where and why' questions for reading comprehension. A final 10 minutes is reserved to award individual and team points.	Delquadri et al. 1986; Greenwood et al. 1999 Research reviews: Greenwood et al. 1989 Greenwood et al. 2001 Utley et al.1997
Peer-assisted learning strategies in reading (PALS)	PALS engages students in three systematic and strategic reading procedures: partner reading with retell, paragraph summary and prediction. PALS provides intensive practice in reading aloud, reviewing and sequencing and summarising the information read, stating main ideas and predicting.	Fuchs et al. 1997 Fuchs et al. 2001

We believe that large numbers of students in inclusive environments can be effectively supported to reach their learning goals with the collaborative instruction alternatives we have described in this chapter. The merits of these alternatives are clear for maximising the engagement and performance of all students, including those with disabilities, compared with more conventional forms of teacher-directed instruction.

KEY TERMS USED IN THIS CHAPTER

Cooperative learning   Collaboration through structured interaction in small groups. It involves students in cooperation for a shared outcome.

Positive interdependence   When the group's goal or product outcome depends upon the actions of all group members.

Peer-mediated instruction and interventions (PMII) Various teaching alternatives that involve students working together to support each other's learning. Students' peer-teaching roles vary from providing direct instruction and modelling (peer tutoring) to encouraging and monitoring performance.

Peer tutoring A general descriptor for cooperative learning strategies that involve pairs of students teaching and learning on a one-to-one basis. In cross-age tutoring arrangements an older student acts as a tutor for a younger student. In reciprocal teaching arrangements students alternate between tutor and tutee roles.

Modelled reading (MR) A paired, cross-age peer-tutoring reading program.

FURTHER READING

Emmer, T. and Gerwels, M. (2002), 'Cooperative learning in elementary classrooms: Teaching practices and lesson characteristics' in *The Elementary School Journal*, 103(1) pp. 75–92.

Fisher, D. (2001), 'Cross-age tutoring: Alternatives to the reading resource room for struggling adolescent readers' in *Journal of Instructional Psychology*, 28(4), pp. 234–41.

Gartner, A. and Lipsky, D. K. (1990), Students as instructional agents. In W. Stainback and S. Stainback (eds) *Support Networks for Inclusive Schooling: Independent Integrated Education*. Grand Rapids, MI: Paul H. Brookes.

Organising the inclusive classroom

Organising children and staff in the classroom is an issue of prime importance for good teachers. The development of clear procedures and structures helps to ensure that a day runs smoothly and that learning is optimised. Often having diverse learners in a class can create significant challenges for the way a teacher runs a classroom. This chapter presents some ways of organising class structures and procedures in a way that is inclusive but that also meets the significant additional needs some children may have. It addresses issues including the physical layout of the classroom, seating plans, classroom procedures, feeding, issues surrounding the scheduling and implementation of a toileting routine, and administering medication.

KEY IDEAS IN THIS CHAPTER
- physical layout of the inclusive classroom
- classroom seating plans
- classroom procedures
  - child tasks
  - emergency plans
  - substitute teacher plans
- feeding children who require special assistance
- toileting children who require special assistance
- medication in the classroom

Physical layout of the inclusive classroom

The primary consideration in an inclusive classroom is the physical layout of the room. All children must be able to access a classroom in order to be involved in learning activities with the rest of the class. Access to the classroom is the most significant prerequisite to learning in an inclusive environment. It is the responsibility of the classroom teacher to ensure that children are able to access the classroom, and that any required modifications to structures are clearly communicated to the appropriate person in the school. These modifications should not be viewed as a 'luxury'—they should be seen as the bare minimum of what is required of a school to meet the needs of its children. Many education systems have special funds set aside and contingency plans for the modification of existing buildings to meet the needs of children with disabilities. Most new school buildings are now constructed with access for people with disabilities.

When we think of classroom access for children with disabilities one of the first things that may spring to mind is the installation of ramps in areas where there are stairs. Ramps are important for access not only for children in wheelchairs, but also for those using walking frames, or those with general mobility difficulties. The installation of ramps is not necessarily an expensive process. Reasonably priced metal ramps that are easy to move and store are now readily available (many parents use these to assist in loading children in wheelchairs into the back of vans). We have also seen examples of ramps constructed from sturdy plywood and painted with a non-slip coating that have adequately met the needs of schools in terms of cost, function and durability. In multi-storey school buildings the installation of a lift may need to be considered. This may take some time to complete. In the meantime, school administration could timetable all classes for children with mobility difficulties in ground-floor classrooms.

Providing access does not, however, stop with the installation of appropriate ramps. Narrow doors may need to be widened. Anyone who has spent a day in a wheelchair can attest to the skinned knuckles that result from doorways being too narrow to fit through easily. How doors open and close also needs to be considered. Doors that are easy to open from a sitting position and will stay open long enough for a child with a mobility difficulty to enter a room may be required. For children with visual impairments, doors should always be left either fully opened or fully closed to ensure that these children do not walk into half-opened doors.

Once in the classroom the child with mobility difficulties needs to be able to freely move around. It is for this reason that the bigger the room, the better it will be for these children. Modern classrooms are often cluttered with chairs, tables, benches, shelves, bags and other learning materials that can represent significant problems for children with mobility difficulties. Children with visual impairments may also be affected by this. Tables may be positioned in such a way that they deny the child with a disability access to all areas of the room. Clutter at below knee level, including mats and rugs, may represent a tripping hazard or cause the wheels of a wheelchair to become stuck. A case study by Loreman (2000) involved a 15-year-old boy, who used a wheelchair, for whom access was a significant issue. This boy was upset by the fact that he was never able to access any other area of a classroom than the front of the room due to the way the desks had been organised. He indicated that this situation had had a significant negative impact on his relationships with his peers, who generally sat away from the teacher, towards the back of the room. Teachers need to consider how their classroom can best be physically structured to meet the needs of all children. Obviously, in a larger room with more area to spread out this will be easier. In smaller classrooms furniture needs and positioning will have to be given more consideration. In classrooms with children who have visual impairments, the frequent moving and reorganising of classroom furniture should be avoided.

Children with attention-related disorders should be seated in areas in which distractions are minimised. For these children, a window seat may not be the best position from which they can concentrate on classroom tasks. Likewise, areas of the room that are full of stimulating materials such as posters, fish tanks, animal cages etc. might be best avoided. High traffic areas such as doors or frequently used shelves are also often not conducive to children with attention difficulties being able to concentrate.

Consideration should also be given to the height of tables and benches in a classroom. In secondary-school science rooms, children with disabilities should also be able to access sinks and other aspects of the room such as gas lines for Bunsen burners. In the inclusive classroom benches may need to be lowered and tables raised. Shelving should also be set at an appropriate height for all children. The lowering of built-in benches (where they are used by children) may entail some significant inconvenience but should be done if they are used to aid teaching. The raising of tables to allow a wheelchair to fit underneath them can be easily done. We have seen examples of metal extensions that fit to the bottom of existing table legs to raise the height, a cheap and effective alternative to purchasing a new adapted student table.

For children with visual impairments, issues of lighting and visibility need to be considered. Specific advice for children with visual impairments will vary according to the individual, but in general these children should be seated in a position that is appropriately lit and from which they are best able to view any instructional materials being used. Children with hearing impairments should be seated in a position that best enables them to hear what is being said; if they are lip-readers they should be seated in a position from which they can clearly see the teacher and other children speaking.

Modifications to provide access for children with disabilities should begin in the classroom, but certainly should not end there. Children with disabilities should be provided with access to all areas of the school that children without disabilities can access (see Box 9.1). This includes the school office, teacher offices, sporting facilities and the playground. Drinking fountains should also be set at an appropriate height so that all children can access them. Children with visual impairments may require hazards such as poles, rails, steps or benches to be painted in a bright colour such as yellow so that they do not accidentally walk into them.

Box 9.1: Physical access to and around classrooms

Things to consider when setting up the inclusive classroom include:

- ramps where there are steps
- width and positioning of doors and doorways; opening and closing speed
- arrangement of furniture
- classroom clutter such as games, bags, rugs, toys, sporting equipment
- table, bench and shelf height
- lighting
- unobscured lines of vision
- distractions
- access to sinks and other specialised classroom equipment
- access to drinking fountains
- access to other areas of the school such as other buildings, sporting fields, playgrounds
- the visibility of hazards.

Child-seating plans

There are many ways of organising how children are seated and grouped for learning in the classroom. In some classrooms, especially those with very young children, more time might be spent engaged in activities out of the childrens' designated seats than in them. In many secondary schools children remain seated for the majority of their classes. This section examines some common ways of organising children for instruction that can be applied to any age group in any setting.

Box 9.2: Advice on setting and space

Mohr (1995) suggests teachers consider the following points when arranging inclusive seating for children with disabilities:

- provide preferential seating
- seat near a 'study buddy'
- seat near a good role model
- place away from distractions
- use study carrels or quiet areas
- match work area to learning styles
- keep desk free from extraneous materials
- ensure barrier-free access
- provide adequate space for movement
- allow for flexible grouping arrangements.

Traditional expository teaching seating plan

Traditionally, children in Western classrooms have been seated in rows of tables or desks facing the teacher, who generally provided instruction from the front of the classroom. This is evident in many early photographs of classrooms. Many teachers continue to seat children of all ages in this way for instruction. Many secondary-school classrooms are set up this way to begin with, offering teachers who work in the room for brief sessions little scope for change.

Diagram 9.1 Traditional expository teaching seating plan

Child	Child	Child	Child	Child	Child
Child	Child	Child	Child	Child	Child
Child	Child	Child	Child	Child	Child
Child	Child	Child	Child	Child	Child

Teacher

The advantage of seating children in this way is that their attention is naturally drawn towards the teacher standing in front of them. The teacher can also see the faces of each of the children to help ensure that each one is listening or is 'on task' (McNamara and Waugh 1993). There are, however, some significant disadvantages associated with teaching children in this way. Instruction becomes teacher focused and the opportunities for learning from peers through discussion are significantly reduced. Classrooms set up in this way tend to encourage 'chalk and talk' type teaching strategies and discourage active involvement in learning (Woolfolk 2001). Individual needs are difficult to address through this type of teaching situation. Children become passive receptors of 'knowledge' rather than active participants in the learning process.

Children with diverse abilities are especially disadvantaged in classrooms set up in this way. As discussed previously, they may be restricted to sitting in the front of the room under the gaze of the teacher rather than with their friends. While there are some academic advantages to sitting near the front (Woolfolk 2001), the social barriers it presents are problematic. More significant, however, is the need for many children with diverse abilities to be more actively engaged in their learning than this mode of instruction allows. Under this model children may only be able to interact with children sitting directly next to them (Woolfolk 2001). All children need to be given the opportunity to interact with one another in order for effective learning to occur at all (McInerney and McInerney 2002).

Ability groups

Some teachers choose to seat their children in groups according to their perceived ability, knowledge or skills in a range of areas. This is known as ability grouping. Children in these groups do not necessarily directly face the teacher, who has more scope to conduct expository sessions or give instructions from any part of the room. This is a significant advantage in having groups organised in this way. With the teacher moving around the room more children can become involved in the teaching session, resulting in better learning (Woolfolk 2001). Children in these groups generally face each other and are able to interact with one another in their learning.

There are some advantages to sitting children in groups according to their abilities, although these are often advantages to the teacher rather than the child. Firstly, with children grouped roughly according to their abilities, teachers can become involved in small-group teaching situations, which they can adjust from group to group depending on levels of ability or need. Children are also able to interact and learn from one another with greater ease than if they were simply seated in rows. Teachers can also access children with greater ease when grouped in this way to provide assistance and individual instruction than when children are seated in rows of desks.

Diagram 9.2   Ability groups seating plan

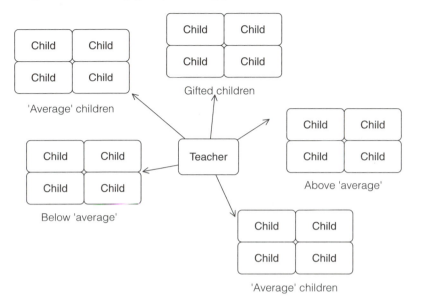

There are, however, some significant disadvantages to grouping children in this way. Firstly, there is almost certainly a social stigma attached to members of various groups, especially those in groups perceived to be struggling with classroom work (McNamara and Waugh 1993). Children might engage in competitive behaviour in order to move 'up' to a 'higher' group. This would have a negative impact on the social atmosphere of the classroom. Secondly, we know that grouping children according to perceived academic ability is not helpful in terms of general academic improvement for all children. While some children might benefit from association with a group of more gifted children, the rest of the class may largely miss out in involvement with this often positive academic and social influence (McNamara and Waugh 1993).

Heterogeneous grouping

Placing children in heterogeneous groups means placing children with mixed abilities in the same group. This is becoming increasingly regarded as an excellent way of grouping children for learning as it avoids many of the difficulties encountered with mixed-ability groups. In heterogeneous groups children with different backgrounds, interests and abilities can interact and learn from one another. Because children are able to easily interact, a variety of constructivist child-centred teaching strategies can be employed, such as peer tutoring and cooperative group work (McInerney and McInerney 2002). Children can also work on individual tasks as required. The advantages to the teacher include being able to facilitate learning for children rather than using teacher-centred instructional techniques, the ability to provide instruction from any point in the classroom and the ability to move around the room with greater ease to assist individual children.

Diagram 9.3   Heterogeneous groups seating plan

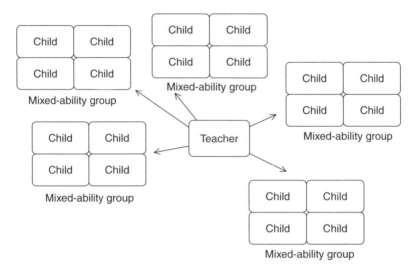

Individual learning spaces

Some teachers set their classrooms up so that children are not grouped at all. Instead, they create a number of small learning spaces to which children can retreat according to their preferences and the task they are supposed to complete. This is more likely to occur in classrooms containing younger children, but even at secondary schools some areas (such as libraries) are often structured according to this model.

The advantages of this model are that children can choose to work in an area that best suits them. Spaces are available for instruction in small or large groups as well as for individual work. A comfortable couch space can be useful for projects involving reading or informal discussion. The teacher is free to move around and address individual needs as required within the various learning environments.

The main drawback to setting up a classroom in this way is a very practical one. For children to benefit from this type of seating plan (where they essentially choose where they want to sit most of the time), they need to be very self-motivated to learn and very self-disciplined. Some children may not be able to deal with the lack of structure that a learning environment like this implies. Children will also need to be able to follow individual courses of study and to some extent manage their own work (McNamara and Waugh 1993).

Diagram 9.4 Individual learning spaces plan

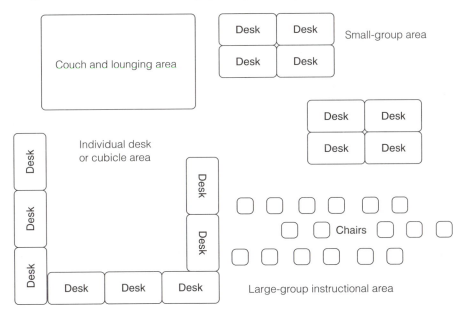

Using a combination of approaches

The reality of the situation is that many teachers are restricted in how they can group children in any given task by a variety of factors, which include the size of the classroom, the resources available, the amount of time spent in one classroom and the nature of the children. In all instances, however, flexibility and the need for children to enhance their learning through social interaction should be considered. Good teachers might use a combination of these seating and grouping models as they construct a learning environment for their children. Classrooms of children who are grouped according to the principles of child-centredness and the need for active social interaction in learning will be structured as good learning environments even if they do not have children with diverse abilities included in them. Classroom practice, according to Alexander et al. (1992, p. 32), will be more effective if teachers:

- have the skills that whole-class teaching, group teaching, and one-to-one work with individuals demand
- exploit the potential of collaborative group work
- use a combination of these strategies, according to the purposes of the task at hand.

Classroom procedures

Aside from structuring the classroom, good teachers generally have established procedures that are clearly communicated to all children in a class. These procedures can range from more mundane, everyday tasks to situations that would only occur in exceptional circumstances. Our experience has been that children of all ages are generally more comfortable within the framework of clearly established routines and procedures. That is not to say that learning should become 'routine', but rather that there is a general framework of procedures that children can reference most times in a classroom.

Student tasks

In most classrooms there are established tasks that children must perform to ensure the smooth running of a class. In classes of younger children these tasks can include any number of activities such as taking attendance, running messages to the office, being responsible for maintaining classroom areas or caring for class pets. Older children, who frequently move from teacher to teacher, are often expected to perform less classroom tasks due to the more transient nature of their contact with staff members. There are, however, areas of responsibility they may still take on, such as organising events or being involved in various school welfare committees. When using an inclusive approach it should be noted that children with diverse abilities should be expected to perform no more or no less tasks than other children. As with other children, the classroom tasks children with diverse abilities perform should be voluntary in nature and should reflect their skills and interests.

Emergency plans

All schools and classrooms should have a clearly set out and understood contingency plan for emergencies. Most schools choose or are required to practice these emergency procedures on a regular basis. Having children with disabilities enrolled requires schools to put extra thought into these plans. Where the evacuation of buildings is required, thought needs to be put into how children with disabilities are going to safely and quickly evacuate a premises. Children with visual impairments may need to be led out of a building. Children in wheelchairs or with mobility difficulties may need special arrangements put in place to assist them to leave a building safely and quickly.

Once children have left a building, safety also needs to be considered. An example of a good evacuation plan follows.

Example: The evacuation

Miss Holly taught a Grade 5 class in an elementary school in Edmonton, Canada. This class of 25 children contained one child in a wheelchair and one child with a moderate to severe visual impairment. One day in mid-January, with outside temperatures of −25°C and snow on the ground, the school alarm system went off, indicating that all children and staff should evacuate the building. The emergency plan Miss Holly had previously developed and communicated to her children was put into practice.

As the children without disabilities went about dressing in their cold-weather clothing and lining up at the door, Miss Holly put on her coat and hat and placed the class attendance list in her emergency basket. As she did this, administrative staff entered her classroom and assisted the child with a visual impairment to put on her coat and hat. The staff laid the coat of the child in the wheelchair over her but did not put it on properly. Dressing this child involved removing her partly from the wheelchair and would have taken more time than would have been wise to spend given the situation. On Miss Holly's instruction, the entire class and staff left the building via the pre-arranged route. One of the administrators pushed the child in the wheelchair. On exiting the building the class quickly assembled at the designated assembly point. Miss Holly removed the blankets from her emergency basket and distributed them to the children, ensuring first that a blanket was given to the child in the wheelchair to compensate for the fact that her coat was not on properly. Miss Holly checked attendance.

Emergency plans should be written and posted in a prominent spot in the classroom so that all children and other adults who may use the room from time to time can familiarise themselves with the required procedure. These plans should fit in with the overall school emergency plan so that staff are not working in isolation during emergency situations.

Emergencies at schools are not limited to incidents affecting the entire school. Emergencies can and do occur in individual classrooms from time to time and contingency plans for these emergencies should also be considered. These are especially important in classes including children with particular medical conditions that make them more liable to the occurrence of a personal emergency, or in classrooms including children with a history of violence. Should any child suffer a medical emergency teachers should have a procedure in place whereby other staff members can be contacted for assistance, and an ambulance can be called without hesitation. If your classroom has a phone, then this is the obvious way to both contact an ambulance and another staff member for assistance. If your room does not have a telephone, a responsible child may need to be designated to go and tell appropriate school staff about the incident and what needs to happen.

Plans for substitute teachers

Almost every teacher will miss days of work through illness at some point in their career. In the inclusive classroom it is important that any absences are planned for in advance. Like it or not, illness often hits us when we least expect it, so a well-constructed plan for the teacher who will replace you will assist your classroom to remain inclusive even when you are not there.

In addition to any plans or information you would ordinarily leave for a substitute teacher, you should also leave some information on the children with diverse abilities in your class and what your expectations are for their involvement in the class. Remember that even though you are absent, your class is still your class and any good substitute teacher will attempt to run it as closely as possible to the way in which you run it. Often teachers do not know who will be taking over their class when they are away. It is for this reason that you should assume in your plans that they know nothing about your children or about inclusion.

A brief information folder, updated by you from time to time, is often helpful to substitute teachers. This folder should contain the following brief information:

- general information on children in your class
- a brief description of your inclusive philosophy and what this means in practice
- your expectations that this philosophy will continue to be practised in your absence
- any important medical or other information.

It is important to keep the information concise. Remember that most substitute teachers do not have the luxury of a lot of time to prepare classes and read information. Two pages is probably a good length. Any additional, non-essential information can be included in the folder as an appendix.

Meeting students' personal care and medication requirements

The remainder of this chapter discusses issues of feeding, toileting and medication, which relate more specifically to children with disabilities. These are issues more pertinent to individual children than the class as a whole, but are important aspects to consider in organising the inclusive classroom.

Helping children who require special assistance to eat

Some children with disabilities will require assistance with eating. As with any area of personal care, teachers and paraprofessionals should ensure that a feeding routine is developed that respects the personal dignity and choices of the student. Steps should also be taken to ensure that snack and meal times take place in an inclusive environment.

In all instances staff working with children who require feeding should seek specialist advice and training from both the parents of the student and relevant professionals, such as doctors or speech-language therapists who have some expertise in swallowing and chewing and who are familiar with the student (Jaffe 1989). Failure to do this can have dire consequences. Children can easily choke when being fed and staff who are unaware of the correct feeding techniques, or what to do in instances when choking occurs, put their children at risk. Some children have gastric feeding tubes (G-Tubes) that are easy to set up and connect (Jaffe 1989), but that also require specialist instruction before a teacher or paraprofessional should use them.

Unless a student with disabilities refuses food, or has a medical reason for eating at different times, they should eat at the same times as other children and in the same environments. In countries such as Australia all children have lunch at school, while in other countries (such as Canada) they may or may not go home for lunch. In most countries children eat morning and afternoon snacks outside. Children requiring feeding should be no different unless there are compelling reasons why this should not occur. Staff feeding the student can go outside with them, feed them in the areas frequented by their friends and peers, clean them up, then leave them to their break. The emphasis is on doing an effective job with feeding while trying not to interfere too much with the social experience of children eating together. Children with disabilities should also have the right to refuse food if they are not hungry and to make choices about what they eat in so far as the other children have choices about the food they eat at school.

Other children may initially have questions about the fact that the feeding of a student by a staff member is taking place. These can be answered frankly in order to demystify the process, but in such a way as to emphasise the similarities and differences in the way all people eat. Our experience has been that peers generally get used to the idea of one of their number being fed by a staff member, and the practice is quickly accepted and swiftly ceases to be an issue. In no circumstances should feeding be delegated to peers. Not only do they not have the on-the-job training provided by allied health professionals to the teacher and/or paraprofessional, but allowing one student to feed another can foster attitudes of dependence that are contrary to inclusive views of children with disabilities as equal and capable members of the school community.

Toileting children who require special assistance

Some children with disabilities require help with toileting. This is usually the result of a physical condition or an intellectual disability that has resulted in the student being delayed in toilet training (Boswell and Gray 1998). Toileting can be a daunting prospect to a teacher who has never had to deal with this before, but by developing a few procedures in the school, toileting issues are easily dealt with. Early research on inclusion showed that teachers who had never taught children with physical disabilities were most concerned about toileting, while those who had taught these children were much more concerned about other issues (Frith and Edwards 1981). This demonstrates that toileting is not as frightening as it might at first seem once you have gained some experience. How much assistance you will get with toileting a student will depend on your school context. In some schools paraprofessionals are assigned the job of toileting children who require it. In other school systems this task is the responsibility of the classroom teacher. In both instances it is the responsibility of the classroom teacher to ensure that toileting is done correctly and with maximum dignity for the student, even if the teacher does not personally do the toileting.

Toileting falls into two main categories. The first is those who are being 'toilet trained', are not in nappies (diapers), but may need to be taken to the toilet and given assistance at designated times. The second category is those children still in nappies (diapers) who will need to be changed regularly. In both cases a private, specially designed toilet room for people with disabilities is appropriate. Careful planning must go into the construction of these toilet rooms to ensure that there is adequate space not only for a toilet, but also for staff, wheelchairs, lifts, an appropriately sized change table and storage areas for changes of clothes, nappies etc. Your school toilet should be set up so that any toileting can be done quickly and with a minimum of fuss. Nappies, cloths, wipes, creams, changes of clothes and other items should be on hand to ensure an efficient and dignified toileting experience. The best way to ensure that student dignity is maintained is to conduct toileting in private (Dalrymple and Boarman 1991). The toilet, with its nappy changing and undressing, is the one area of a school where an inclusive environment with other children is not appropriate.

Any staff involved in toileting children should follow what are known as 'universal precautions' in order to maintain the health of all involved. Universal precautions come from a 'worst-case scenario' perspective and operate under the assumption of the presence of disease. This means that even if you think you know that the children you are dealing with have no communicable diseases, when it comes to toileting you should treat them as if they do. Conversely, the adoption of universal precautions also protects the student from any diseases the caregiver may have. In the case of toileting, universal precautions usually only amount to washing hands before and after toileting and the wearing of new disposable gloves with each student. If any other measures are required to ensure that body fluids do not come in contact with staff or other children then they should be taken (Tetlow 1990). Any spills of bodily fluids (such as urine) should be cleaned using gloves and a 1:10 bleach/water solution, and any cloths used disposed of in a plastic-lined bin and professionally cleaned. Surfaces such as change tables should also be disinfected between uses.

Children being toilet trained often go to the toilet on a time schedule or immediately on their request to avoid accidents. Where this is the case a teacher may need to discreetly remind the student to go to the toilet on, for example, an hourly basis. Generally having a paraprofessional on hand to quietly slip out of class with the student ensures minimal disruption to the class. If becoming toilet trained at school is an individual program plan goal for a student, then toileting success should be assessed and documented on a form (see Form 17 in Useful forms). Gathering data is an essential part of encouraging toilet training (Dalrymple and Boarman 1991). Toilet-training programs will differ according to the individual student but should be designed according to the assessment, programming and instructional procedures covered in earlier chapters.

In scheduling regular toilet times a teacher needs to keep discretion in mind. Toileting should be done at times that draw minimum attention to the student and ensure minimum disruption to the school day. The best times to implement a toileting regime are generally during class transitions. This can mean between classes, just prior to or towards the end of break times, or just before or after school. These times are frequently busy and hectic, and thus withdrawal to use the toilet is less noticeable. Children without disabilities also tend to use the toilet at these times, so in this sense the timing is nothing out of the ordinary.

Medication in the classroom

Frequently teachers are called on to administer medication to children in schools. The prevalence of conditions such as seizure disorders and Attention Deficit Disorder (ADD), which are often treated with medication, means that the administration of medication is increasingly becoming an issue in schools. A considerable amount of debate as to the appropriateness of the practice of teachers administering medication has been taking place around the world for a number of years (Gadow and Kane 1983; McCarthy et al. 2000). Some argue that teachers are not medical practitioners and thus should not be administering medication. Others argue that when children are at school, teachers must act *in loco parentis*, that is, in the place of parents, and thus should ensure the well-being of children in their care by administering medication (Morse et al. 1997). Some schools are large enough to have a school nurse employed, but these schools are certainly in the minority and the reality is that, like it or not, teachers often have no choice but to administer medication to children during the school day. Teachers in this position need to take measures to ensure not only that medication is administered in a safe and appropriate way, but that adequate records are kept of this administration should a problem occur. Under no circumstances should teachers administer needles or perform any invasive medical procedures on any student.

We recommend that teachers only administer medication to children if there is no other alternative. You may also wish to seek advice from your professional association regarding the administration of medication. In some instances dosages and administration times can be adjusted by the family doctor so that all medication can be administered at home, outside school hours (Gadow and Kane 1983). We recommend that in all cases the family doctor be consulted to see if this is a possibility. If this is not possible then doctors should consider administration times that interfere as little as possible with class times. Furthermore, procedures at the school level need to be developed and implemented to ensure that student safety is not compromised.

Storage of medication
We have seen many examples of medication being stored in unlocked filing cabinets or desk drawers in classrooms. In some cases we have seen children keeping and administrating their own medication. Both scenarios entail a significant amount of risk if dosages become confused or if other children take medications that are not prescribed to them. The best policy is for all medication, however innocuous, to be collected and held in a secure location by school staff. This includes over-the-counter medications such as some cold or headache remedies.

In storing medication, schools have two options. The first, and probably the preferred option, is for all medication for all children in the school to be stored in the one secure location, perhaps the school office or another area constantly attended by staff. Medications in these areas should be stored in a locked cupboard fixed to the wall, clearly marked, and used only for the storage of medication. Keys to this cupboard should be limited to only a few staff members. Lockable boxes such as cash boxes, that are not fixed to the wall, are not appropriate for the storage of medication as they can be easily carried away. As some medications require refrigeration, a small lockable refrigerator (you may have to install a locking system yourself), once again used only for the storage of medications, should also be in the same area (Biggs et al. 1998; McCarthy et al. 2000). When it is time for medication to be administered, children can be met in this area by designated staff members who administer and record the medication.

The second option is for each classroom to have its own fixed, lockable medication cabinet, with refrigerated medications being stored in a locked central location. This option is less preferred because it results in medication being scattered across many locations in the school, which might pose security problems. It is, however, preferable to medications being stored in unlocked locations in a classroom.

Administration of medication

Before any medication can be administered, the school should be provided with appropriate documentation from medical professionals authorising the use of the medication with the student and outlining dosage and times, conditions under which the medication should be taken, and any possible side-effects or negative reactions that school staff might need to watch for. We recommend that school staff are in receipt of this written documentation from the family doctor before administration commences. Further to this, schools should seek written permission from the parent of the student before administration commences (Biggs et al. 1998; McCarthy et al. 2000). Gathering this documentation might seem time consuming and pedantic in many cases, but it is an important part of the process in ensuring that everything is well documented should a problem occur. A sample of a permission form for use with parents is provided as form 18 in Useful forms.

Once the relevant documentation and the actual medication has been forwarded to the school, protocols should be in place for its administration. As mentioned above, in schools where all medication is administered from a central area it is probably best to have a single staff member designated to take on that role. Ideally and wherever possible a second staff member should be designated to assist with the administration of medication (with a third and fourth staff member designated as back-up should any of the designates be away from school on any given day). School staff must be aware of the need to respect medical confidentiality (Biggs et al. 1998), and the less staff involved the better. It is sometimes possible to take short courses and in-services on medication administration, and wherever this is possible we suggest that all staff involved in this practice attend such a course. It is appropriate to have nurses or other medical professionals assess the protocols and training put in place with respect to medication administration prior to its taking place (Morse et al. 1997). Ideally the administration of medication should take place in a private area so as not to embarrass a student. Medication must be administered within 30 minutes before or after the prescribed time (Biggs et al. 1998). Any longer than this and medical advice from the prescribing doctor and verbal permission from the parent should be sought.

When administering medication, staff should observe the protocol in Box 9.4, which should be displayed prominently in the area where medication is administered.

Box 9.4: Protocol for administering medication

1 Wash hands/put on gloves.
2 Check medication name, use-by date, times and dosage on bottle/package against details on the medication administration form (Form 19 in Useful forms).
3 Where possible ask a second staff member to confirm the details on the package match those on the medication administration form.
4 Check that you have the correct student for the correct medication.
5 Have a second staff member check that the correct medication is going to the correct student.
6 Place the required dosage of the medication in a small clean plastic medication cup (or measuring cup/spoon in the case of liquids).
7 Have a second staff member check that this is the correct dosage.
8 Supervise the administration of the medication. Check that the student has swallowed the medication. Often having a student drink a glass of water (where permitted) is a good way of ensuring this.
9 Dispose of the plastic cup.
10 Record the administration of the medication (once again checking medication information against the form before placing back in storage area) on the form and sign off.
11 Wash hands/dispose of gloves.

Record keeping

It is extremely important that accurate, up-to-date records are kept of all medication administration (Biggs et al. 1998). Good records not only help to ensure that medication is not 'missed' (or conversely, that two doses are not given) but they also provide documentation that the school has been fulfilling its obligations with respect to administering medication to children. We suggest that all information pertaining to the medication for a student be kept together in a folder that is stored in the direct vicinity of the medication storage area. The folder should contain all permissions, information on the medication/s, and sheets for recording the administration of the medication/s. (Form 19 in Useful forms will assist you in doing this.)

Administration away from school

On some occasions children will be away from the school building on educational field trips or sports days when it is time for medication to be administered. In this instance the staff member responsible for giving the medication should take the required medication on the outing, keeping it in the most secure location possible (generally the staff member's bag). A field-trip medication form (such as Form 20 in Useful forms) should be filled out prior to leaving the school and completed at the actual time of administration. This record can then be kept on file and the usual documentation filled out on the return to school to reflect the fact that the medication was administered. As far as is possible staff should follow the same medication administration protocol when they are on trips outside of the school.

Errors in medication administration

Any error in the administration of medication is a serious matter and medical advice should be sought immediately, preferably from the prescribing doctor. Medication errors can include (Biggs et al. 1998):

- an omitted dose
- wrong student
- wrong dose
- wrong medication
- wrong time
- wrong method of ingestion (route).

Following the seeking of medical advice and notification of the parent of the student, an incident report (such as Form 21 in Useful forms) should be completed and filed, with a copy made and sent home.

This chapter has examined practical aspects of inclusion, including how to modify and adapt your classroom for children with diverse abilities, as well as some important aspects relevant to individuals with disabilities, such as feeding, toileting and the administration of medication. The next chapter discusses how to promote positive social relationships for diverse learners.

KEY TERMS FROM THIS CHAPTER

Ability grouping Placing children in groups according to their perceived ability, knowledge or skills in a range of areas.

Heterogeneous groups Placing children with mixed abilities in the same group.

FURTHER READING

Alexander, R.J., Rose, J. and Woodhead, C. (1992), *Curriculum Organisation and Classroom Practice in Primary Schools: A Discussion Paper,* London: Department of Education and Science.

Jaffe, M.B. (1989), 'Feeding at-risk infants and toddlers' in *Topics in Language Disorders*, 10(1), pp. 13–25.

McCarthy, A.M., Kelly, M.W. and Reed, D. (2000), 'Medication administration practices of school nurses' in *Journal of School Health*, 70(9), pp. 371–76.

10

Promoting positive behaviour

At some point in their career all teachers are faced with children who present with challenging behaviour in their classroom. It is a fact that these children will be there and that they are entitled to our attention and the same standard of education as any other child in a class. Challenging behaviour can be viewed as an annoyance and source of irritation in the classroom, or as an opportunity to develop new skills and understandings about teaching and learning. This chapter focuses on positive ways of dealing with children whose behaviour is challenging through a whole-school and an individual-classroom approach.

KEY IDEAS IN THIS CHAPTER
- defining challenging behaviour
- developing school behaviour policy
- the sources of challenging behaviour
- violence and touching
- class meetings
- teaching tips that work
- developing an 'action plan'

What is challenging behaviour?

Challenging behaviours can be thought of as being the result of conflict between a child and the environment. These can occur when a child responds to his or her educational environment in ways that differ significantly from age-appropriate expectations and interfere with his or her own learning or that of others (Educational Response Centre 1992). Types of challenging behaviour might include but are not limited to:

- the inability to maintain satisfactory relationships with peers or adults
- episodes of physical violence towards people or property
- the use of poor or hostile language
- resistance to following rules or expectations
- general unwillingness to follow instructions from those in authority
- self-harming behaviour
- a general mood of anger or unhappiness.

These behaviours often present themselves to teachers in the context of a learning situation, and are often a sign that the student is having difficulty coping in that particular situation. It is the job of the teacher and the school to find and address the reasons for misbehaviour in order to present all children with an optimal learning environment.

Responding to challenging behaviour

The behaviour of students in schools is the result of many different influences. However, when order breaks down in a school the typical response is to blame and focus attention on the 'behavioural-problem students' or 'trouble-makers'. This over-simplified response overlooks the importance of the school context in which the behaviour occurs.

Box 10.1: Checklist for promoting positive behaviour in schools

This checklist provides a listing of beliefs, policies and practices important for schools in providing an infrastructure that supports belonging, order and learning. Tick those applicable to your school. Those not ticked need to be addressed by the school community as a whole.

1 Values
   1.1 The principal and teachers know students as individuals
      (e.g. their names, interests, peer group, personalities). ❐
   1.2 This school has a positive climate for supporting both teacher
      and student learning. ❐

2 Policies
   2.1 This school has policies that promote belonging and acceptance
      and support diversity. ❐
   2.2 This school has a bullying policy. ❐

2.3 This school has behaviour policy that includes clearly articulated practices for promoting acceptable behaviour. (See Box 10.2 School Behaviour policy.) ❐

3 Practices

3.1 This school actively encourages members to respect one another. ❐

3.2 This school has an inclusive and evidenced-based approach to the improvement of organisational and classroom practices. ❐

While there will always be some students with emotional and behavioural issues that will need extraordinary approaches beyond those generally available, there is much that can be done at the school level to minimise the need for these individual approaches. Every aspect of a school's social climate—the leadership, the way it operates and the way it interacts with the wider school community—influences the behaviour of its students. These influences can create successful learning environments for disadvantaged schools and, conversely, create environments without order and standards for acceptable behaviour and lower learning outcomes in schools considered to be more advantaged.

Behaviour policies alone are not the answer. The school community must actively promote, encourage and model the value and respect for all members. Policies themselves must be integrated and consistent with one another. Schools need to ensure that new members are informed through student- and staff-induction programs.

Box 10.2: Fifteen steps to developing a school behaviour policy

The school behaviour policy should:

1 help promote a positive environment for student and parent involvement
2 be written so it is easy to understand by the whole school community
3 inform students, teachers and parents
4 involve students, parents and teachers in its development and ongoing monitoring and evaluation
5 integrate with other policies such as welfare, inclusion, bullying and staff development
6 be informed by the monitoring of school and classroom practices.

The behaviour policy should include:

7 a statement of values and principles
8 an outline of the roles and responsibilities for students, school leadership, teaching staff, parents and outside professionals

9   clearly stated standards for acceptable behaviour for both students and school staff
10 guidelines for parent behaviour and outside professionals
11 explicit rules for acceptable behaviour and expected practices for compliance and non-compliance
12 steps for regular monitoring, evaluation and modification
13 steps for induction of new teaching staff and new students
14 steps for providing positive support to teaching and other staff at the first point of concern
15 steps for informing and modifying related policies.

Most importantly, the implementation of the policies into practices needs to be monitored regularly to ensure that all members of the community are responding in the same way and that the school organisation supports the practices and informs modification of policies, practices and staff professional development. There are many different ways that members of a school might monitor and evaluate their policies and practices. The choice of tools for gathering the evidence will vary in response to the questions asked.

Questions for analysing why there is a particular ongoing 'problem behaviour' in a school might include:

- When does the behaviour occur?
- Are there any patterns, e.g. same activity, same time, same student/s, same teacher/s, same location?
- What exactly happens? Describe precisely the verbal and/or non-verbal components.
- What are the consequences for the student/s, the teacher, the class, the school?
- Do all teachers respond to the behaviour in the same way or do the consequences vary? Do consequences reflect school values and/or policies?

In order to answer these questions teachers may need to collect and monitor school behaviour and responses for several weeks or a school term. Evidence could include:

- asking teachers and students to record their answers to some of the above questions immediately after an incident
- interviewing students and teachers
- systematically observing students and teachers
- keeping diaries
- photography
- video recording
- examining policy documents

- reviewing curriculum
- conducting a survey of students and/or parents and teachers.

Data should reflect different viewpoints and the values espoused by the school policy.

Once data has been collected, a team of teachers and students can meet to sort and critically analyse the data. It may also be appropriate at specific points in the analysis to engage a 'critical friend' in the process. A critical friend is someone who has expertise or special skills relevant to the problem but is external to the school. The key issue is to look for patterns. Discussion should elicit strategies and the evaluation should be used positively to improve practices and where appropriate be supported through staff development.

While many schools have developed school-wide strategies and procedures for promoting positive behaviour and dealing with children with challenging behaviour, you will be called on to deal with misbehaviour in your classroom in the context in which it occurs. In the majority of schools this means that most frequently this will be when you are alone with your class. Dealing with misbehaviour in the context of teaching an entire class can be a frightening proposition, but if it is approached in an organised and planned way you can be prepared to deal with most misbehaviour in a way that ensures the dignity of all involved is kept intact. Being organised can help to reduce the stress that children with difficult behaviours can introduce to a teaching and learning situation.

The sources of challenging behaviour

In order to successfully manage the behaviour of children we must first view all behaviour, good or bad, as a choice made by the child. This is a very important way of looking at behaviour. If we do not believe that behaviour is a choice, then what we are saying is that the actions of a child are out of his or her control, and therefore nothing the child and teacher can do will change that behaviour. We are saying that it is essentially innate and therefore not influenced by the conscious mind. While there are some examples of children not being able to exercise choice over the way in which they behave (for example, some medical conditions involving psychosis), these are certainly in the minority and should be addressed by the medical profession as they present. In the majority of cases we simply must begin with the premise that a child is choosing his or her behaviour if we are to successfully intervene and change the way in which they behave.

Albert (2003) presents a useful frame in which to view the misbehaviour of children, according to which the sources of misbehaviour fall into four categories: attention seeking; avoidance of failure; power; and revenge. It is difficult to imagine any misbehaviour that does not have its roots in one of these four categories.

Attention-seeking behaviour

As the term suggests, attention-seeking behaviour occurs when students are trying to fulfil a need for extra attention. Even if you feel that these students already get plenty of extra attention, they feel they need more, and sometimes this need is never completely fulfilled no matter what you try! Attention seekers can operate in two modes. 'Active' attention seekers are those students who engage in behaviour that often lacks subtlety. These are the students who do things such as making faces at their peers, calling out in class, or pulling the hair of the child in front of them. Anything to get people to notice them. 'Passive' attention seekers are those who, as Albert decribes it, engage in 'one pea at a time' behaviour. They rarely disrupt, but are those students who work on 'slow, slower, and slowest speeds' (Albert 2003). They get our attention by not cooperating and deliberately not reacting to our instructions. Both active and passive attention seekers prefer positive attention, but often their behaviour is so irritating to teachers and peers that the feedback they get is negative. To the attention seeker, however, negative attention is better than none at all and will only serve to reinforce the misbehaviour. Albert (2003) suggests that we deal with attention seekers by rewarding instances of appropriate behaviour and by teaching children appropriate ways of asking for extra attention when they need it.

Avoidance of failure

Avoidance of failure behaviour is another self-evident term. When avoidance of failure is the cause of misbehaviour, children tend to withdraw from classroom activities in order to avoid the possibility of performing poorly. These are children with low self-esteem and little confidence in their own abilities. According to Albert (2003), these children tend to procrastinate, do not complete work, develop temporary incapacities such as headaches, or assume traits associated with children who have learning disabilities. We can help these children through improving their self-esteem by providing them with learning situations in which they can experience success, and by drawing them into congenial relationships with ourselves and peers. If we can assist these children to reflect on their successes then their concept of themselves as effective learners should improve.

Power behaviour

Children who engage in power behaviour are constantly trying to challenge our authority as teachers. They want to engage us in public power struggles and have a need to be seen as being 'in charge'. This can be very threatening to teachers. If we are seen to have lost a power struggle with a student, then from that point on our authority is questioned not only by that student, but also by the rest of the class. The consequences for a teacher who is perceived by the majority of a class to have no authority in the classroom are obvious and authority, once lost, is a very difficult thing to rebuild. Albert (2003) lists two types of power behaviour. A student can exhibit 'active' power behaviour by throwing physical or verbal tantrums, showing both disrespect and defiance towards the teacher, or demonstrate 'passive' power behaviour by quiet noncompliance with instructions while continuing to outwardly act friendly, which is often little more than a thin veneer covering a seething resentment underneath.

Revenge behaviour

Revenge behaviour occurs 'when students misbehave to get revenge . . . they are retaliating for real or imagined hurts' (Albert 2003). Students exhibiting revenge behaviours want to hurt their teacher as much as possible. They do this through physical or verbal attacks or by deliberately violating the values held by a teacher through their comments or actions. According to Albert (2003), students who are exhibiting revenge behaviour have 1001 ways of saying 'I hate you'.

The principles of prevention for both power and revenge behaviour are similar. The most important, and often the most difficult, thing to do is to avoid confrontation and power struggles altogether with children exhibiting these types of behaviours. You cannot win, as these battles are generally continued until they are settled on the child's terms. Even if you do eventually get your way you have probably lost your cool and some of your dignity in achieving that. The best solution is to diffuse any potential confrontations by:

1 becoming aware of situations where confrontation might occur and changing your approach to teaching accordingly
2 when confrontations do occur employ strategies that will help you to avoid a pitched battle (some of these techniques will be addressed in the section 'Teaching tips that work' later in this chapter).

You should also find ways of helping these students to legitimately hold some power or, in the case of revenge behaviour, to express dissatisfaction in a constructive way with something that has happened. You can do this by developing a relationship with these students and negotiating the holding of power through special 'jobs' they can be responsible for, and by opening up a two-way dialogue for the expression of any real or imagined hurts. In this way you are not engaging yourself in public power struggles.

Violence and touching

It is our view that physical violence in any form should not be tolerated in schools. Notwithstanding our commitment to inclusion, we believe that any students who pose an immediate and present physical danger to themselves or to others as a result of their behaviour do not belong at school until that immediate risk has been adequately dealt with. Any removal of a child for reasons of violence should only be for a very short period of time to enable that child to seek the appropriate medical or psychological intervention before returning to the classroom. Safety must always be our first consideration as teachers.

Teachers often speak of their frustration at no longer being allowed to touch students. This is a frequent misconception and misinterpretation of the 'no touching' rule. The general practice of limiting physical contact between teachers and students has been introduced in order to protect students from physical and sexual harassment and abuse. It is wise not to unduly touch the children you are teaching. This can, however, be taken too far. In situations where students are behaving in such a way as to pose a physical risk to themselves, other children, staff or valuable property, a teacher is morally (and often legally) obliged to step in and control that behaviour, even if it means touching the child concerned. Of course the amount of force you use needs to be reasonable and appropriate to the situation, and based on the principle of minimum intervention. This means using the least intrusive means necessary to control a given situation.

We strongly advise you to check with your school jurisdiction, and consult and follow their policies and the law on the issue of dealing with instances of classroom violence. Furthermore, there are a variety of different courses available to teachers, such as 'non-violent crisis intervention' courses, which can teach you not only how to diffuse potentially violent situations, but also how to not hurt children or yourself if a situation does get physical.

Class meetings

Regular class meetings are an excellent way of promoting positive behaviour in your classroom, and to help children to think about their behaviour and take responsibility for it. Class meetings should be scheduled on at least a weekly basis, and possibly more frequently if required. Class meetings are criticised by some practising teachers as taking too much time out of an already overloaded schedule. While this is a legitimate concern, in most instances class meetings contribute to the promotion of good behaviour in the classroom, which then enables the teacher to concentrate on teaching the curriculum. Generally, the time investment required for class meetings is more than compensated for by the time that is freed up through improved behaviour. Children of all ages, including those in high school and very young children, can successfully participate in class meetings, although the terminology and process may need to be simplified for younger children.

Class meetings can be adapted to suit your own classroom context, but there are some features that other teachers have found helpful in running their own class meetings that you might wish to adopt (see Box 10.3).

Box 10.3: Eight building blocks of successful class meetings

Eight building blocks of successful class meetings as put forward by Nelsen et al. (1993) are:

1   forming a circle
2   practising compliments and appreciation
3   creating an agenda
4   developing communication skills
5   learning about separate realities
6   solving problems through role-playing and brainstorming
7   recognising the four reasons people do what they do
8   applying logical consequences and other non-punitive solutions.

Children need to be specifically taught what the eight building blocks mean in order to be successful participants in class meetings. This can be done while holding your initial meetings.

Forming a circle
Wherever possible class meetings should be conducted with everyone seated in a circle. This feels more democratic and egalitarian. All students and the teacher need to be included in the circle.

Practising compliments and appreciation
Complimenting others in the class on things they have done well is an essential part of keeping your class meetings positive in nature and boosting the self-

esteem of your students. Giving compliments, however, does take practice for some children so modelling how to give sincere compliments is important. It is also important for all students to receive compliments, not necessarily at every class meeting, but on a regular and frequent basis.

Creating an agenda

An important feature of class meetings is that the children have the opportunity to place items for discussion on the agenda. In fact, it should primarily be the children who place items on the agenda, rather than the teacher, who has the opportunity to discuss discipline issues on other occasions. When children form the agenda it helps them to 'buy in' to the process and take some responsibility for and ownership of the class meetings. An agenda notebook or noticeboard should be placed in the room where children can access it at specific times designated by you to contribute items. They may remove items they themselves put on, but not the items of others, and there needs to be a clear rule that the issues placed on the agenda are not to be discussed outside the times allocated for class meetings. This will help to avoid arguments. The list of agenda items should be reviewed by the teacher at each meeting and the child who contributed the item should be asked if it still needs to be discussed (often problems are resolved prior to the class meeting).

Developing communication skills

An ineffective class meeting involves a class of children sitting in a circle, all talking at once and not listening to anything. Children need to learn and develop communication skills that are appropriate for class meetings. This means that children need to be able to express their concerns as well as listen to the concerns of others. A good way to ensure that this happens is to use a small bean bag or 'talking stick'. Only the person with the bean bag is allowed to talk, and everyone else may listen. If someone wants to respond to a comment or contribute to the discussion they must raise their hand and the teacher will indicate that the bean bag be given to them. Children who choose not to follow this rule can be given one warning before being asked to leave the meeting or sit in a 'penalty box' type situation where they can observe but not participate for a set period of time. Children should be frequently reminded that the purpose of the meeting is not to blame others, but to find solutions to problems in a mature way.

Learning about separate realities

Through class meetings children will learn that not everybody sees things the same way. They need to be prepared to accept that different people will have different perspectives and views, and develop the skills to negotiate an outcome that benefits everyone.

Solving problems through role-playing and brainstorming
The purpose of class meetings is to solve problems. The best ways for children to do this are to either act out the scenario and its possible other solutions, or to brainstorm possible solutions. These solutions should be discussed without judgment. The child who put the item on the agenda can then pick the best solution from the list devised by the class. In instances where that student is unable to select a solution, the entire list of possible solutions can be put to a vote by the entire class. The selected solution should be tried for a week and then discussed again if it has not worked. It is then important for reasons of preserving healthy self-esteem that the concept of appreciations and giving compliments is briefly revisited, particularly for those involved in placing the item on the agenda and the child who made the mistake.

Recognising the four reasons people do what they do
Before consequences and solutions are applied, it is important for children to reflect on the reasons for misbehaviour as identified by Albert (2003). This should help to develop some empathy and enable children to come up with more sensitive and appropriate consequences.

Applying logical consequences and other non-punitive solutions
All problems require solutions, and all instances of misbehaviour should be met with appropriate consequences. The final 'building block' children need to develop in order to participate in effective class meetings is that of applying these solutions and consequences. In devising consequences, children need to be reminded that the consequence must meet three criteria. Any consequence must be related to the misbehaviour. For example, if a child has vandalised another child's property, then a related consequence may be to spend time in at recess to repair the damage. A consequence must also meet the criterion of being respectful. A child should not be demeaned as a result of the consequence. Thirdly, a consequence needs to be reasonable. Being asked to write a 20-page paper over two full weeks of recess may not be a reasonable consequence for a child who litters, but spending two recesses cleaning up in the school may. All consequences devised by children need to be compared against each criterion before being applied.

Box 10.4: Class-meeting format

This simple format for a class meeting was devised by Nelsen et al. (1993, p. 90):

1   compliments and appreciations
2   follow-up on past solutions

3   agenda items:
   (a)   share feelings while others listen
   (b)   discuss without fixing
   (c)   ask for problem-solving help
4   future plans (field trips, parties etc.).

Sometimes, despite our best efforts as teachers, our classroom management does not have the impact we desire. At this point it is a good idea to reflect and take stock of the situation. Is there something missing? The following questions can be used to help you guide self-evaluation and critical reflection of your approach to classroom management:

* How much teacher-talk was there compared with student-talk? Which students talk? Who listens? When do they talk?
* Who is off task? On task?
* Were the instructions presented so that all the students could understand?
* Was the task too easy? Too difficult?
* Was there enough time for students to complete the activity?
* Were distractions and disruptions minimised?
* Were some students provided with alternatives?
* Were students who did not have the prerequisite skills given scaffolds to support their participation and learning?

Box 10.5: Teaching tips that work

These 'quick tips' might help you to promote better behaviour in your classroom.

1   Get to know your **students as individuals** and develop a personal relationship with them. Friends and common interests can be a focus for conversation.
2   **Be positive!** Make constant attempts to build on each student's success—encourage, reward and praise their appropriate actions. Help them see how good they are at what they do.
3   **Model** the standards for behaviour that you expect. At all times be polite and courteous and expect the same of your students.
4   Regularly **observe** the behaviour of the classroom. Try to be aware of a number of behaviours that are occurring simultaneously. **Record** incidents of ongoing 'problem' behaviour.
5   Make all **classroom rules explicit** and list three important, reasonable class rules clearly on the wall. Communicate your expectations clearly. Involve students in establishing the rules for classroom behaviours.

6   Implement strong, predictable **routines**.

7   Plan and **organise the lesson and the classroom** to **minimise disruption** and maximise students' interest. Seating layout, student grouping, pacing, humour are all vital in minimising opportunities for disruption. Avoid down time and boredom—this can lead to trouble. Expect your students to be on task. Use humour in your teaching.

8   Seating and grouping. Some students do not work well together. Do not seat easily distracted students near windows, doors or high-traffic areas.

9   **Pace** your lessons appropriately. Too quick and students may get left behind and give up. Too long and they may become bored.

10 Be careful, cautious and consistent in using **reprimands**—choose private over public reprimands. Be fair and firm, never sarcastic. Never make empty threats—ensure your reprimand is appropriate and you can carry it out. Pick your battles. Some small details are not worth fighting for. Know when to ignore and when to step in. Avoid reprimanding or punishing a class or group.

11 **Use non-verbal gestures**. Maintain a high rate of **eye contact**. Use a signal that all students know means 'Silence, please'. Give 'the eye' and use silence and facial expressions to put some misbehaviour back in check. Smile and nod positively. Use 'proximity control'. Move near students acting disruptively.

12 Don't yell. Students can become 'teacher deaf' after a while. Save raising your voice for rare occasions when you really need to make an impact. Speaking softly can help keep the classroom calm.

13 Give students special responsibilities around the classroom or school.

14 Require students to say three nice things ('put ups') for each time they 'name call' or 'put down' another student.

15 Display student work samples to promote self-esteem and confidence.

16 Be a physical presence during times of transition between activities. The absence of structure at these times can sometimes create problems.

17 Monitor and critically reflect on your classroom management and identify areas for improvement. Monitor your handling of the beginning, transition and ending of a lesson as well as responses to an unexpected event or a classroom crisis.

Developing an action plan

Earlier in this chapter we discussed the need to tackle misbehaviour in a positive but also structured and planned way. One of the best ways to build this structure is to come up with an action plan to deal with specific behaviour being exhibited by a particular child. It is wise to involve the child in this process so that your action plan also becomes a type of social contract between you and the student.

The first step in this process is to ensure the child is aware of what the misbehaviour is, and that he or she is willing to commit to improving their behaviour. There are many ways you can make the prospect of behaviour improvement attractive. These can range from discussions about how grades and reports home will improve to more concrete rewards. Once a child has accepted that a behaviour needs changing and is willing to work on it, then an action plan can be drawn up (see Form 22 in Useful forms for 'Positive behaviour action plan'.) The stages in drawing up that plan are:

- identify behaviours
- identify reasons
- identify solutions
- identify consequences and rewards.

Identify behaviours

At this stage you need to identify what the misbehaviour is. The idea is to extinguish this behaviour. Extinguishing a behaviour is, however, rarely enough. A list needs to be drawn up of alternative, positive behaviours that can replace the negative behaviour once it is gone. Failure to replace negative behaviours with positive ones can lead to a behaviour vacuum in which the child simply finds an alternate negative behaviour to replace the last one. An example may be a child who identifies speaking out of turn as a behaviour he wishes to extinguish. Positive alternatives to this behaviour which he can adopt might include putting up his hand or placing his hand on his head.

Identify reasons

The next stage is to identify the reason for this misbehaviour based on Albert's (2003) goals of misbehaviour discussed earlier. Make the child aware of what these four goals are and then ask him or her to identify why they are demonstrating a particular poor behaviour.

Identify solutions

This stage involves brainstorming possible solutions for the problem. You might want to involve parents or other children (with the focus child's consent) in the process. Discuss, negotiate, and select the 'best' solution with the child.

Identify consequences and rewards

The final stage involves you and the child negotiating consequences for continued misbehaviour as well as rewards for improved behaviour. Remember that consequences should be reasonable, respectful and related (Nelsen et al. 1993). You can use Form 22 in Useful forms to develop your action plan.

KEY TERMS FROM THIS CHAPTER

Challenging behaviour   When a child responds to his or her educational environment in ways that differ significantly from age-appropriate expectations and interfere with the child's own learning or that of others.

Minimum intervention   The least intrusive means necessary to control a given situation.

Critical friend   Someone who has expertise or special skills relevant to the problem but is external to the school.

FURTHER READING

Albert, L. (2003), *A Teacher's Guide to Cooperative Discipline* (2nd edn), Minnesota: AGS Publishing.

Mishna, F. (2003), 'Learning disabilities and bullying: Double jeopardy' in *Journal of Learning Disabilities*, 36(4), pp. 336–48.

Nelsen, J. et al. (1993), *Positive Discipline in the Classroom*, Rocklyn, CA: Prima.

Slee, R. (1996), 'Bullying in the playground: The impact of inter-personal violence on Australian children's perceptions of their play environment' in *Children's Environments*, 12, pp. 320–27.

11

Promoting social competence

As explained in Chapter 1, creating an inclusive classroom environment that is respectful and accepting of all students is one of a teacher's most important roles. This chapter outlines some of the things a teacher can do to convey acceptance of all students in the classroom and to promote positive social interaction among the students. All students will further develop their social competencies throughout their school years. Some students will not acquire these skills as easily as their peers. Teachers may need to include specific strategies and classroom programs to facilitate the development of their social competencies.

KEY IDEAS IN THIS CHAPTER
- defining social competence
- creating friendships
- developing social skills
- social-skills program and resources

What is social competence?

Social competence has long been recognised by educators and researchers as vital for successful and productive participation in society. It is a process that begins at birth and continues throughout life. Social interactions are considered to be important for cognitive development (Vygotsky 1978) and academic performance (Welsh et al. 2001; Wang et al. 1994) and have been linked to resiliency (Benard 1993) and 'real-world' success.

Individuals with intellectual disabilities or with learning difficulties often have associated difficulties with social competence, particularly with social interactions with peers (Haager and Vaughn 1995; Kavale and Forness 1996; Gresham and MacMillan 1997; Mishna 2003; Nowicki 2002). Peer interactions and friendships have been found to play an important role in facilitating the personal, social and moral development of individuals (Hall and McGregor 2000).

We mostly live as members of various social groups, for example, the classroom, our work environment, family/living group, sporting groups, etc. An individual's social competence will determine how he or she participates in these groups. Positive changes in the quality of an individual's participation will also improve their sense of well-being, feelings of belonging and sense of adjustment. This is a most important goal for all educators.

Social competence can be described as the ability to integrate thinking, feeling and behaviour to achieve social tasks and outcomes valued in the host context and culture (University of Dundee 1998). Social competencies require an individual to:

- be motivated to seek interaction with others
- be knowledgeable about the rules and ways of interacting
- have a set of social skills and know where and when to use these effectively and appropriately
- modify behaviour in response to changes in the context, situation and/or relationship.

Although different cultures and contexts value different social competencies, there is some general consensus across most societies as to what is acceptable and valued in positive social interaction. There may also be several different and individual approaches and attributions to the same outcome in any context, and a number of chance or environmental variations. Therefore it is impossible to view social competence in terms of a limited range of social skills and/or social goals. It is the ability to flexibly modify a range of behaviours in a number of different contexts that determines the extent of an individual's social competence.

Social competence allows us to achieve socially appropriate goals.

Motivation to communicate

Social competence requires that we must be motivated to socially interact with others. Shultz (1988) has identified three basic needs that motivate communication:

- a need for identity—to belong and to be involved
- a need to be accepted—to fit in, make friends and be liked and accepted
- a need for control—to initiate action and respond to others, to determine

who we speak to and what we say, and to have some influence on our environment.

Knowledge

Social competence requires that we must be knowledgeable about the rules and ways of interacting with others and for solving social problems. Knowledge plays an extremely important part in memory and problem-solving performance and development. Research has demonstrated many problem-solving strategies cannot be executed without a well-developed knowledge base. An extensive and well-organised knowledge base about social conventions and skills is essential for successful social-problem solving. The success of social-competence programs are therefore highly dependent on the knowledge the student has about each social problem in the specific social context.

Box 11.1: Knowledge about social competence

Knowledge about social competence includes:

- rules and conventions
- routines and rituals
- verbal and non-verbal cues
- expectations
- behavioural patterns
- strategies (both successful and unsuccessful).

Brainstorming is one activity often suggested for identifying and discussing student knowledge. For example, brainstorming with students to discover what they know about friendship can be very useful when students have had substantial friendship experiences. A student who has had many different experiences of friends will have a well-developed knowledge base about the topic and will readily be able to generate ideas and contribute to any discussion. Some students, however, have had very limited experiences interacting with peers and may never have experienced a friend. Because of their limited knowledge about friendship, these students will be unlikely to generate ideas or make meaningful contributions to discussion. Other students, for example those diagnosed with autism or asperger syndrome, may not maintain eye contact during social interactions. As a consequence, these students will have limited visual knowledge of the non-verbal behaviour of social interactions. Their opportunities for gaining non-verbal knowledge will have been limited by their lack of eye contact. While it is important to identify what a student knows about social competence, it is equally important to find out what opportunities he or she may have had for learning this information.

Box 11.2: Limiting factors to knowledge about social competence

A student's social understanding and knowledge may be limited because of a lack of appropriate learning experiences, including:

- inadequate opportunities for social-learning experiences
- memory difficulties for storing and retrieving social-learning experiences
- learning difficulties (including perceiving and interpreting cues, and attention)
- inappropriate models of social behaviour.

Remember, it is not only important to identify what a student knows, but also what opportunities he or she may have had for learning this information.

Friendships

Peer interactions and friendships play an important role in facilitating the personal, social and moral development of all students. Students with disabilities or with learning difficulties can often experience difficulties in socially interacting with their peers.

Some students may choose social isolation while others appear to be rejected by their peers. Students who choose social isolation are not as likely to be vulnerable to distress or anxiety in their relations with others, as they are protecting themselves by rejecting social interactions. Alternatively, students who wish to be included and seek interaction, but who are rejected by their peers, are vulnerable to distress and anxiety, which is pervasive in terms of their adjustment to school and learning.

The outcomes of rejection or social isolation can be victimisation, bullying, teasing, physical or verbal threats or exclusion from games. A student may respond with an increase in acting-out behaviours, anger and loss of control. A student may also respond by 'living in their private fantasy world' or even take their anger out on parents or siblings at home. Other responses can include health problems, increased vulnerability to psychopathology, physical aggression and lowered academic performance. The occurrence of problem behaviours will further significantly disadvantage the student in all social settings including the classroom.

Box 11.3: Outcomes of social isolation or rejection

Students who are rejected by their peers may experience:

- bullying
- teasing
- physical and/or verbal threats
- exclusion from games
- victimisation.

Students who are rejected by their peers may respond with:

- acting-out behaviours
- physical aggression
- anger and loss of control
- 'living in a private fantasy world'
- physical and/or mental health problems
- lowered academic performance.

The occurrence of any of these behaviours will further significantly disadvantage the student in all social settings.

Social skills

While the terms 'social competence' and 'social skills' are often used interchangeably, there are in fact a range of models, definitions and assessment and training approaches distinguishing the two. Social-skill models are primarily concerned with identifying the specific behaviours that are needed for successful performance of social tasks. Social competence requires that we not only have a repertoire of social skills but that we know where and when to use these skills effectively and appropriately. Social skills are behaviours that assist individuals to successfully interact with others and respond to the expectations of society. Social skills can be simple or complex. Social skills include both verbal and non-verbal behaviour.

In school, social skills can include solving disagreements that arise in informal games, setting interpersonal goals, accepting compliments and criticism, expressing opinions in socially acceptable ways and initiating interaction and behaviours associated with winning and losing games. Riches' (1996a) training approach is consistent with the relational-competence model (Spitzberg and Cupach 1984) and is much broader than simple social-skill routines, taking account of the crucial issues of motivation, knowledge, context and outcomes (see Box 11.4).

Difficulties in social-skill routines occur if a student:

- omits one or more of the steps
- performs one or more steps incorrectly
- adds inappropriate steps
- lacks automaticity or fluency of performance.

Box 11.4: Training units essential for everyday social interaction

Riches' (1996a) training units identify the rules, the verbal and non-verbal behaviours, that are linked together into a meaningful sequence of steps for several social-skill routines, along with problem-solving exercises. They include:

1 key components—relational competence
2 greetings, non-greetings and partings
3 request and inquiries
4 handling refusals
5 social courtesies
6 apologies
7 conversational skills
8 conversation topics
9 handling praise and criticism
10 friendships.

Observation of students is important for several purposes. Systematic observation can be used to:

- identify what social skills a student is using
- specify difficulties that he or she may be experiencing
- correct social-skill performances
- indentify particular skills that require practice to improve automaticity and fluency.

You may wish to observe and evaluate the social-skill behaviours and levels of social competence of a student in your school. Form 23 in Useful forms lists specific examples of social skills to target for student observation. For evaluation purposes you can rate your observations of each behaviour (e.g. never, sometimes, often, always).

Box 11.5: Instructional approaches for developing social competence

Some instructional strategies known to be effective for developing social competence in schools are (see also Chapter 8):

- modelling
- direct instruction, behavioural intervention
- brainstorming with students about:
  - positive and negative feelings
  - problems that frequently happen between students at school
  - behaviours that interfere with classroom participation, such as aggression, non-compliance, out-of-seat behaviours
- cooperative and partnered learning strategies (see Chapter 8)
- discussion groups
- teaching the rules, routines and verbal and non-verbal conventions for social behaviour
- rehearsing and practicing social-skill routines
- including 'real life' opportunities for learning and practice in natural environments
- matching expressions with feeling words, using photographs, videos, drawings for stimuli
- using role play and simulations
- using word finds or crosswords and close procedures with social content
- using prediction activities (e.g. What feelings will be expressed by the different protagonists, characters in story-problem situations?)
- teaching self-control/self-monitoring strategies (e.g. stop and think before acting)
- teaching social problem-solving strategies
- establishing individual goals for each student
- discussing likely consequences of various strategies, solution options
- implementing strategies and plans of action
- reviewing and evaluating the outcomes of student action plans
- supporting student learning with teacher cues and prompts (verbal and non-verbal). Include ongoing direct observation and evaluation into the design of all teaching programs
- playing social-skill games.

Real-life instructional environments

Since different social skills are required according to the particular context and situation, it makes sense that instruction is most effective when provided in real-life environments. In the past, social-skill instruction has often taken place in training or simulated settings, using role-play, discussion and rehearsal techniques. This has typically resulted in poor transfer of skills to natural settings. Social-skills instruction can be enhanced by:

- including as many elements of the real-life setting as possible
- substantial practice, varying both situations and contexts
- using real-life reinforcers and rewards.

Remember, social-skills instruction will be most effective if sufficient practice is provided in the real-life environment in which it naturally occurs. Some social skills to target for instruction include:

- greetings
- listening
- ways to join a group
- self-monitoring and/or self-control strategies
- strategies for maintaining friendships
- personal responsibility
- conversational skills
- responding to criticism and praise
- questions for clarifying understanding.

Programs and resources

Several published social-skills and social problem-solving programs are available to educators that may also support this process. Life games such as the Social Skills Game provide some good discussion starters on topics such as being assertive without appearing aggressive, and responding in various social contexts, and provide valuable practice in playing cooperatively and interacting appropriately with peers (Searle and Streng 1996).

Social competence and social problem-solving can often be included as components of the teaching program. For example, the understanding of concepts related to feelings—both positive and negative, in ourselves and in others—can be incorporated into the daily classrooom discussion of events. Similarly, everyday social problems that occur at school between students and students, and students and teachers and that result in upset feelings can be used as a platform for extending students' understanding of social concepts. A number of instructional responses to these social situations can be employed, including:

- discussion
- establishment of rules to guide social behaviour
- role-play, modelling of skills

- rehearsal of skills
- guided feedback
- opportunities for generalisation.

Discussion topics might include:

- friendship
- various persons' roles (e.g. parent or teacher)
- moral dilemmas
- problems with peers
- using humour to maintain relationships.

Additionally, generating a list of rules associated with a selected discussion topic can often help students to focus on desirable behaviours. For example, friendship rules might include:

- share information and news with your friend
- show support for your friend when he/she is having problems
- have fun when you and your friend are together
- repay debts or favours to your friend
- don't try to own your friend
- don't criticise your friend to other people
- take turns, be a good sport
- say nice things to and about your friend.

Modification in response to change

Social interaction takes place in an ever-changing environment. Various changes can affect the appropriateness and the effectiveness of our social behaviour at any given time for that situation, including the:

- moods and expectations of other persons
- nature of the relationship
- standards for behaviour
- age and/or gender of the other persons
- physical environment
- cultural context
- purpose or goal of the communication
- previous events and interactions that have occurred in that environment.

Knowledge about social situations is often specific to particular contexts and situations. Teaching activities should always ensure that the learning of social skills addresses the knowledge that may be required for different contexts and different situations.

KEY TERMS FROM THIS CHAPTER

Social competence The ability to integrate thinking, feeling and behaviour to achieve social tasks and outcomes valued in the host context and culture.

Social skills Behaviours that assist individuals to successfully interact with others and respond to the expectations of society.

FURTHER READING

Odom, S.L., McConnell, S.R. and McEvoy M.A. (1992), *Social Competence of Young Children with Disabilities: Issues and Strategies for Intervention*, Baltimore, MA: Paul H. Brookes.

Reflection: The key to lasting change

Chapter 3 closed off with the assertion that, when it comes to making classrooms work, two attitudes that matter most are the belief that all children can learn, and that teachers who believe they can make a difference, do. In a sense those two statements sum up the purpose and function of this book—that inclusive classrooms can work and the teachers who believe they can make them work, will do so. Along the way the hints and ideas put together here will make it easier for you to plan and implement procedures or organisation that will allow you to meet your objectives as a teacher who matters.

KEY IDEAS IN THIS CHAPTER
- reflecting on practice
- using reflective diaries
- the effects of reflective teaching

There is no doubt that teachers today face far more complex problems than did teachers in times gone by. Tyler (1995), an international figure in the field of the study of individual differences, noted:

> Human diversity constitutes [a] greater challenge in the complex societies of our time than it did in simpler societies of the past. Our society could not function without the unique contributions of unique individuals. Its members cannot be considered to be identical, interchangeable parts. They do not just compete with one another; they complement one another (p. 12).

The advent of the inclusive classroom is a continuation of that trend from simpler societies to more complex, but along with the challenges of the complexities go the possibilities of greater and more extensive successes.

A lecturer in architecture, a friend of one of the authors, used to bemoan the difficulties inherent in inducting budding architects into the mysteries and challenges of professional practice. He claimed his first task when faced with a class of keen young architects was to convince them that being a good and creative architect was not a matter of sitting in a comfortable chair with a warm moist cloth placed across the forehead and dreaming dreams of new buildings or fantastic new ways of designing structures. There are always times for standing back and looking and thinking and dreaming, but mostly it is a case of working at designs, modifying them to meet new needs, and constantly evaluating the concepts and their implementation.

So it is with classrooms. An important key to successful implementation of good teaching ideas is to use reflection and reflective practice as the means whereby educational and learning goals are met.

Reflecting on practice

PAVOT is the acronym for an international approach to encourage teachers to take a researcher's view of their own teaching. Standing for 'Perspective and Voice of the Teacher', it arose out of another teacher-based research orientation to teaching, PEEL, or 'Project for the Enhancement of Effective Learning', which has active groups in Canada, Australia, New Zealand, Sweden and Denmark and is still growing into other countries.

Whether one wants to join any particular group is not important, but the lessons learned by the many teachers of all school levels and types who are involved in either PEEL or PAVOT can be put into practice in any school or formal learning situation. Initially interested in why some students did not learn, the analysis of poor learning tendencies by the teachers who started the group led to the identification of good learning behaviours. The teachers identified six major behaviours that indicated good learning (Baird and Northfield 1992). They are:

- seeks assistance—tells the teacher what they do not understand
- checks progress—refers to earlier work before asking for help
- plans work—anticipates and predicts possible outcomes
- reflects on work—makes links between activities and ideas
- links ideas and experiences—offers relevant and personal examples
- develops a view—justifies opinions.

These behaviours will be shown by any learner, although how they display them will vary according to the developmental age of the student concerned. Very young learners will go through all these phases as they move on from one experience to another even if they cannot explain what is happening. Some older students may be able to articulate what is happening but, for most, the processes will not be at the level of overt awareness. Indeed, it was only through discussing, observing and analysing that the teachers were able to make up their lists of what constitutes good learning.

Teachers want all their students to learn everything they have been taught. That seems very natural. If teachers did not want the children to learn then they wouldn't bother teaching in the first place. But not all children learn at the same pace or in the same quantities. That is a truism about teaching that has always been the case but with homogeneous groupings of children, it can sometimes be overlooked. The policies of inclusion mean teachers have to think more carefully about the issue.

Amanda Berry (Berry and Milroy 2002), teaching a regular science class of 15-year-olds, found that she could no longer teach as if the tacit assumption that everyone in the class was learning at the same pace were in any sense true. That assumption she termed the 'big comfortable lie'. She wrote:

> The biggest shift [in thinking about student learning] for me has been in scrapping any assumptions I had about the whole group moving *en masse*. It's a big lie. It's important to 'pick on' individuals (in the nicest possible way) to understand where they're at. I understand concepts in much greater depth than before because we're going slowly and coming at them again and again. If it is so for me then surely it must be the same for my students (p. 199).

One of the ways we understand our world is by categorising everything and being able to distinguish one set of phenomena from another by means of a defining characteristic or set of characteristics. If we could not do this everything would be a blur and everything would be the same. It is impossible even to imagine what our life experiences would be like if this were the case. Hence almost all language and understanding of the world is based on the capacity to group ideas into concepts.

These concepts are abstract, they are mental, they are real but not observable and they begin at the most basic levels. Light and dark, hard and soft, tangible and abstract, and so on through all the things we know. Everything fits into one category or another and with increasing sophistication and experience our concepts reflect out individual experiences. For example, the words most people have for snow are fairly limited but it is reported that the Inuit, in the snowy regions of Canada, have many words to describe it. Concepts are many-faceted and hierarchical in their order. Being able to work through these orders is often taken as an indication of intellectual ability. The Wechsler Intelligence Scales include a subtest that asks the examinee to say in what way numerous pairs of ideas or objects are alike, even though in normal life we think of them as being completely different from one another. This subtest asks for an explanation of the way in which item a is similar to item b, items that can be as close as two colours or as distant as an animal and a plant. The task involves the examinee 'stepping back' from the two items and working through their orders of concepts until they can find a link. The more facility people have in doing this task, the more intellectually able they are considered to be.

We use individual names to differentiate and identify individuals. As teachers we also use personal characteristics or physical characteristics to do something similar. But it is not only to identify individuals that we make use of information about these individual characteristics or physical states. We also use these characteristics to determine what we should teach and how we should go about our teaching. How we use them determines whether we can claim to be teaching all our students or just some of them; how we use them displays our attitudes to our profession and our responsibilities as teachers of all students.

We cannot live without categorising and giving labels to things, but at the same time this phenomenon can be taken too far. If it is true that without categorisation everything would be a blur, it is also true that at some point we must join things together to form homogeneous or like-minded groups. Our minds cannot cope with everything being different. Individual characteristics can separate but they can also be used to collect or join things together. Age and sex are common categories with which we are all familiar. Common categories also apply in almost all aspects of teaching. But groupings become much more sophisticated when learning needs of identified age groups are concerned. An important task facing all teachers is to know when it is appropriate to put all students into one group and when to separate out the individual student.

Separation of students will normally be based on learning needs or accomplishments but discussions of difference and the identification of those with needs that differ from the rest leads us again into the problems associated with labelling, as discussed earlier. Teachers' use of labels or 'diagnostic tags' is often a clear indicator of attitudes to their profession. Is a label used as a reason for not doing something or is it used as an insight into where the educational plans must be focused?

On the positive side, the labels can be used to find out what is known about the learning needs of special groups where there are some common characteristics. When learning groups of words most of us will automatically reorder the words into similar groups. If our task is to learn and recall a list of ten words—cat, rose, cream, crocodile, bread, lily, horse, tulip, parrot and cake—we would group the animals together, and the flowers and the foods. In that way we would be able to cope with the range of items more easily. Some children with intellectual disabilities tend not to group things together in this way automatically, but they can be taught this strategy. In discussion, the three different kinds of objects can be highlighted and then grouped together with effectively only three categories of items needing to be recalled. Knowing this about children with intellectual disabilities is an example of a label being used to the child's advantage. On the other hand, failure on the part of the child with the intellectual disability to pick up on the strategy automatically could lead to the teacher explaining (read 'excusing') the failure to complete the task satisfactorily on the grounds that the child has 'an intellectual disability'.

Diagnostic categories are useful when they alert teachers to learner characteristics associated with a category but they do not tell all about either an individual child or the category into which the child might fit. The *Diagnostic and Statistical Manual of Mental Disorders (DSM)*, an official publication of the American Psychiatric Association (APA), first appeared in 1952 and is now in an updated, text-revised fourth edition (American Psychiatric Association 2000). It contains many indicators of a range of disorders, including intellectual disability and learning disorders, but it is neither complete nor fully informed in all its categories. What is noticeable about many of the entries is the range of indicators that can be used to diagnose a condition, of which only a few are required in order to complete the diagnosis. The authors of the *DSM* are also keen to point out that there is no assumption that individuals sharing a diagnosis are alike in all important ways, and encourage professionals to view disorders in terms of information that exceeds the mere lists of behaviours given in their text. The APA continues to view the manual as being in need of constant revision and more versions can be expected as information and more data accumulate.

The process of differentiating mental conditions is complex, and although the *DSM* is an invaluable asset to the medical and psychological professions, it reminds teachers that categories of disability give us only very general definitions and only broadly indicate where instructional needs might lie. A category or diagnosis will give us hints, but only by understanding the individual student will we be able to understand where our teaching efforts should be placed.

Where knowledge of specific conditions may be helpful is in reflecting on our teaching goals and linking these in with the curriculum standards that guide our classroom work. Even where adaptations are required, they are unlikely to apply only to the one child in the class, and even then only in very specific areas. What is more likely to happen is that in considering the needs of a particular child our habits of grouping things and people together will come to our aid and we will begin to see how commonly within a certain group, particular learning gaps or particular strengths are to be found. Once we do that sort of grouping we can be really aware that we are inclusive teachers, looking to each student's advantage, not using excuses for failing to achieve our goals.

There is nothing new about the attitudes and approaches we advocate. Research over recent years has consistently highlighted the fact that teachers at all levels have significant effects on their students. Teachers, say this research, are not simply implementers of administrative policies but are active agents, thinking professionals, who have important effects on student learning (see, for example, Good and Brophy 1990; Feiman-Nemser and Floden 1986).

Brophy and Everston (1976) investigated the differences between relatively effective and relatively ineffective teachers, judged in terms of learning outcomes for students. Successful teachers saw teaching as an interesting and worthwhile challenge that they approached by assuming personal responsibility for the learning of their students. They believed that problems could be overcome by searching for solutions and were courageous enough to test their solutions in the classroom. Less successful teachers saw teaching as merely a dull job, discussed problems as if they were too serious to be solved and behaved in ways that ensured they were not solved. This group did not believe they could make a difference and therefore did not. Good attitudes need to be backed up by professional knowledge, but professional knowledge without commitment is of little use. This research was conducted in the 1970s but there has been nothing since to show that a teacher's role has changed from what they found.

If the PAVOT and PEEL experiences teach us anything, they show that just thinking that some time should be spent reflecting on one's teaching is not enough. To do this successfully there is a need to approach the task in a systematic and continuous way. An integral part of teacher training is to spend time in schools observing teachers at work. Most practicum programs expect student teachers to keep some sort of a diary and to record their impressions and ideas about teaching on a daily basis. Those techniques need not be restricted to pre-service training but can be used as the basis of your own continued professional development. An example of how a reflective diary may be used is outlined below.

Reflective diaries

A reflective diary should contain ideas, questions and reflections that arise as the result of your everyday experience. We suggest that a 'reflection' should be written up on each occasion when you notice or do something 'critical'. How you define the critical moments of your teaching or child learning is up to you, but clearly completing any more than one reflection sheet per day, or a few per week, will quickly become onerous and unrealistic given time constraints. Simply record the events that really matter in your view. Your reflections should include questions that arise out of your practice as well as steps you will take to answer those questions. Two examples of reflective diary entries are given below.

Example: Diary entries

Entry 1

Date: 21/8   **Setting:** Art session, my school

Reflections:
Helping children with severe language impairment to express themselves. Expressing feelings through art.

I have been watching a class that included a child with a severe language disorder participate in an art session.

Students who have difficulties expressing themselves using verbal language may find an outlet for their inner thoughts and feelings through art. There are a number of different forms of art. A trained art therapist may be able to help a child with special needs find the arts form that best suits his or her interests, abilities and needs.

Creating visual art such as drawing, painting or making objects allows the artist to express themselves in visual ways, which are often a release for strong emotions that they can't put into words. Children may also choose music as an outlet for their feelings. Music has a universal quality that links people together and helps the children overcome their feelings of isolation.

Questions arising:
Some children with severe physical disabilities may not be able to manipulate art tools or musical instruments. Can they still express themselves through the arts? Do they need to find other alternatives?

Next steps:
Observe music and another art class to see how children with limited motor control learn about music and art.

Entry 2

Date: 25/8   **Setting:** Local business trip

Reflections:
More accepting community attitudes for people with special needs. Views of business people towards persons with intellectual disabilities as customers.

The class went on a school trip that included a visit to some local businesses. I noticed that some of the people we met were uncomfortable talking to one of the students who has Down syndrome.

The views of business people towards the presence of persons with intellectual disabilities as customers were investigated by Parsons et al. (2000) in Queensland, Australia.

They investigated 89 individuals representing a range of convenience stores, video rental shops, fast-food restaurants, pharmacies, hairdressers, newsagents and a variety of other businesses. Eighty-five per cent of the interviewees expressed positive responses about people with intellectual disabilities coming to their stores, such as, 'Love it', 'Good customers' and 'Good to see them getting out'. There were a few other responses; for example, one respondent said he felt 'impatient if it is busy', and one expressed his concern that other customers may 'prefer not to shop with them'.

Very little is known about the community's reaction to people with disabilities using local amenities and resources. The above research was conducted to provide additional supporting data to the research by Saxby et al. (1986) who found attitudes towards persons with intellectual disabilities as customers in shops, pubs and cafes in the United Kingdom were favourable.

As a teacher in my town I think I need to think about whether I will take a class that includes a child or two with intellectual disabilities into town shops. I want to treat everyone in my class as important and accepted and I will take them anywhere as a group but I think I need to be aware that I don't put any of them in situations where they might be embarrassed by the reactions of people in shops or anywhere else.

Questions arising:
How can I ensure I treat all my children as equals but not allow myself to over-compensate for the one or two who may be different? How can I work out ways to ensure that everyone in my class thinks everyone else in the group is just as important as them?

Next steps:
Talk this over with other colleagues and the principal.

The effects of reflective teaching

What will be the outcome for you, the teacher, if you embark on the practices we have been advocating in this book? We believe you will find that there are four things that will happen; they are the same as Mitchell (2002) argues will be the effects on teachers who develop a reflective, thinking, research-oriented approach to their work.

You will be willing to take risks

Often there is comfort in just doing the same old things day after day. This is not a crime, because we know that stability and security are based on being able to predict outcomes, but stability and security for their own sakes also blight progress. Sometimes there is a need to step outside our comfort zones and try new ways of doing things, for only in this way will we progress.

Courage is needed to take these steps. Courage is not the same as just doing something different for the sake of it. That could well be credulity, or foolhardiness. The courage to try something new in the present context is based on the needs for change that become apparent as you reflect on present practice and see where gaps are obvious. Continual evaluation of teaching outcomes will provide the knowledge we need to have in order to find out what works and what doesn't. Spending time working out what will enhance the learning of students with special needs will also show us ways that will work with those who do not have obvious difficulties in learning. That is one of the real gains of the movement from special schools to inclusive schools.

You will learn to generalise from the particular to the larger group and be able to articulate your practice

A success of the inclusive-schools movement has been the necessity to take accepted patterns of work that appear to have worked with homogeneous groups of average students and reflect on how they need to be changed in order to meet the needs of all students. These needs include not only those recognised as gifted and talented but also those with intellectual or physical disabilities.

The wider range of needs means new frames of reference are required in order to grasp the magnitude of the task. These can only come about through paying attention to the special-needs groups, identifying common factors that apply to them initially but may also apply to the rest of the class, and being able to say what is required and how the new ways of thinking can be implemented.

Consider the reflective diary entries on pages 228 and 229. Here we see how the questions arose from regular school activities, there was some delving into known research on the issue(s), there was reflection on the individual teacher's response, and there were questions to ask about how action was to take place in the future. It is important to note that they are written out, not just thought about. They are observable, permanent and able to be modified.

Throughout this book we have reiterated that writing down ideas, thoughts, reflections, lessons, etc., is a key to successful and thoughtful implementation of good teaching. Language is our means of communicating and written language is our means of ensuring ideas are not lost, that others can contribute to their further development, and they can be implemented when appropriate. Writing is a skill, and a skill that improves with practice. Writing helps us define our terms, our ideas and our hopes. The more we can write, the more easily and efficiently we can articulate our ideas and share our insights.

Your perceptions of your role will change

Writing down what you believe, what you do and why you think you are teaching will change your self-image as a teacher. Being thoughtful and reflective about your work may initially make you wonder why you do the job you do because inevitably you will begin to notice gaps in your practice that might otherwise have escaped your attention.

As you get more confidence in being self-critical and using the information to seek improvements in your practice and planning, the sense that your opinions are valuable will increase. This increase in confidence will be evidence based, that is, your own journals will map out the development of your thinking and the manner in which your practice has changed. The experience of systematic data collection of your own practice is to increase self-confidence and the enhancement of learning outcomes in your class.

Your journey will be irreversible

Mitchell (2002) makes the point that the PAVOT teachers who continued on with the tasks of becoming teacher-researchers found that their classroom practices changed in ways that were permanent and important, and notes: 'Even though teaching in some ways becomes more demanding, with higher standards for a "good" lesson, there is no going back' (p. 254).

The satisfaction and pride in a good job, the joy of seeing progress in one's students and the knowledge that these students, some of whom may well have been overlooked for years, are learning and growing, are the reasons for us doing what we do—for all our students.

KEY TERMS FROM THIS CHAPTER

PAVOT (**Perspective and Voice of the Teacher**)   An international approach to encouraging teachers to take a researcher's view of their own teaching.

PEEL (**Project for the Enhancement of Effective Learning**)   An international approach to encourage teachers to take a researcher's view of their own teaching. It has active groups in Canada, Australia, New Zealand, Sweden and Denmark and is still growing into other countries.

FURTHER READING

Loughran, J., Mitchell, I. and Mitchell, J. eds (2002), *Learning from Teacher Research*, Sydney: Allen & Unwin.

Useful forms

These blank forms are designed for you to photocopy and complete for your inclusive school activities. You may wish to modify them for your own specific requirements. You can also download PDFs of these forms from the website: www.allenandunwin.com/InclusiveEducation.asp

Data collection coding sheet

Student:	Date:
Observer Name:	Starting Time:
Setting:	Activity:

Comments	4 Minute		8 Minute		16 Minute	

Form 2

Interview analysis sheet

For _____ Date _____

Question	Parent response	Child response	Staff response	Summary of all responses

Therapy implementation permission form

I, _____ , give permission for staff at _____ school

to implement the therapy listed below to my child _____

Therapy type _____

Description _____

_____

_____

_____

_____

_____

_____

_____

_____

_____

_____

_____

_____

Supervising therapist name _____ Phone contact _____

Staff member implementing therapy _____

The supervising therapist has outlined the assessment and treatment to me. I am aware that the staff member implementing the therapy has been shown the correct procedure by the therapist. The therapist will review the program and the progress of my child on a regular basis and will inform me of the results. I will notify the school, in writing, if there are any changes to the conditions listed above.

Signed _____ (Parent/Guardian) Date _____

Form 4

Daily therapy plan

For _____ Date _____

Daily classroom activity	Therapy opportunity?	Person to implement therapy	Brief description of therapy

Daily plan schedule

Teacher _____ Class _____ Date _____

Time	Lesson	What teacher does	What paraprofessional does

Form 6

Single lesson plan

Subject area/grade _____ Date and time _____

Lesson topic

Lesson goal:	
Materials:	
Procedure:	
Homework task:	
Teacher does:	
Paraprofessional does:	
Assessment:	

Learning at home planning sheet

For _____

Objective	What happens at school	What can happen at home

Form 8

Agenda for meeting of Program Support Group

Child: _____ Date of meeting: _____

Place: _____ Time: _____

PSG members:

Purpose: _____

Status _____

Time	Activity	Program Support Group members responsible

Form 9

Medical advice form

Any specific medical considerations?   Yes   No
Description/action required: _____

_____

Level and type of extra supports to be provided
(e.g. Therapy, teachers aide, personal care, accommodations in exams etc.):

Review dates:

Program support group signatures: Date: _____

_____ _____ _____ _____

Form 10

Individual program plan

Child name:		Age:	Grade/Year
Coordinating Teacher		Date:	

Vision Statement:

Assessment Results summary:

Assessment Type	Description of Results

Long-term goals

Individual list   Group list   (please circle whichever applies)

Child name:	Date:

Learning Priorities
(in order of most important to least important)

1)	
2)	
3)	
4)	
5)	
6)	
7)	
8)	
9)	
10)	
11)	
12)	
13)	
14)	
15)	

Form 12

General task analysis

Child: _____

Task:	Progress (Date)						
Step							

Note: ✔ means 'achieved'
✗ means 'not yet achieved'

Indicators of achievement

Long-term goal:			
Behavioural objective 1:	Inclusive teaching strategies for this objective:	Indicators of achievement:	Date achieved:
Behavioural objective 2:	Inclusive teaching strategies for this objective:	Indicators of achievement:	Date achieved:
Behavioural objective 3:	Inclusive teaching strategies for this objective:	Indicators of achievement:	Date achieved:
Behavioural objective 4:	Inclusive teaching strategies for this objective:	Indicators of achievement:	Date achieved:
Modified materials required for this goal—summary:			

Form 14

Unit planner

Dates:	Class:

Subject area:

Central issues/problems

Opening grabber/motivator:

Summary of series of linked lessons:

Culminating projects:

Ongoing assessments (additional to culminating projects):

When?	What content/skills?	What form will it take?	How did student/s demonstrate learning?

Form 15

Unit planner—Infusing individual targets

Dates:	Child:	Class:

Subject area:		

Central issues/problems	Relevant goals:

Summary of series of linked lessons:	Relevant linked individual objectives:

Suggested culminating project:

Form 16

Individual lesson planning form

Subject area/grade _____ Date and time _____

Lesson topic

Lesson goal:	
Central problem:	
Materials:	
Procedure:	
Homework task:	
Diverse learner objectives for this lesson:	
Inclusive materials and procedures:	
Alternative assessment:	
Teacher does:	
Paraprofessional does:	
Assessment:	

Form 17

Toilet training documentation form

Child Name: _____

Date	Time	Pants: wet/dry?	Result in toilet?	Notes	Date	Time	Pants: wet/dry?	Result in toilet?	Notes

Form 18

Medication administration permission form

I, _____ , give permission for staff at _____ school

to administer the medication listed below to my child _____ .

This medication has been prescribed to my child by the family doctor listed below. I have disclosed, in writing, all relevant information pertaining to this medication, such as possible side-effects and negative reactions, to school staff.

Medication name _____

Dosage _____

Date authorised administration begins _____

Days of the week medication is to be administered _____

Administration time _____

Special conditions under which the medication should be administered

_____

_____

Name of family doctor _____ Phone number_____

Emergency contact _____ Phone _____

I agree that I will provide the medication to the school staff in person and not permit my child to be in possession of the medication at any time, including to and from school. I will also notify the school, in writing, if there are any changes to the conditions of medication administration listed above.

Signed _____ (Parent/Guardian) Date _____

Form 19

Medication administration form

Child name _____

Medication _____

Dosage _____

Administration times & days _____

Special Conditions/information_____

_____

Written permission for administration on file from: ❐ family doctor?   ❐ parent?

Medication name	Dosage	Time	Date	Administerd by (print name)	Initials	Checked by (print name)	Initials

Form 20

External school trip medication form

Child name _____   Grade/Year _____

Teacher _____

Date _____

Medication name _____

Dosage _____

Time to be given _____

Person giving medication _____

Date and time medication actually given _____
(signature)

Please return this paper to school office on return. Ensure that child medication administration records are updated.

(Adapted from Briggs et al. 1998, p. 42)

Form 21

Medication incident report

Child _____   D.O.B _____

School _____

Date of incident _____

Medication(s) _____

Dosage _____   Time administersed _____

Incident description (e.g. missed medication). Please provide detailed account.

_____

_____

_____

_____

_____

_____

Action taken _____

_____

_____

(Adapted from Briggs et al. 1998, p. 72)

Form 22

Positive behaviour action plan

Student _____ Teacher _____ Date _____

The behaviour that needs changing is:

I would like to change that behaviour and do the following instead:

The reason for that behaviour is:

The best solution to this problem is:

What the student will do:	What the teacher will do:

The consequences for continued misbehaviour are:

The rewards/benefits of improved behaviour are:

Social skill behaviour rating scale

The following areas are suggested as a focus for your observations.

Self control	Never	Sometimes	Often	Always
1 Can cope with criticism or direction from adults	☐	☐	☐	☐
2 Can wait for needs to be met	☐	☐	☐	☐
3 Responds appropriately when peers push or hit	☐	☐	☐	☐
4 Controls temper in problem situations	☐	☐	☐	☐

Peer interaction	Never	Sometimes	Often	Always
5 Initiates conversations or interactions with peers	☐	☐	☐	☐
6 Can compromise when others wish to change an activity	☐	☐	☐	☐
7 Invites others to join in activities	☐	☐	☐	☐
8 Makes friends easily	☐	☐	☐	☐
9 Can respond to good-natured teasing from peers	☐	☐	☐	☐
10 Gets along with others who are different	☐	☐	☐	☐
11 Can give compliments appropriately	☐	☐	☐	☐
12 Volunteers to help peers when necessary	☐	☐	☐	☐
13 Cooperates with peers on class activities without direction	☐	☐	☐	☐
14 Seeks company from peers	☐	☐	☐	☐
15 Can stick up for him/herself with peers	☐	☐	☐	☐

Work habits	Never	Sometimes	Often	Always
16 Can use free time appropriately	☐	☐	☐	☐
17 Finishes school work in reasonable time	☐	☐	☐	☐
18 Takes pride in school work	☐	☐	☐	☐
19 Looks after own belongings	☐	☐	☐	☐
20 Can change from one activity to the next without upset	☐	☐	☐	☐
21 Follows instructions carefully	☐	☐	☐	☐
22 Ignores distractions from peers when doing class work	☐	☐	☐	☐
23 Copes with moments of embarrassment	☐	☐	☐	☐
24 Acts as if self-esteem is high	☐	☐	☐	☐
25 Is invited to join in group activities	☐	☐	☐	☐

Identify areas for further observation and for specific social skills instruction.

	Never	Sometimes	Often	Always
26 _____	☐	☐	☐	☐
27 _____	☐	☐	☐	☐
28 _____	☐	☐	☐	☐
29 _____	☐	☐	☐	☐
30 _____	☐	☐	☐	☐

Bibliography

Ainscow, M. and Sebba, J. (1996), 'International developments in inclusive schooling: Mapping the issues' in *Cambridge Journal of Education*, 26(1), pp. 5–18.

Albert, L. (2003), *A Teacher's Guide to Cooperative Discipline* (2nd edn), Minnesota: AGS Publishing.

Alexander, R.J., Rose, J. and Woodhead, C. (1992), *Curriculum Organisation and Classroom Practice in Primary Schools: A Discussion Paper*, London: Department of Education and Science.

Allport, G.W. (1954), *The nature of prejudice*, Cambridge, MA: Addison-Wesley.

Alper, S. and Ryndak, D.L. (1992), 'Educating students with severe handicaps in regular classes' in *Elementary School Journal*, 92(3), pp. 373–87.

Alter, M. and Goldstein, M.T. (1986), 'The "6-S" paradigm: A tool for IEP implementation' in *Teaching Exceptional Children*, 18(2), pp. 135–38.

American Psychiatric Association (2000), *Diagnostic and Statistical Manual of Mental Disorders* (4th edn), *Text Revision*, Washington, DC: American Psychiatric Association.

Americans with Disabilities Act 1990, 42 USCA, available at http://www.usdoj.gov/crt/ada/adahom1.htm

Ames, C. and R.I.C. Ames (1989), 'Perspectives on motivation' in *Research on Motivation in Education, Volume 3: Goals and Cognitions*, C. Ames and R. Ames, San Diego: Academic Press, pp. 1–10.

Ashman, A. and Elkins, J. eds (1998), *Educating Children with Special Needs*, Sydney: Prentice Hall.

Baird, J.R. and Northfield, J.R. eds (1992), *Learning From the PEEL Experience*, Melbourne: Monash University.

Barth, R. (1990), 'A special vision of a good school' in *Phi Delta Kappa*, 71, pp. 514–15.

Bellanca, J., Chapman, C. and Swartz, E. (1994), *Multiple Assessments for Multiple Intelligences*, Palatine, Illinois: IRI/Skylight Publishing.

Benard, B (1993), 'Fostering resiliency in kids' in *Educational Leadership*, 51(3), pp. 44–49.

Bernell, S.L. (2003), 'Theoretical and applied issues in defining disability in labor market research' in *Journal of Disability Policy Studies*, 14(1), p. 36.

Berry, A. and Milroy, P. (2002), 'Changes that matter' in J. Loughran, I. Mitchell and J. Mitchell eds, *Learning from Teacher Research*, Sydney: Allen & Unwin, pp. 196–221.

Biggs, A., Long, P., Perreault, C., Ritchen, B. and Hertel, V. eds (1998), *Guidelines for School Medication Administration*, Denver, CO: Colorado State Board of Nursing.

Bjorklund, D.F. and Harnishfeger, K.K. (1990), 'The resources construct in cognitive development: diverse sources of evidence and a theory of inefficient inhibition' in *Development Review*, 10, pp. 48–71.

Bjorklund, D.F. and Schneider, W. (1996), 'The interaction of knowledge, aptitude, and strategies in children's memory performance' in *Advances in Child Development and Behaviour*, 26, pp. 58–89.

Blackman, H.P. (1992), 'Surmounting the disability of isolation' in *School Administrator*, 49(2), pp. 28–29.

Bloom B.S. (1984), 'The 2 sigma problem: The search for methods of group instruction as effective as one-to-one tutoring' in *Educational Researcher*, 13, pp. 4–16.

Blumenfeld, P.C., Marx, R., Soloway, E and Krajcik, J. (1997), 'Learning with peers: From small group cooperation to collaborative communities' in *Educational Researcher*, 25, pp. 37–40.

Bodenheimer, A.R. (1974), *Doris: The Story of a Disfigured Deaf Child*, Detroit: Wayne State University Press.

Borkowski, J.G. (1992), 'Metacognitive theory: a framework for teaching literacy, writing and math skills' in *Journal of Learning Disabilities*, 25(4), pp. 253–57.

Boswell, S. and Gray, D. (1998), 'Applying structured teaching principles to toilet training' in *ERIC Document 430362*.

Bounds, J. (2001), The modeled reading program used with students identified as having a specific learning disability and cross-age peer tutors: A study of its effects on reading ability and an exploration of its effects on motivation in terms of self-efficacy and attitude, a research paper for Master of Education (Special Education) thesis, Melbourne: Monash University.

Brophy, J. and Everston, C. (1976), *Learning from Teaching: A Developmental Perspective*, Boston: Allyn & Bacon.

Brown, A.L., Bransford, J.D., Ferrara, R.A. and Campione, J.C. (1983), 'Learning, remembering, and understanding' in *Handbook of Child Psychology: Cognitive Development*, vol. III, P.H. Mussen ed., New York: Wiley, pp. 77–166.

Carpenter, B. (1997), 'The interface between the curriculum and the code' in *British Journal of Special Education*, 24(1), pp. 18–20.

Cattell, R.B. (1963), 'Theory of fluid and crystalized intelligence: A critical experiment' in *Journal of Educational Psychology*, 54(1), pp. 1–22.

Ceci, S.J. (1990), '*On Intelligence . . . More or Less: A Bio-ecological Treatise on Intellectual Development*, Century Series in Psychology, Englewood Cliffs, NJ: Prentice-Hall.

Cheney, C. and Demchak, M. (1996), Providing Appropriate Education in Inclusive Settings: A Rural Case Study, Washington, DC: Office of Special Education and Rehabilitative Services, pp. 10.

Chi, M.T. and Ceci, S.J. (1987), 'Content knowledge: Its restructuring with memory development' in *Advances in Child Development and Behavior*, H. Reese and L. Lipsett, 20, pp. 91–146.

Clough, P. (1988), 'Bridging "mainstream" and "special" education: A curriculum problem' in *Journal of Curriculum Studies*, 20(4), pp. 327–38.

Coenen, M. (2002), 'Using gifted students as peer tutors: An effective and beneficial approach' in *Gifted Child Today*, 25(1), pp. 48–56.

Cohen, E.G. and Lotan, R.A. (1995), 'Producing equal-status interaction in the hetrogeneous classroom' in *American Educational Research Journal*, 32(1), pp. 99–120.

Cohen, E.G., Lotan, R. and Catanzarite, L. (1990), 'Treating Status Problems in the Cooperative Classroom' in *Cooperative Learning Theory and Research*, S. Sharan ed., NY: Praeger Publishers.

Cohen, P., Kulik, J. and Kulik, C. (1982), 'Educational outcomes of tutoring' in *American Educational Research Journal*, 19, pp. 237–48.

Cole, C.M. and McLeskey, J. (1997), 'Secondary inclusion programs for students with mild Disabilities' in *Focus on Exceptional Children*, 29(6), pp. 1–15.

Collet-Klingenberg, L. and Chadsey-Rusch, J. (1991), 'Using a cognitive-process approach to teach social skills' in *Education and Training in Mental Retardation*, (26), pp. 258–70.

Cook, L. and Friend, M. (1995), 'Co-teaching guidelines for effective practice' in *Focus on Exceptional Children*, 28(2), pp. 1–12.

Cooper, P.C., Davies, B.R., Holderness, J., Hudson, G.A., Peterson, R.M., Topp, R.K. and Topp, R.J. (1986), 'Peer tutoring' in *Getting it Together: Organising the Reading-Writing Classroom*, W. McVitty, V. Nicoll, J. Vaughan and L. Wilkie eds, Rosebery, NSW: Primary English Teaching Association, p. 121.

Corbett, J. (1993), 'Postmodernism and the "special needs" metaphors' in *Oxford Review of Education*, 19(4), pp. 547–53.

Cosden, M.A., Iannaccone, C.J. and Wienke, W.D. (1990), 'Social skills instruction in secondary education: Are we prepared for integration of difficult-to-teach students?' in *Teacher Education & Special Education*, 13(3–4), pp. 154–59.

Dalrymple, N. and Boarman, M. (1991), *Functional Programming for People with Autism: Toileting*, Bloomington, IND: Indiana Resource Center for Autism.

Danforth, S. (1997), 'On what basis hope? Modern progress and postmodern possibilities' in *Mental Retardation*, 35(2), pp. 93–106.

Davern, L. and Schnorr, R. (1991), 'Public schools welcome students with disabilities as full members' in *Children Today*, 20(2), pp. 21–25.

Davidson, G.R. and Freebody, P.R. (1986), 'Children and adults or novices and experts? A dilemma for cross-cultural developmental research' in *Special Issue: Contributions to Cross-cultural Psychology. Australian Journal of Psychology*, 38, pp. 215–29.

Davidson, G.R. and Freebody, P.R. (1988), 'Cross-cultural perspectives on the development of metacognitive thinking' in *Hiroshima Forum for Psychology*, 13, pp. 21–31.

Davidson, N. (1994), 'Cooperative and collaborative learning: An intergrative perspective' in *Creativity and collaborative learning. A practical guide to empowering students and teachers*, J.S. Thousand, R.A. Villa and A.I. Nevin eds, Baltimore: Brooks, pp. 13–30.

Davis, S. (1995), *Report Card on Inclusion in Education of Students with Mental Retardation*, Arlington, TX: The Arc: A National Organization on Mental Retardation. p. 22.

Delaney, E.A. and Hopkins, T.F. (1987), *The Stanford-Binet Intelligence Scale: Fourth Edition. Examiner's Handbook*, Itasca, ILL: Riverside Publishing.

Delquadri, J., Greenwood, C.R., Whorton, D., Carta, J.J., and Hall, R.V. (1986), 'Classwide peer tutoring' in *Exceptional Children*, 52, pp. 535–42.

Dembo, T., Leviton, G.L. and Wright, B.A. (1956), 'Adjustment to misfortune: A problem of social–psychological rehabilitation' in *Artificial Limbs*, 3, pp. 4–62.

Denzin, N.K. (1978,) *The research act: A theoretical introduction to sociological methods*, New York: McGraw-Hill.

Department of Education, Victoria (1998), *Program for Students with Disabilities and Impairments*, Melbourne: Community Information Service, Department of Education.

Deppeler, J.M. (1994), Characteristics of Empirically Derived Subgroups of Gifted Children Based on Cognitive Processing Patterns, an unpublished doctoral thesis, Melbourne: Monash University.

Deppeler, J.M. (1998), *Professional Development Workshops: Supporting People with Disabilities*, Melbourne: Impact printing.

Deppeler, J.M. (2003), *Improving inclusive practice through collaborative inquiry: A university and school-system professional development project*, a paper presented at the ICET Teachers as Leaders: Teachers Education for a Global Profession Conference, Melbourne, 20–25 July.

Deppeler, J. and Gurry, P. (1994), *Helping You and Your Partner: Modelled Reading Resource Kh*, Melbourne. Education. Curriculum & Resources.

Dettmer, P., Dyck, N. and Thurston, L.P. (1999), *Consultation, Collaboration, and Teamwork for Students with Special Needs*, Needham Heights, MA: Allyn & Bacon.

Devin-Sheehan L., Feldman R. and Allen, V. (1976), 'Research on children tutoring children: A critical review' in *Review of Educational Research*, 46, pp. 355–85.

Dinsmore, C., Daugherty, S. and Zeitz, H. (2001), 'Student responses to the gross anatomy laboratory in medical curriculum' in *Clinical Anatomy*, 14, pp. 231–36.

Disabilities Discrimination Act (1992), Commonwealth of Australia, available at http://www.austlii.edu.au/au/legis/cth/consol_act/dda1992264/

Doyle, M.B. and Lee, P.A. (1997), 'Creating partnerships with paraprofessionals' in *Quick Guides to Inclusion: Ideas for Educating Students with Disabilities*, M.F. Giangreco ed., Baltimore: Paul H. Brookes, pp. 57–84.

Dunn, R. (1983), 'Learning style and its relation to exceptionality at both ends of the spectrum' in *Exceptional Children*, 49, pp. 496–506.

Dunn, R. (1989), 'Individualizing instruction for mainstreamed gifted children' in *Teaching Gifted and Talented Learners in Classrooms*, R. Milgram ed., Springfield, ILL: Charles C. Thomas, pp. 63–111.

Dunn, R. and Price, G.E. (1980), 'Identifying the learning style characteristics of gifted children' in *Gifted Child Quarterly*, 24, pp. 33–6.

Educational Response Centre (1992), *Behavior Challenges: A Shared Approach*, Alberta Education: Edmonton.

Emmer, T. and Gerwels, M. (2002), 'Cooperative learning in elementary classrooms: Teaching practices and lesson characteristics' in *The Elementary School Journal*, 103(1), pp. 75–92.

Erwin, E.J. and Soodak, L.C. (1995), 'I never knew I could stand up to the system: Families' perspectives on pursuing inclusive education' in *Journal of the Association for Persons with Severe Handicaps*, 20(2), pp. 136–46.

Evans, J. and Vincent, C. (1997), 'Parental choice and special education' in *Choice and Diversity in Schooling: Perspectives and Prospects*, R. Glatter, P.A. Woods and C. Bagley eds, London: Routledge, pp. 102–15.

Farmer, S. (1996), 'Finding Amy's voice: A case for inclusion' in *Voices From the Middle*, 3(4), pp. 27–31.

Feiman-Nemser, S. and Floden, R. (1986), 'The cultures of teaching' in *Handbook of Research on Teaching* (3rd edn), M. Witrock ed., New York: Macmillan.

Feldhusen, J.F., Proctor, T.B. and Black, K.N. (1986), 'Guidelines for Grade Advancement of Precocious Children' in *Roeper Review*, 9, pp. 25–27.

Fillenworth, C., Rouch, M. (1985), *Pairing Content and Process: some observations*, paper presented at the 13th Annual Meeting of the Plains Regional Conference in Reading, Minneapolis, MN. (ERIC Document 267392).

Fisher, D. (2001), 'Cross-age tutoring: Alternatives to the reading resource room for struggling adolescent readers' in *Journal of Instructional Psychology*, 28(4), pp.234–41.

Foreman, P. (2000), 'Disability, integration and inclusion: Introductory concepts' in *Integration and Inclusion in Action* (2nd edn), P.J. Foreman ed., Melbourne: Nelson, pp. 3–34.

Foreman, P.J. (2001), *Integration and Inclusion in Action*, Sydney: Harcourt Brace & Company.

Forlin, C., Douglas, G. and Hattie, J. (1996), 'Inclusive practices: How accepting are teachers?' in *International Journal of Disability, Development and Education*, 43(2), pp. 119–33.

Fox, N.E. and Ysseldyke, J.E. (1997), 'Implementing inclusion at the middle school level: Lessons from a negative example' in *Exceptional Children*, 64(1), pp. 81–98.

French, N. (2001), 'Supervising paraprofessionals: A survey of teacher practices' in *Journal of Special Education*, 35(1), pp. 41–53.

Frey, N. (2001), 'Tying it together: Personal supports that lead to membership and belonging' in *Inclusive Middle Schools*, C.H. Kennedy and D. Fisher eds, Baltimore: Paul H. Brookes.

Friend, M. and Bursuck, W.D. (1999), *Including Students with Special Needs: A Practical Guide for Classroom Teachers*, Boston: Allyn & Bacon.

Friend, M. and Cook, L. (1996), *Interactions: Collaboration Skills for School Professionals*, White Plains, NY: Longman.

Frith, G.H. and Edwards, R. (1981), 'Misconceptions of regular classroom teachers about physically handicapped students' in *Exceptional Children*, 48(2), pp. 182–84.

Fuchs, D., Fuchs, L.S., Mathes, P.G., and Simmons, D.C. (1997), 'Peer Assisted Learning Strategies: Making classrooms more responsive to diversity' in *American Educational Research Journal*, 34, pp. 174–206.

Fuchs, D., Fuchs, L.S., Thompson, A., Svenson, E., Yen, L., Al Otaiba, S., Yang, N., McMaster, K.N., Prentice, K., Kazdan, S. and Saenz, L. (2001), 'Peer-assisted learning strategies in reading: Extensions for kindergarten, first grade, high school' in *Remedial and Special Education*, 22(1), pp. 15–21.

Fuchs, D., Fuchs, L.S., Thompson, A., Svenson, E., Yen, L., Al Otaiba, S., Yang, N. and Nyman, K. (2001), 'Peer-Assisted Learning Strategies: Extensions downward into kindergarten/first grade and upward into high school' in *Remedial and Special Education*, 22.

Gadow, K.D. and Kane, K.M. (1983), 'Administration of medication by school personnel' in *Journal of School Health*, 53(3), pp. 178–83.

Gardner, H. (1983), *Frames of Mind: The Theory of Multiple Intelligences*, New York: HarperCollins.

Gardner, H. (1993), *Multiple Intelligences—The Theory in Practice: A Reader*, New York: Basic Books.

Gardner, H. (1999), *Intelligence Reframed: Multiple Intelligences for the 21st Century*, New York: Basic Books.

Gartner, A. and Lipsky, D.K. (1990), 'Students as instructional agents' in *Support Networks for Inclusive Schooling: Independent Integrated Education*, W. Stainback and S. Stainback eds, Grand Rapids, MI: Paul H. Brookes.

Gerardi, R.J., Grohe, B., Benedict, G.C. and Coolidge, P.G. (1984), 'I.E.P.—More paperwork and wasted time' in *Contemporary Education*, 56(1), pp. 39–42.

Gersten, R., (2001), 'Sort out the roles of research in the improvement of practice' in *Learning Disabilities. Research and Practice*, 16(1), pp. 45–50.

Giangreco, M., Broer, S.M. and Edelman, S. (1999), 'The tip of the iceberg: Determining whether paraprofessional support is needed for students with disabilities in general education settings' in *Journal of the Association for Persons with Severe Handicaps*, 24(4), pp. 281–91.

Giangreco, M., Cloninger, P., Mueller, S. and Ashworth, S. (1991), 'Perspectives of parents whose children have dual sensory impairments' in *Journal of the Association for Persons with Severe Handicaps*, 16(1), pp. 14–24.

Giangreco, M.F., Dennis, R., Cloninger, C., Edelman, S. and Schattman, R. (1993), '"I've counted Jon": Transformational experiences of teachers educating students with disabilities' in *Exceptional Children*, 59(4), pp. 359–72.

Giangreco, M., Edelman, S. and Broer, S.M. (2001), 'Respect, appreciation, and acknowledgment of paraprofessionals who support students with disabilities' in *Exceptional Children*, 67(4), pp. 485–98.

Giangreco, M.F., Edelman, S.W., Evans Luiselli, T. and MacFarland, S.Z.C. (1997), 'Helping or hovering? Effects of instructional assistant proximity on students with disabilities' in *Exceptional Children*, 64(1), pp. 7–18.

Gilliam, J.E. (2001), *Gilliam Asperger disorder scale*, Austin, TX: PRO-ED.

Goessling, D.P. (1998), 'The invisible elves of the inclusive school—Paraprofessionals' in *Annual Meeting of the American Educational Research Association*, San Diego, CA: AERA.

Good, T.E. and Brophy, J.L. (1990), *Educational Psychology: A Realistic Approach*, New York: Longman.

Goodman, J.F. and Bond, L. (1993), 'The individualized educational program: A retrospecive critique' in *Journal of Special Education*, 26(4), pp. 408–22.

Gormley, K.A. and McDermott, P.C. (1994), 'Modifying primary grade classrooms for inclusion: Darrell's 3 years of experience' in *American Educational Research Conference*, New Orleans, LA: ERIC document, pp. 29.

Gow, L., Ward, J., Balla, J. and Snow, D. (1988), 'Directions for integration in Australia: Overview of a report to the Commonwealth Schools Commission Part II' in *Exceptional Child*, 35(1), pp. 5–22.

Grbich, C. and Sykes, S. (1992), 'Access to curricula in three school settings for students with severe intellectual disability' in *Australian Journal of Education*, 36(3), pp. 318–27.

Greenway, A.P. and Harvey, D.H.P. (1980), 'Reaction to handicap' in *Problems of handicap*, R.S. Laura ed., Melbourne: MacMillan, pp. 27–32.

Greenwood, C.R. (1997), 'Classwide peer tutoring' in *Behaviour and Social Issues*, 7(1), pp. 53–57.

Greenwood, C.R., Arreaga-Mayer, C.A., Utley, C., Gavin, K.M. and Terry, B.J. (2001), *Classwide peer tutoring learning management system*, 22(1) p. 34.

Greenwood, C. R., Delquadri, J. C., and Carta, J. J. (1999), *Class Wide Peer Tutoring (CWPT) for Teachers*. Longmont, CO: Sopris West.

Greenwood, C.R., Delquadri, J.C., and Hall, R.V. (1989), 'Longitudinal effects of class-wide peer tutoring' in *Journal of Educational Psychology*, 81(3), p. 371(13).

Grenot-Scheyer, M., Fisher, M. and Staub, D. (2001), *At the End of the Day: Lessons Learned in Inclusive Education*, Baltimore: Paul H. Brookes.

Gresham, F. and MacMillan, L. (1997), 'Social competence and affective characteristics of students with mild disabilities' in *Review of Educational Research*, 67(4) pp. 377—420.

Griffin, J. (1989), *Well-being,* Oxford: Oxford University Press.

Griggs, S.A. (1991), 'Counselling gifted children with different learning-style preferences' in *Counseling Gifted and Talented Children: A Guide for Teachers, Counselors and Parents*, R.M. Milgram ed., Norwood, NJ: Ablex, pp. 53–74.

Haager, D. and Vaughn, S. (1995), 'Parent, teacher, peer, and self-reports of the social competence of students with learning disabilities' in *Journal of Learning Disabilities*, 28, p. 205.

Hacker, D and Tenent, A. (2002), 'Implementing Reciprocal Teaching in the Classroom: Overcoming Obstacles and Making Modifications' in *Journal of Educational Psychology*, 94(4), pp. 699–718.

Hadadian, A. and Yssel, N. (1998), 'Changing roles of paraeducators in early childhood special education' in *Infant-toddler Intervention: The Transdisciplinary Journal*, 8(1), pp. 1–9.

Hahn, H. (1985), 'Towards a politics of disability: Definitions, disciplines, and policies' in *Social Science Journal*, 22, pp. 87–105.

Hall, L. and McGregor, J. (2000), 'A follow-up study of the peer relationships of children with disabilities in an inclusive school' in *Journal of Special Education*, 34(3), p. 114.

Hargreaves, A. (1997), 'Introduction' in *1997 ASCD Yearbook. Rethinking Educational Change with Heart and Mind*, A. Hargreaves ed., Alexandria, VA: Association of Supervision and Curriculum Development, pp. vii–xv.

Hayes, A. (1998), 'Families and disabilities: Another facet of inclusion' in *Educating Children with Special Needs*, A. Ashman and J. Elkins eds, Sydney: Prentice-Hall, pp. 39–66.

Hedin, D. (1986), *Students as teachers: A tool for improving school climate and productivity*, a paper prepared for the Task Force on Teaching as a Profession, Carnegie Forum on Education and the Economy, New York.

Higgins, M. (1985), 'Beginning reading' in *Teaching Reading: A Language Experience*, G. Winch and V. Hoogstad eds, Melbourne: Macmillan, pp. 68–82.

Hill, C.A. and Whiteley, J.H. (1985), 'Social interactions and on-task behavior of severely multihandicapped and nonhandicapped children in mainstream classrooms' in *Canadian Journal for Exceptional Children*, 1(4), pp. 136–40.

Hobbs, T. and Westling, D.L. (1998), 'Promoting successful inclusion through collaborative problem solving' in *Teaching Exceptional Children*, 31(1), pp. 12–19.

Hollinger, C.L. and Koesek, S. (1986), 'Beyond the use of full scale IQ scores' in *Gifted Child Quarterly*, 34, pp. 21–26.

Hollins E.R., Smiler H., and Spencer K. (1994), 'Benchmarks in meeting the challenges of effective schooling for African American youngsters' in *Teaching Diverse Populations: Formulating a Knowledge Base*, E.R. Hollins, J.E. King and W.C. Hayman (eds), Albany: State University of New York Press.

Hollowood, T.M., Salisbury, C.L., Rainforth, B. and Palombaro, M.M. (1995), 'Use of instructional time in classrooms serving students with and without severe disabilities' in *Exceptional Children*, 61(3), pp. 242–53.

Human Rights and Equal Opportunity Commission Act (1986), Commonwealth of Australia, available at http://www.austlii.edu.au/au/legis/cth/consol_act/hraeoca1986512/

IDEA, *Individuals with Disabilities Education Act 1997*, available at http://www.ideapractices.org/law/index.php

Idol, L. (1997), 'Key questions related to building collaborative and inclusive schools' in *Journal of Learning Disabilities*, 30(4), pp. 384–94.

Jaffe, M.B. (1989), 'Feeding at-risk infants and toddlers' in *Topics in Language Disorders*, 10(1), pp. 13–25.

Jakupcak, J., Rushton, R., Jakupcak, M. and Lundt, J. (1996), 'Inclusive education' in *Science Teacher*, 63(5), pp. 40–43.

Jeon, Y and Haider-Markel, D.P. (2001), 'Tracing issue definition and policy change: An analysis of disability issue images and policy response' in *Policy Studies Journal*, 29(2), p. 215.

Johnson, D.W. and Johnson, F.P. (1994), *Joining Together*, Boston: Allyn & Bacon.

Johnson, D.W. and Johnson, R.T. (1989), *Cooperation and Competition: Theory and Research*. Edina, MN: Interaction Books.

Johnson, D.W., Johnson, R.T. Waring, D. and Maruyama, G. (1986), 'Different cooperative learning procedures and cross-handicap relationships' in *Exceptional Children*, 53(3), pp. 247–52.

Jorgenson, C.M. (1996), 'Designing inclusive curricula right from the start: Practical strategies and examples for the high school classroom' in *Inclusion: A Guide for Educators*, S. Stainback and W. Stainback eds, Sydney: Paul H. Brookes, p. 400.

Jorgensen, C.M. ed. (1998), *Restructuring High Schools for All Students: Taking Inclusion to the Next Level,* Baltimore: Paul H. Brookes.

Kagan, S. (1992), *Cooperative learning* (7th edn), San Juan Capistrano, CA: Resources for Teachers.

Kauffman, J.M. and Hallahan, D.P. (1995a), 'From mainstreaming to collaborative consultation' in *The Illusion of Full Inclusion: A Comprehensive Critique of a Current Special Education Bandwagon,* J.M. Kauffman and D.P. Halloran eds, Austin, TX: Pro-ed, pp. 5–17.

Kauffman, J.M. and Hallahan, D.P. eds (1995b), *The Illusion of Full Inclusion: A Comprehensive Critique of a Current Special Education Bandwagon,* Austin, TX: Pro-ed.

Kavale, K. and Forness, S. (1996), 'Learning disability grows up: Rehabilitation issues for individuals with learning disabilities' in *The Journal of Rehabilitation,* 62(1), pp. 34–42.

Kennedy, C.H. and Fisher, D. (2001), *Inclusive Middle Schools,* Baltimore: Paul H. Brookes.

Koegel, R. and Kern Koegel, L. (1996), *Teaching Children with Autism: Strategies for Initiating Positive Interactions and Improving Learning Opportunities,* Baltimore, MA: Paul H. Brookes.

Kubany, E.S. and Sloggett, B.B. (1973), 'Coding procedure for teachers' in *Journal of Applied Behaviour Analysis 6,* pp. 339–44.

Lamont, I.L. and Hill, J.L. (1991), 'Roles and responsibilities of paraprofessionals in the regular elementary classroom' in *B.C. Journal of Special Education,* 15(1), pp. 1–24.

Lederer, J. (2000), 'Reciprocal teaching of social studies in inclusive elementary classrooms' in *Journal of Learning Disabilities,* 33(1), p. 91.

Leighton, M., O'Brien, E., Walking Eagle, K., Weiner, L., Wimberly, G. and Youngs, P. (1997). *Roles for Education Paraprofessionals in Effective Schools: An Idea Book,* Washington, DC:Policy Studies Associates, Inc.

Lewis, M. (1992), *Parent Involvement in the Special Education Process: A Synopsis of Exemplary Models,* Bloomington, IND: Indiana University.

Lincoln, Y.S. and Guba, E.G. (1985), *Naturalistic Inquiry,* Beverley Hills, CA.: Sage.

Lipsky, D.K. (1989), 'The roles of parents' in *Beyond Separate Education: Quality Education for All,* D.K. Lipsky and A. Gartner eds, Baltimore: Paul A. Brooks, pp. 159–79.

Lipsky, D.K. and Gartner, A. (1994), 'Inclusion: What it is, what it's not and why it matters' in *Exceptional Parent,* September, pp. 36–38.

Lloyd, A. (1987), *Payment by Results: Kew Cottages' First 100 Years 1887–1987,* East Burwood, Vic: Kew Cottages and St Nicholas Parents' Association.

Lloyd, C., Wilton, K. and Townsend, M. (1996), 'Children at high risk for mild intellectual disability in regular classrooms: Six New Zealand case studies' in *10th World Congress of the International Association for Scientific Study of Intellectual Disability,* Helsinki: ERIC, pp. 16.

Loreman, T.J. (1997), *Improving the Implementation of Individualized Education Programs in Edmonton Public Schools,* Geelong: Faculty of Education, Deakin University.

Loreman, T. (1999), 'Integration: Coming from the outside' in *Interaction*, 13(1), pp. 21–23.

Loreman, T. (2000), 'School inclusion in Victoria, Australia: The results of six case studies' in *International Special Education Congress 2000*, M. Ainscow and P. Mittler eds, Manchester: Inclusive Technology and the University of Manchester.

Loreman, T.J. (2001). *Secondary School Inclusion for Students with Moderate to Severe Disabilities in Victoria, Australia*, Clayton: Faculty of Education, Monash University.

Loreman, T. and Deppeler, J.M. (2001), 'Working towards full inclusion in education' in *Access: The National Issues Journal for People with a Disability*, 3(6), pp. 5–8.

Loughran, J., Mitchell, I. and Mitchell, J. eds (2000), *Learning from Teacher Research*, Sydney: Allen & Unwin.

MacMullin, et al. (1992), *The Sheidow Park Social Problem Solving Program*, Adelaide: Flinders University of South Australia.

Madden, N.A. and Slavin, R.E. (1983), 'Mainstreaming students with mild handicaps: Academic and social outcomes' in *Review of Educational Research*, 53(4), pp. 519–69.

Maheady, L., Harper, G.F. and Mallette, B. (1991), 'Peer-mediated instruction: A review of potential applications for special education' in *Reading, Writing, and Learning Disabilities International*, 7, pp. 75–103.

Maheady, L., Harper, G.F. and Mallette, B. (2001), 'Peer-Mediated Instruction and Interventions and Students with Mild Disabilities' in *Remedial and Special Education*, 22(1), pp. 4–15.

Maheady, L., Harper, G.F., Sacca, K.C. and Mallette, B. (1991), *Classwide Student Tutoring Teams (CSTT)*, instructor's manual and video package, Fredonia, NY: SUNY-Fredonia, School of Education.

Manley, S. and Levy, S. (1981), 'The IEP organizer: A strategy for turning IEPs into daily lesson plans' in *Teaching Exceptional Children*, 18(1), pp. 70–72.

Margolis, H. and Truesdell, L. (1987), 'Do special education teachers use IEPs to guide instruction?' in *The Urban Review*, 19(3), pp. 151–59.

Mastropieri, M.A. and Scruggs, T.E. (1987), *Effective Instruction for Special Education*, Boston: College-Hill.

Mastropieri, M. A. and Scruggs, T.E. (2000) *The Inclusive Classroom: Strategies for Effective Inclusion*, Englewood Cliffs, NJ: Prentice-Hall.

McCarthy, A.M., Kelly, M.W. and Reed, D. (2000), 'Medication administration practices of school nurses' in *Journal of School Health*, 70(9), pp. 371–76.

McGregor, G. and Vogelsberg, R.T. (1998), *Inclusive Schooling Practices: Pedagogical and Research Foundations*, Baltimore: Paul H. Brookes.

McGuire, W.J. (1989), 'The structure of individual attitudes and attitude systems' in *Attitude, Structure and Function*, A.R. Pratkanis, S.J. Breckler and A.G. Greenwald eds, Hillsdale, NJ: Erlbaum, pp. 37–69.

McInerney, D.M. and McInerney, V. (2002), *Educational Psychology: Constructing Learning*, Sydney: Prentice-Hall.

McNamara, D.R. and Waugh, D.G. (1993), 'Classroom organisation: A discussion of grouping strategies in the light of the "Three Wise Men's" report' in *School Organisation*, 13(1), pp. 41–50.

Meijer, C.J. W., Pijl, S.J. and Waslander, S. (1999), 'Special education funding and integration: Cases from Europe' in *Funding Special Education: Nineteenth Annual Yearbook of the American Education Finance Association*, T.B. Parrish, J.G. Chambers and C. Guarino eds, CA: Corwin Press.

Mishna, F. (2003), 'Learning disabilities and bullying: Double jeopardy' in *Journal of Learning Disabilities*, 36(4), pp. 336–48.

Mitchell, I. (2002), 'Learning from teacher research for teacher research' in *Learning from Teacher Research*, J. Loughran, I. Mitchell and J. Mitchell eds, Sydney: Allen & Unwin, pp. 249–66.

Mohr, L.L. (1995), 'Teaching diverse learners in inclusive settings: Steps for adapting instruction' in *Annual International Convention of the Council for Exceptional Children*, Indianapolis: Council for Exceptional Children.

Morse, J.S., Colatarci, S., Nehring, W., Roth, S.P. and Barks, L.S. (1997), 'Administration of medication by unlicensed assistive personnel to persons with mental retardation and developmental disabilities' in *Mental Retardation*, 35(4), pp. 310–11.

Natasi, B. and Clements, D.H. (1991), 'Research on cooperative learning: Implications for practice' in *School Psychology Review*, 20, pp. 110–31.

National Board of Employment Education and Training (1992), *Curriculum Initiatives: Commissioned Report No. 12*, Canberra: Australian Government Publishing Service.

Nelsen, J., Lott, L. and Glen, S.H. (1993), *Positive Discipline in the Classroom*, Rocklyn, CA: Prima.

Nowicki, E.A. and Sandieson, R. (2002), 'A meta-analysis of school-age children's attitudes towards persons with physical or intellectual disabilities' in *International Journal of Disability, Development and Education*, 49(3), pp. 243–65.

Odom, S.L., McConnell, S.R. and McEvoy M.A. (1992), *Social Competence of Young Children with Disabilities: Issues and Strategies for Intervention*, Baltimore, MA: Paul H. Brookes.

OECD (1994a), *The Curriculum Redefined: Schooling for the 21st Century*, Paris: Organisation for Economic Co-operation and Development.

OECD (1994b), *The Integration of Disabled Children into Mainstream Education: Ambitions, Theories and Practices*, Paris: Organisation for Economic Cooperation and Development, p. 55.

OECD (1999), *Inclusive Education at Work: Students with Disabilities in Mainstream schools*, Paris: OECD Publications.

O'Grady, C. (1990), *Integration Working*, London: Centre for Studies on Integration in Education, p. 28.

Onosko, J.J. and Jorgenson, C.M. (1998), 'Unit and lesson planning in the inclusive classroom: Maximising learning opportunities for all students' in *Restructuring High Schools for All Students: Taking Inclusion to the Next Level*, C.M. Jorgensen ed., Baltimore: Paul H. Brookes, p. 273.

O'Shea, D.J. and O'Shea, L.J. (1998), 'Learning to include: Lessons learned from a high school without special education services' in *Teaching Exceptional Children*, 31(1), pp. 40–8.

O'Toole, T.J. and Switlick, D.M. (1997), 'Integrated therapies' in *Teaching Students in Inclusive Settings: From Theory to Practice*, D.F. Bradley, M.E. King-Sears and D.M. Tessier-Switlick eds, Needham Heights, MA: Allyn & Bacon, pp. 202–24.

Pallincsar, A.S. and Brown, A.L. (1984) 'The reciprocal teaching of comprehension-fostering and comprehension-monitoring activities' in *Cognition and Instruction*, 1, 117–75.

Pallincsar, A.S. and David, Y.M., and Brown. A.L. (1989), *Using reciprocal teaching in the classroom: A guide for teachers*, unpublished manual.

Pallincsar, A.S. and Herrenkohl, R. (2002), 'Designing collaborative learning contexts' in *Theory into Practice*, 41(1), pp. 26–33.

Pallincsar, A.S. and Klenk, L. (1992), 'Fostering literacy learning in supportive contexts' in *Journal of Learning Disabilities*, 25, pp. 221–25.

Parsons, G., Elkins, J. and Sigafoos, J. (2000), 'Are people with intellectual disabilities just another customer? Interviews with business owners and staff' in *Mental Retardation*, 38, pp. 244–52.

Pendarvis, E.D., Howley, A.A. and Howley, C.B. (1990), *The Abilities of Gifted Children*, Englewood Cliffs, NJ: Prentice-Hall.

Peterson, L. and Gannon, A. (1992), *The Stop, Think, Do, Teachers' Manual for Training Social Skills while Managing Student Behaviour*, Hawthorn, Vic: ACER.

Phinney, M.Y. (1988), *Reading with the Troubled Reader*, Scholastic, Toronto.

Pickett, A.L., Vasa, S.F. and Steckelberg, A.L. (1993), *Using Paraeducators in the Classroom: Fastback 358*, Bloomington, IND. Phi Delta Kappa

Pinnell G.S., Lyons C.A., DeFord, D.E., Bryk, A.A. and Seltzer, M. (1994), 'Comparing instructional models for the literacy education of high-risk first graders' in *Reading Research Quarterly*, 29, pp. 9–40

Pressley, M. (1998), 'Comprehension strategies instruction' in *Literacy for all: Issues in teaching and learning*, J. Osborn and F. Lehr, eds, pp. 113–33.

Pressley, M. (2002), 'Reading Instruction That Works: The Case for Balanced Teaching' in *Solving Problems in the Teaching of Literacy*, New York, NY: Guilford Publications.

Pressley, M., Borkowski, J. G. and Schneider, W. (1987), 'Cognitive strategies: Good strategy users coordinate metacognition and knowledge' in *Annals of Child Development* (vol. 4), R. Vasta and G. Whitehurst eds, Greenwich, CT: JAI Press, pp. 89–129.

Pugach, M. (1982), 'Regular classroom teacher involvement in the development and utilization of IEPs' in *Exceptional Children*, 48(4), pp. 371–74.

Redding, R.E. (1990), 'Learning preferences and skill patterns among underachieving gifted adolescents' in *Gifted Child Quarterly*, 34, pp. 72–75.

Riches, V. (1996a), *Everyday Social Interaction: A Program for People with Disabilities*, Sydney: McLennan & Petty.

Riches, V. (1996b), 'A review of transition from school to community for students with disabilities in NSW, Australia' in *Journal of Intellectual and Developmental Disability*, 21(1), pp. 71–88.

Riggs, C.G. (2001), 'Ask the paraprofessionals: What are your training needs?' in *Teaching Exceptional Children*, 33(3), pp. 78–83.

Robinson, R. (1964), *An Atheist's Value*,. Oxford: Blackwell.

Rogan, J., LaJeunesse, C., McCann, P., McFarland, G. and Miller, C. (1995), 'Facilitating inclusion: The role of learning strategies to support secondary students with special needs' in *Preventing School Failure*, 39(3), pp. 35–39.

Rowe, H.A. (Australian Council for Educational Research) (1985), *Problem Solving and Intelligence*, Hillsdale, NJ: Erlbaum.

Ryba, K., Curzon, J. and Selby, L. (2002), 'Learning partnerships through information and communication technology' in *Educating Children with Diverse Abilities*, A. Ashman and J. Elkins eds, Frenchs Forest, NSW: Pearson Education, pp. 500–29.

Ryndak, D. and Alper, S. (1996), *Curriculum Content for Students with Moderate and Severe Disabilities in Inclusive Settings*, Needham Heights, MA: Allyn & Bacon.

Sailor, W. and Skrtic, T.M. (1995), 'American education in the postmodern era' in *Integrating School Restructuring and Special Education Reform* (vol. 1), L. Paul, D. Evans and H. Rosselli eds, Orlando: Brace Coll, pp. 214–36.

Salvia, J. and Hughes, C. (1990), *Curriculum based assessment: Testing what is right*, New York: Macmillan.

Saxby, H., Thomas, M., Felce, D. and De Kock, U. (1986), 'The use of shops, cafes and public houses by severely and profoundly mentally handicapped adults' in *British Journal of Mental Subnormality*, 32, pp. 69–81.

Schneider, W. and Weinert, F.E. eds (1990), *Interactions Among Aptitude, Strategies, and Knowledge in Cognitive Performance*, New York: Springer-Verlag.

Searle, Y. and Streng, I. (1996), *The Social Skills Game*, London: Taylor & Francis.

Sharma, U. and Desai, I. (2002), 'Measuring concerns about integrated education in India' in *Asia & Pacific Journal on Disability*, 5(1), pp. 2–14.

Sharpe, M.N., York, J.L. and Knight, J. (1994), 'Effects of inclusion on academic performance of classmates without disabilities: A preliminary study' in *Remedial and Special Education*, 15(5), pp. 281–87.

Shultz, W. (1988), 'The interpersonal world' in *Understanding Human Communication* (3rd edn), R.B. Adler and G. Rodman eds, London: Holt Rinehart & Winston.

Slater, W. and Horstman, F. (2002), 'Teaching reading and writing to struggling middle school and high school students: The case for reciprocal teaching' in *Preventing School Failure*, Summer, 46(4), p. 163.

Slavin, R.E. (1990), *Cooperative learning: Theory, research, and practice*, Englewood Cliff, NJ: Prentice Hall.

Slavin, R.E. (1995), 'Research on cooperative learning and achievement: What we know, what we need to know' at http://www.successforall.net/cooplear.html

Slee, R (1996), 'Bullying in the playground: The impact of inter-personal violence on Australian children's perceptions of their play environment' in *Children's Environments*, 12, p. 320–27.

Slee, R. and Cook, S. (1994), 'Creating cultures of disability to control young people in Australian schools' in *Urban Review*, 26(1), pp. 15–23.

Sommerstein, L.C. and Wessels, M.R. (1996), 'Gaining and utilising family and community support for inclusive schooling' in *Inclusion: A Guide for Educators*, S. Stainback and W. Stainback eds, Sydney: Paul H. Brookes, pp. 367–82.

Spinelli, C.G. (2002), *Classroom Assessment for Students with Special Needs in Inclusive Settings*, Englewood Cliffs, NJ: Merrill Prentice Hall.

Stainback, S. and Stainback W. (1996), *Inclusion: A Guide for Educators*, Sydney: Paul H. Brookes.

Staub, D. and Peck, C. A. (1995) 'What are the outcomes for nondisabled students?' in *Educational Leadership*, 54 (4), pp. 36–40.

Sternberg, R.J. (1986), 'A triarchic theory of intellectual giftedness' in *Conceptions of Giftedness*, R.J. Sternberg and J.E. Davidson eds, New York: Cambridge University Press, pp. 223–43.

Sternberg, R.J. and Davidson J.E. eds (1986) *Conceptions of Giftedness*, New York: Cambridge University Press.

Strickland, B. and Turnbull, A. (1990), *Developing and Implementing Individualized Education Programs*, Ohio: Merrill.

Tannenbaum, A.J. (1986), 'Giftedness: A psychosocial approach' in *Conceptions of Giftedness*, R.J. Sternberg and J.E. Davidson eds, New York: Cambridge University Press, pp. 21–52.

Taylor, R.L. (2000), *Assessment of Exceptional Students: Educational and Psychological Procedures* (5th edn), Needham Heights, MA: Allyn & Bacon.

Tetlow, P. (1990), *Health Care: Infection Control, Medication Administration, and Seizure Management*, Miami, FLA: Dade County Public Schools.

Tomlinson, C.A., Moon, T.R. and Callahan, C.M. (1997), 'Use of cooperative learning at the middle level: Insights from a national survey' in *Research in Middle Level Education Quarterly*, pp. 37–55.

Tonn, N. (2002), 'Reading change during and following modeled reading using cross-age peer tutors', an unpublished research thesis, Monash University Melbourne, Australia.

Topping, K. (1987), 'Peer Tutored Paired Reading: Outcome Data from Ten Projects' in *Educational Psychology*, 7(2), pp. 133–45.

Topping, K. and Ehly, S. (1998), 'Introduction to peer-assisted learning' in *Peer-assisted learning*, K. Topping and S. Elby eds, Mahwah, NJ: Erlbaum, pp. 1–23.

Topping, K. and Lindsay, G. (1993), 'Paired reading: A review of the research' in *Research Papers in Education*, 7, pp. 199–246.

Turnbull, A.P. and Turnbull, H.R. (1982), 'Parent involvement in the education of handicapped children: A critique' in *Mental Retardation*, 20(3), pp. 115–22.

Tyler, Leona (1995), 'The challenge of diversity' in *Assessing Individual Differences in Human Behavior*, D. Lubinski and R.V. Dawis eds, Palo Alto, CA: Davies-Black, pp. 1–14.

Utley, C.A., Mortweet, S.L. and Greenwood, C.R. (1997), 'Peer-mediated instruction and interventions' in *Focus on Exceptional Children*, 29(5), pp. 1–23.

Vaughan G.M. and Hogg, M.A. (2002), *Introduction to Social Psychology*, Frenchs Forest, NSW: Pearson Education.

Vaughn, S., Klingner, J.K. and Bryant, D.P. (2001), 'Collaborative strategic reading as a means to enhance peer-mediated instruction for reading comprehension and content-area learning' in *Remedial and Special Education*. 22(2), pp. 66–75.

Vaughn, S. and Schumm, J.S. (1995), 'Responsible inclusion for students with learning disabilities' in *Journal of Learning Disabilities*, 28(5), pp. 264–70.

Vislie, L. and Langfeldt, G. (1996), 'Finance, policy making and the organisation of special education' in *Cambridge Journal of Education*, 26(1), pp. 59–70.

Wade, A., Abrami, P., Poulsen, C and Chambers, B. (1995), *Current Resources in Cooperative Learning*, Lanham, MD: University Press of America.

Walker, H., Todis, B., Holmes, D. and Horton, G. (1988), *The Walker Social Skills Curriculum*, Austin, TX: Pro-Ed.

Wallace, T., Shin, J., Bartholomay, T. and Stahl, B. (2001), 'Knowledge and skills for teachers supervising the work of paraprofessionals' in *Exceptional Children*, 67(4), pp. 520–33.

Wang, M.C., Haertel, G.D. and Walberg, H.J. (1997), 'Fostering resilience: What do we know?' in *Principal*, 77(2), p. 18.

Warren, Bill (1980), 'Some thoughts towards a philosophy of physical handicap' in *Problems of Handicap*, R. Laura ed., South Melbourne: MacMillan, pp. 76–85.

Wasik, B.A. and Slavin, R.E. (1993), 'Preventing early reading failure with one-to-one tutoring: A review of five programs' in *Reading Research Quarterly*, 28(20) pp. 178–200.

Webb, N.M., Troper, J.D. and Fall, R. (1995), 'Constructive activity and learning in collaborative small groups' in *Journal of Educational Psychology*, 87(3), pp. 406–23.

Weisenfeld, R.B. (1987), 'Functionality in the IEPs of children with Down syndrome' in *Mental Retardation*, 25(5), pp. 281–86.

Wells, T., Byron, M., McMullen, S. and Birchall, M. (2002), 'Disability teaching for medical students: Disabled people contribute to curriculum development' in *British Journal of Medical Education*, 36, pp. 788–92.

Welsh, M., Parke, R.D., Widaman, K. and O'Neil, R. (2001), 'Linkages between children's social and academic competence: A longitudinal analysis' in *Journal of School Psychology*, 39(6), p. 463.

Westwood, P. (1997), 'Moving towards inclusion: Proceed with caution' in *Australian Journal of Learning Disabilities*, 2(3), pp. 18–20.

Whitmore, J.R. (1980), *Giftedness, conflict, and underachievement*, Boston: Allyn & Bacon.

Woolfolk, A. (2001), *Educational Psychology*, Needham Heights, MA: Allyn & Bacon.

Wright, B.A. (1983), *Physical Disability: A Psychosocial Approach* (2nd edn), New York: Harper and Row.

Yasutake, D. and Lerner, J. (1997), 'Parents' perceptions of Inclusion: A survey of parents of special education and non-special education students' in *Learning Disabilities: A Multidisciplinary Journal*, 8(2), pp. 117–20.

Yong, F.L. and McIntyre, J.D. (1992), 'A comparative study of the learning style preferences of students with learning disabilities and students who are gifted' in *Journal of Learning Disabilities*, 25, pp. 124–32.

Index